What Others are Saying Ab

" I've spent many hours traveling with Gig Gwin and even more hearing of his travels, always an entertaining and informative experience. Readers of this book now get to enjoy and learn from this world explorer just as I've been able to for the last 38 years! Open it, and see the world!"

John Bottchen, Project Manager and Travel Director

" *Travel Dreams Sold Here* is not only a fun read, but very helpful. Having also traveled extensively overseas, I found Mr. Gwin's advice about "attitude" to be right on target: a healthy sense of adventure goes a long way to making an enjoyable trip. Gig translates his experiences into useful information. A nice surprise was his extensive use of humorous anecdotes to illustrate the various regions of the world, and the questions regarding the type of vacation you will enjoy points you in the right direction —adventure is great, but a soft bed and a glass of wine are even better. With great lists of places to go on all continents, sights to see, and even cocktails to sample - whether you are planning a vacation, traveling for work, or simply want to dream about far-off lands; *Travel Dreams Sold Here* is a must-read."

Ray Scott, Vice President, Supply Chain Management

" Someone who's been to every country in the world! Who better to give travel advice and recommendations—for those who are already sophisticated travelers as well as for the novice with an itch and a desire."

Glenn Detrick, President, Educational Benchmark Inc.

" I have traveled with Gig to the corners of the world, we have seen the best and the worst. His book is full of travel facts and inspiring stories."

Dr. Alexander Gushansky, Traveled to 300 countries

" Gig Gwin is the 'go to guy' for the best, most-comprehensive information on any destination in the world! As a history teacher I could depend on Gig to know the cultural and historical significance of sites all over the world. I didn't need the internet with Gig on my speed-dial!"

Donna Picataggio, Educator 31 years

TRAVEL DREAMS SOLD HERE

Crafting an Extraordinary Vacation

Graydon "Gig" Gwin

TRAVEL DREAMS SOLD HERE:
Crafting an Extraordinary Vacation

Unattributed quotations are by Graydon "Gig" Gwin

Cover Design: Todd Gwin

Library of Congress Cataloging-in-Publication Data
Gwin, Graydon "Gig"
Travel Dreams Sold Here: Crafting an Extraordinary Vacation / by Graydon "Gig" Gwin
          p. cm.
Includes Index
ISBN 9780615360133
1. Travel—Guidebooks. I. Title
Library of Congress Control Number: 2010904106

FIRST EDITION • Printed and bound in the U.S.A.
14   13   12   11   10   5   4   3   2   1

Published by:

Lyneildon Publishing
111 N. Taylor Ave.
Kirkwood, MO 63122
314-822-1993
www.gwins.com/gig

This Book Is...

For my parents, Helen and Jimmy, who fostered my love of travel ...

For my wife, Terrie, and sons, Aaron, Kyle & Todd, who stood with me ...

For my cat, Sasha, who stepped on my papers and slept nearby while I wrote.

Gig and Terrie Gwin on the Orient Express.

Travel Memories

The travel adventures in our lives are well-cherished memories ... trips only once lived, but many times remembered.

Yet, this Earth will change and with that change will be lost experiences ... civilizations never discovered, gourmet dishes never tasted, bargains never bought. Renew your spirit ... see this world soon, for travel is the building block of our memories.

—Gig Gwin

Itinerary Overview

Itinerary Details

Far away places
with strange-soundin' names,
Far away over the sea.
Those far away places
with the strange-soundin' names,
Are callin', callin' me.

—Bing Crosby

Introduction

In September 1999, I stepped off a commuter plane onto Lampedusa. This tiny island in the Mediterranean Sea had recently been placed on the Travelers' Century Club list of world countries. Though it was one small step onto a runway, it was a giant leap in my travel career. It signified the completion of a life-long goal of visiting every country on earth; at that time the list was at 313.

Later in the afternoon I dug my feet into the sand at a beach-side Italian café and, to celebrate, indulged in pasta and vino, kicked back and slipped into a spiritual calm. It was a time of peace and reflection, interrupted only by European sunbathers strutting past my table. Only a handful of travelers have touched them all, but now was not the time for high-fives – just the inner satisfaction of being there, completing my personal quest, overcoming eons of flight time, fighting jetlag, being denied entrance into Third World countries, then sucking it up and slaying travel dragons, just so I could check one more country off the list. Was it worth the journey? Absolutely!

Fulfilling my own travel dreams makes it possible for me to help fellow travelers fulfill theirs. The creation of this book was developed over 40 years of counseling clients. Granted, people have different dreams, yet I've noticed a curious phenomenon, a repetition of the same questions regarding planning vacations. As a travel agent, my responsibility has been to ask questions, listen to clients' needs and share destination knowledge.

As a travel explorer and journalist, I've wandered to exotic cities and remote countries—always taking notes and photos, making word memory lists and indulging in the sights, cultures and local cuisine.

After completing a lifetime goal of visiting all the countries of the world, I settled into a comfortable chair and began putting facts and experiences into a keynote speech—"The Top Ten Grand Tours of the World." The recurring questions that followed my speeches and travel counseling made it clear that I needed to get out of my chair and write a planning book for travelers— dedicated to answering the most often asked questions and highlighting the great destinations of the world.

Travel Dreams Sold Here answers the most frequently asked questions and hopefully shares knowledge through stories and examples. Here's an overview:

Chapter One, "Why We Travel," looks into the motivation that calls people to explore this compelling planet. Learning more about the spectacular landmarks and gems expands your view of the world. The survey I use for my travelers is included in the first chapter, to set a direction for your future trips.

Writing Chapter Two, "Tourism Through the Ages," utilizes my college history degree along with some storytelling and a little tongue-in-cheek humor. The foundation of travel was set by the early Greeks, Romans, European Crusaders, pilgrims and adventurers. Marco Polo opened the eyes of the western world, and soon seafaring explorers followed the four winds and the seven seas to unknown lands. Tourism began the path of enlightenment and education that blossomed in the 20th century, thanks to new technology and forward thinkers like Lowell Thomas.

Chapter Three, "Travel Tips for the Mind & Spirit," shares the travel tips that I've recorded over the years. Pre-trip planning sets the stage for an enjoyable trip full of lifelong memories. For example, shopping can be a great joy with just a little research.

Great photography can turn into a work of art, but you do not need an easel—you can create a snapshot and hold a memory in your hands.

Chapter Four, "The Grand Tours of the World," is the next natural step to expand a person's mind; it's a discussion of the best-of-the-best destinations ranked by travelers who have visited most, if not all, 320 countries. I've crafted this list taking into consideration the components that bring joy and fulfillment into people's lives. Yes, it is subjective, but many experienced eyes other than mine have reviewed and added their advice. Let the Grand Tours stand as a solid reference in selecting upcoming travel.

Chapter Five covers "Planes, Trains, Ships & Cars." If a reader fancies the drop-dead beauty of any of these modes of transportation, then this is your chapter.

Lodging is like a box of chocolates—you never know what you're going to get. Chapter 6, "Lodging Made Memorable," shares great places to rest your head. With multiple selections in mind, it is my resolve to clarify the many choices and present to you some memorable properties where I've stayed throughout the world.

A good travel planning book should not exclude our extraordinary US national parks. For Chapter 7, "America's National Parks," I've asked a true expert in the field, Bob Hoelscher, to explain the parks and their recent improvements. Bob is the past president of the National Tour Association and in his 40 years in the travel business has traveled to 90 percent of the national parks.

One of the greatest experiences on any trip is enjoying the local food and beverage. Chapter 8, "Dining Around the World," describes many of the wonderful places where a traveler can experience the joy of new foods and beverages in their local setting. The dining experience may start before your trip by making reservations at a restaurant in your neighborhood that specializes in regional or international cuisine. I've assembled a list of memorable restaurants in great locations, plus added notable drinks from around the world. Relax and enjoy this chapter—it should be fun, not a sobering experience.

Chapter 9, "Museums That Inspire," opens the door to an area of tourism that is sometimes overlooked and deserves more attention, particularly for curious minds. Returning travelers give high marks to these best-in-class museums.

Chapter 10, "Tourism's Shining Future," closes the book with some thoughts on giving the gift of travel.

I'm always asked by clients about the total number of countries in the world. The answer can be found in the appendix, "All Countries Great and Small," which includes the Travelers' Century Club list. Because I've also traveled extensively for business purposes, the appendix includes some road-warrior tested tips in "Gig's Tips for Business Travel."

To top off the book, I've added a touch of quotations and musical lyrics sprinkled throughout the chapters. Travel writing is the ideal venue for great words of wisdom. I'd like to thank Mark Twain, Frank Sinatra and all the supporting cast for their brilliant thoughts and memorable music.

Knowledge is such a gift; I hope this book brings you joy and inspiration, whether an armchair traveler or an adventurous trekker.

—Gig Gwin

Note: Throughout this book, areas of the world are listed in the following order and using the color-coding shown here.

North America

Caribbean

Central America

South America

Antarctica

Atlantic Ocean

Europe

Africa

Middle East

Indian Ocean

Asia

Pacific Ocean

Twenty years from now
you will be more disappointed
by the things you didn't do
than by the ones you did do.
So throw off the bowlines.
Sail away from the safe harbor.
Catch the trade winds in your sails.
Explore. Dream. Discover.

–Mark Twain

Chapter 1:

Why We Travel

A re vacations plans in your future? Because if they are, fairy tales can still come true and magical moments are waiting at your beck and call. Start with your travel dreams and let them evolve into vacations of a lifetime, trips to inspire and fulfill your life. Throughout this book, I hope to expose you to the wonders of the world, allowing you to benefit from my years of exploration and create a picture-perfect grand tour of your own making. You should find it to be time well spent, as the chapters on travel style and choice will help you filter the options to best suit your personal travel lifestyle. The short section on tours from a historical perspective may add understanding and foster a better balance of selections for your next trip.

We, of course, are not all alike. I have spent 40 years coaching travelers with the goal of placing them on the path that will satisfy their greatest expectations. The joyful art of planning vacation dreams might lead you to a grand tour that showcases, for example, the rich cultural feast of Europe.

Once you have taken the step of considering options, you may find yourself preparing for a stroll down a medieval street, taking in the spires, gables, arches and palaces. But tours come in different-size packages. Some are filled with historical landmarks; others are wrapped with flower leis and coconut palm beaches. Some trips pulsate with the samba drums of Carnival on a sensual night in Rio; other tours might center on an evening of elegant dining. The five travel options in this book are: Touring, Romance, Relaxing, Adventure and Special Interests. You can decide which of the five travel choices best fit your style.

Touring—Discoveries for a Lifetime

Somewhere over the rainbow, way up high
— there's a land that I heard of once in a lullaby.

— Judy Garland

By the numbers, touring or sightseeing ranks at the top of most travelers' wish list. You may choose cruising, motorcoach tour packages or individual explorations. Each of these means of travel can enrich your life and etch a permanent memory of special stories and places revisited many times on your past grand tours. Sightseeing experiences plant deep roots in your mind ready for recall. Your memory, if it's akin to mine, may play silly games. I vividly recall the beef and wine lunch alfresco on a corner street café in Buenos Aires but occasionally forget the last name of my neighbors, two houses down. When I recall tours of Cooperstown or Canton, every sports legend is crystal clear in my mind–yet a moment later I'm befuddled as to where I left my car keys. The great bonus of touring is the almost permanent memory bank of travel adventures.

We travel the globe to explore times past and modern marvels. At the heart and soul of travel is the uncovering of historical and geographical gems from around the world. That thirst for knowledge entices many to travel to the ends of the earth. Have you not yearned to wander the temples of Greece where Western history comes alive? The great landmarks of the world become a library of knowledge for our minds. Riding a camel to the base of the pyramids in the land of the Pharaohs is an unforgettable experience. It adds to the treasure-trove of experience that we may bring back from trips both near and far.

A defining moment in your life can begin with a nod of your head and a commitment to a tour experience. I share opinions and experiences with people who visit me at my travel agency. Often I pull out my photo albums to help the client visualize and select that perfect "blue chip" trip. If touring is in the cards, we review cruises and motor coach options. Most cruises offer luxury at sea combined with entertainment and fine dining. I tell my client that getting the best bang for the buck involves choosing an itinerary that will whet the appetite at each and every port of call. The proper itinerary is a vital step in trip planning, and I can't emphasize this point too much. My first love in counseling is to make sure the travel selection is an itinerary to remember. Reviewing the brochures and choosing the best itinerary for the traveler, should be joyful homework.

Travel with a Touch of Romance

I see trees of green, red roses too — I see them bloom for me and you and I think to myself, what a wonderful world — Oh yeah.

—Louis Armstrong

I openly confess I am a romantic soul and a seeker of beauty. I'm that person who stays up into the night in Agra, India, waiting in anticipation for the full moon to shine down upon the Taj Mahal. After a welcome nod to the moon, my eyes wander across the white silhouette of the Taj and I sit in awe of the graceful domes and balancing minarets. After quiet moments, I reach the conclusion that while man has constructed countless buildings dedicated to beauty, this one he got absolutely right! The story is told that Emperor Shah Jahan ordered the marble tomb built in loving memory of his wife, who died in childbirth. Their bodies lie in the center vault in silent repose.

Saying good night to the Taj, I stroll down the center walkway as moonbeams dance across the reflecting pools. The beauty of the night is a gathering of impressions–one piled upon another. In the spirit of harmony the full moon plays its role, providing revealing light on an otherwise dark Indian night. The symmetrical dome contributes a stunning centerpiece, and a warm breeze wafts across the sitting area, allowing me to drink in the moment like something out of a Neverland fairy tale.

What constitutes a romantic setting?

Sometimes it's a state of mind, or it may be the presence of another person who means very much to you. Just standing beside that special someone, engaging in conversation, walking down a peaceful path, holding hands, a soft kiss or warm hug is all it takes to illuminate the night.

A romantic destination allows all of us to place ourselves outside the normal routine of life. When I enjoyed the impressions of the Taj, my wife was 8,000 miles away and my thoughts of romance had to wait until I returned home. This, then, deserves a moment of reflection about what elements are part of a romantic setting. If someone yearns for inner happiness, several sensations must be present. I do believe, first and foremost, our senses of taste, touch, sound, smell and vision play a vital role in our emotional reactions.

Our sense of smell, with those every-ready olfactory nerves, alerts us to our surroundings. Maybe it's as simple as a lady's perfume or a gentleman's alluring cologne. Romance is in the air the moment a pretty Hawaiian girl presents a flower lei. The white plumeria and the tube rose flowers burst with a delight-ful bouquet offering the spirit of aloha. Japanese gardens rotate seasonal flowers to heighten one's senses, and of all things, the city hotels in Tokyo and Osaka take pride in their gardens, which help relax the busy traveler. I recall the transformation from the busy city street traffic to the inner garden of calming fragrances.

I also remember driving to the end of Long Island and breath-ing the brisk ocean breeze wafting over land's end at Montauk —it's a rejuvenating scent that reminded me of my youth, when I would jump into the waves on the beaches of the eastern sea-board. Other romantic aromas drift from the perfume shops in Cairo, Egypt. These are fascinating specialty shops with multi-colored apothecary jars full of potent, uncut floral essences. The highlight of perfume shopping is the factory outlets in Grasse, France near Monte Carlo–the hub of the perfume industry. This is where Coco Chanel created her famous Chanel No. 5. Give your nose a treat … inhale the scents that can inspire romance–or allergic reactions.

Not all smells conjure up romance. Here are a few love-stopping, pungent moments still lucid in my mind and my nose. Let's start with communist Russia—I led a Carrier Corporation group of 900 to Moscow and Leningrad during the years of the old Soviet Union. The propaganda said, "It was a worker's paradise, the people's government, the people's country." But they failed to mention … no one ever, ever cleaned those "people's" restrooms. In Saigon, during the war, street odors were a mixture of cheap diesel fuel, water buffalo droppings, elephant dung, human urine and exposed garbage. As a young soldier, I concluded that "war is smell." I also should mention the penguin guano hills of Antarctica–a not to be forgotten experience, testing your love of wildlife vs. the stench of nesting birds. And who could forget limburger cheese—it actually smells worse than it tastes. If one party eats it and the other doesn't, it's a mood-breaker of the first order. What medieval sadist came up with that smelly concoction? Yet, keep in mind that good fragrances are the start of a romantic experience.

Touch is another way to draw the opposite sex. Holding hands and hugging don't require an exotic journey to Venice, but as it works out, warm weather is a great way to rev up the libido. Working bridal shows, I interview thousands of prospective brides, and almost all requested warm-weather destinations as their favorite honeymoon choice. They dream of walking hand in hand with their sweetheart, basking in the warm tropical sun.

Many a travel experience began with my ears alerting me to the surrounding noises. Here is an example: I flew halfway around the world to witness a once-a-year Temple of the Tooth parade and experience a peaceful evening under the full moon. Peaceful? Not by a long shot. At the annual parade of Asala Perahara in Kandy, Sri Lanka, the beating of ceremonial drums pounds through your body, and you almost become part of the temple ceremony. The cacophony of sounds pulse high, then low, while local village dance teams compete for your approval. The dancers in multi-colored outfits blow whistles and smack their bare feet on the pavement. Asian elephants, three abreast, lumber down the street bedecked in fanciful ceremonial headdress. Torch bearers with crackling dried coconut poles flank the parade, providing firelight and adding to the mystical event. Sometimes the torch bearers get a little too enthusiastic with their dancing, and cinders come to rest on innocent bystanders, who jump to quickly smother the hot ashes. This Temple of the Tooth festival assaults the ears and may leave you with a ringing for a day or two – exciting yes, romantic, no. The sounds are too intense and overpowering.

For a sound-pleasing experience, a cruise on Lake Geneva is an ideal setting. Standing on the bow of the lake cruiser, one can barely hear the chug of the engine. On a distant hillside, a train passes by without a whisper of noise. In Switzerland, loud noises are frowned upon. Traffic on the roads is quiet, and virtually no one honks a horn–people even speak in pleasant tones and probably the cows are trained not to moo. Now take this halcyon setting, which includes crystal-clear water, green hills and dramatic alpine mountain peaks, and you have an almost idyllic romantic setting. Always keep in mind that first and foremost, our senses play a key role in choosing the perfect location when planning for that special romantic trip.

The Art of Relaxing

Sittin' in the morning sun, I'll be sittin' when the evening comes
Watching the ships roll in, Then I watch them roll away again ...

–Otis Redding

Any reference material about a relaxing vacation must include the pristine island getaways of the world. To many, any thought of travel dreams starts and ends with that sound of water splashing gently on a sandy beach. Add graceful palm trees and warming sunshine then kick back in an oversized beach chair and let the rest of the world go by.

No high adventure here. It's time to unwind and smell the roses—or if you're on a Pacific island, smell the white and yellow plumeria as you relax. Images of the workplace fade away, the toil and tribulation of daily responsibilities seem not so urgent, or even possibly for the time being are forgotten. A new set of tasks are now in place before you. Your tranquil soul now ponders questions of the sun and surf set. Did the beach boy turn on the Jacuzzi this morning? Do I recline on the beach blanket or by poolside? I left my watch in the room ... do I care? And the quintessential question for beach lovers–is it too early in the morning to order a margarita?

Dream Beaches of the World—Relaxing Getaways

Catch a wave and you're sitting on top of the world.
–The Beach Boys

Soft white sand and calm tropical water are the perfect ingredients for a relaxing vacation. When it's time to unwind and rejuvenate the spirit, it's time to hop on a fast plane, then slow down by the beach bar, or dig your toes into the sand.

On the next page is a collection of my favorite dream beaches, from all corners of the globe. Here is how I came to choose these beaches. 1) A year-round warm climate is essential, so many northern beaches, although appealing, are not included in this list. 2) If the beach area is too commercial or too busy, or if the beach is so remote that it lacks decent resorts, it also does not make the final cut. Surprisingly, many countries are not blessed with great, relaxing beaches.

Many of the island nations abound with relaxing beaches. The Bahamas are convenient to the United States, and their 700 islands of white and pink sand glisten in turquoise waters. Another island nation is the Seychelles in the Indian Ocean, where you find dramatic, gray granite boulders as a background to the clear beaches. If you travel to Indonesia, Bali is most noted for its unique culture, intriguing group festivals and dance, but particularly the spectacular beach sunsets that can last for an hour. The Philippines are blessed with palm beaches, and Tahiti offers dramatic mountain peaks and crystal clear lagoons.

Dream Beaches

North America
North Carolina–Cape Hatteras, Outer Banks
South Carolina–Kiawah, Hilton Head
Georgia–Sea Pines, St. Simon, Jekyll, Sea
Florida (most Florida beaches are relaxing)–Amelia, St. Augustine, West Palm
Beach, Boca Raton, Florida Keys, Marco,
Naples, Ft. Meyers, Sanibel, Captiva,
Sarasota, St. Petersburg, Clearwater,
Destin, Pensacola
Texas–South Padre
California - Beaches from San Diego to
Monterey including: Laguna, La Jolla,
Malibu, Santa Barbara
Mexico - Los Cabos (beaches can be
rough), Puerto Vallarta, Cancun, Riviera
Maya, Cozumel

Caribbean
Bahamas
Turks & Caicos
Cuba–Varadero
Grand Cayman
Jamaica–Montego Bay, Ocho Rios, Negril
Dominican Republic–Punta Cana
Puerto Rico
Virgin Islands–Trunk Bay, St. John

Caribbean (cont.)
British Virgin Islands
Anguilla
Antiqua
St. Martin/St. Maarten
St. Kitts & Nevis
Guadeloupe
Martinique
St. Lucia
St. Vincent
Barbados
Tobago
Aruba
Bonaire

Central America
Costa Rica–West Coast

South America
Brazil–Rio, Copacabana & Ipanema
Uruguay–Punta del Este
Chile–Viña del Mar

Atlantic Ocean
Bermuda
Canary Islands–Gran Canaria, Tenerife
Madera–Porto Santo

Dream Beaches (Cont.)

Europe
France–Biarritz, French Riviera (Côte d'Azur), Cannes, St. Tropez
Balearic Islands–Mallorca, Menorca, Ibiza
Spain–Malaga, Costa del Sol
Portugal–Algarve
Italy–Santa Margarita, Capri, Amalfi, Sicily
Sardinia–Costa Esmeralda
Malta
Greek Islands–Corfu, Crete, Rhodes, Mykanos, Santorini
Cyprus

Africa
Morocco–Casablanca
Egypt–Sharm el Sheikh Red Sea
Kenya–Mombassa
Tanzania–Zanzibar
South Africa–Cape Town, Garden Route, Wild Coast, Durban

Middle East
Turkey–Kusadasi
Lebanon–Beirut
Jordan–Aqaba
United Arab Emirates–Dubai

Indian Ocean
Seychelles
Mauritius
Comoros
Maldives

Asia
India–Goa
Thailand–Phuket, Pattaya
Philippines
Malaysia–Penang
Vietnam–Vung Tau & Nha Trang
China–Sanya, Hainan Island
Hong Kong–Repulse Bay

Pacific Ocean
Australia–Lord Howe Island, Gold Coast, Great Barrier Reef Islands & Bondi Beach Sydney
Fiji
Kiribati–Tarawa
Tonga
Vanuatu–Port Villa
Northern Marianas–Saipan
Guam
Okinawa–Miyaki and Yoron Islands
Hawaii– Waikiki (crowded but beautiful), Hanauma Bay, Big Island, Kona, Kauai, North Shore, Po'ipu, Lanai, Manele Bay, Maui, Kaanapali, Kapalua, Wailea, Hana
Micronesia–Truk
Tahiti–Moorea & Bora Bora, Raiatea, Tahaa, Huahine
Easter Island–Anakena
Cook–Rarotonga
Marquesas
Galapagos

Note: Many nice beaches didn't make the final cut, so use this list as a general reference guide when you plan a relaxing vacation.

Special thanks to Christine Huffman, Jim Patecha and Paul Bickham–all lifetime administrators and travel directors–for their review of this list.

Adventure Travel

Life is either a daring adventure or nothing.

–Helen Keller

Does adventure travel call to everyone? Not really. That fire in the belly to climb or hike, bike or raft is limited to a select audience. Being young or young at heart is not enough; you've "gotta wanna" – overcoming fear with victory, the self-imposed hero's journey. But if you yearn for adventure, sometimes your answer—"because it's there"—just sounds right. It's risk vs. reward. As one of my climbing buddies puts it, "Sometimes you get the mountain; sometimes the mountain gets you."

At any age, I love the guys and gals who have a spirit of adventure. As a travel counselor, I tend to break down the journey not by location, but by natural setting. I start the general questions with a survey of land, water and air and ask, "What are your dreams? Are you content with your present type of adventure or do you seek new worlds to conquer? Are you a light, medium or vigorous player?"

A few years back, I set a goal of traveling to Tanzania and taking an adventure safari on the Serengeti Plains. I pre-planned the trip during the summers Great Migration. Who would not want to stand on a hillside overlooking a million animals as they follow the fresh plains grass that recently sprouted from the monsoon rains? On the way to the Serengeti, Tanzania also offers a once in a lifetime experience–a safari jeep excursion

down switch-back trails into the Ngorongoro Crater. This menagerie of animals does not migrate and the crater floor is plen-
tiful with large-tusked elephants, rare rhinos, huge flocks of
pink flamingos and lion prides with playful cubs.

Knowing this trip would kick up some dust and dirt, I called
my favorite adventure partner, Bill Droege, who lives in the
Hudson Valley of New York. He'll go anywhere ... anywhere
that offers exotic cultures or far-out hiking. We've traveled to
the five Stans of Asia, weathered monsoons in Bhutan, climbed
an Inca trail above Machu Picchu and slid down snow peaks
in Antarctica. So I called and nimbly got past Bill's concerned
wife Susan, then sprang the next great adventure trip on Bill,
"Picture watering holes with angry hippos, birds in full plumage, blood-thirsty hyenas, waterbucks and leaping impalas."
Bill paused a moment then answered with dry humor, "I'll look
at your stupid animals, then we'll climb Kilimanjaro." I thought
a moment and informed Bill that I was getting too old for that
mountain, my belly is portly and my legs feel like rubber. After
some diplomatic negotiations, we agreed on a week's safari and
a five-day ascend — it was unforgettable!

I remember the struggle up the mountain; my gentle Tanzanian
guide looked me in the eye and strongly suggested it was time
to go back down the mountain. "You have made it to the rim of
Kilimanjaro and you look tired." Yes, I had rubber legs and I was
sucking air, but I felt the inner need to reach Uhuru, the highest point in Africa. Reluctantly, my guide joined me for a two-
hour snow march around the rim to the top of Africa — 19,300
feet. My chest felt compressed, waiting for the imminent heart
attack, the irritating headache persisted and I noticed a swelling in my right ankle. What price glory? I took stock of my surroundings: Hemingway's snow covered the mountaintop crater
and I was well above the clouds. Then another thought flashed
into my mind: I was not in my Lazy Boy in the den, not hanging
out by the pool, not just a fan — I was a player. Only then did I
agree that the reward was worth the sacrifice.

Land Adventures

Hiking, Skiing, Bungee Jumping

Hiking: Walks, hikes and treks find great popularity among travelers curious about exploring the lay of the land. Surprisingly, cruise ship ports of call present a wonderful opportunity aside from the standard cruise tour. Cruise directors may not encourage walks and hikes, as there is not much profit for the ship, but some of my greatest experiences have come with setting out on my own for a self-guided walking tour. So, if you're cruising, do your homework. I took a walk in the woods with my son in Ketchikan, Alaska, where gigantic pines grow to massive heights. The girth of the tree was so large that when we hugged it, our fingers did not touch. It was great!

My friend Glenn Detrick is a retired educator and entrepreneur. He claims to be just an ordinary guy, yet he has enjoyed hiking on all seven continents. Yearly, he takes several grand hikes to special places around the world. I've asked him for his "A-List,", and here are some of his favorites.

Hiking is only one of the many adventure activities available to willing travelers. Medium to heavy adventures include ATV safaris, rock climbing and zip lines. A zip-line ride traverses a long cable stretched between two points, usually centered over a deep valley. My wife and I strapped up at Whistler Resort north of Vancouver; we zipped from station to station, and I loved the rush and wished the ride would never end. She looked at this adventure from a different perspective – questioning why clear-minded people pay good money to be attached to a thin-looking cable and repeatedly tortured.

The "A" List of Hiking

North American
Lake Louise, Alberta, Canada–The two teahouses above the Chateau Lake Louise and Moraine Lake to Wenkchemna Pass

Waterton Lakes, Alberta, Canada

Glacier National Park, Montana–The Highline Trail and Avalanche Canyon

Yellowstone National Park, Wyoming

Grand Teton, Wyoming–Cascade Canyon to Lake Solitude and Holly Lake

Zion, Bryce and Arches National Parks, Utah

The Grand Canyon (rafting/hiking), Arizona

Long's Peak, Estes Park, Colorado

Yosemite, California–4-mile trail to Glacier Point, Vernal Falls, and Half Dome

Olympic National Park, Washington

Acadia National Park, Maine

South America
The Inca Trail, Peru

Europe Hikes
Switzerland–In and around Wengen/Grindelwald and Zermatt/Matterhorn

The Highland Way, Scotland

Asia Hikes
The Annapurna Circuit, Nepal

Pacific Ocean Hikes
New Zealand–The Milford Track and The Grand Traverse (Routeburn and Greenstone Tracks)

Australia–Daintree National Forest and The Sydney Bridge Climb

–List compiled by Glenn Detrick

Skiing: Winter can be a melancholy time of year; it shuts down most adventure sports. But as the snow falls, skiing begins in earnest. A whiteout on the slopes means lights out in most classrooms. There is no better example than the University of Colorado, where students are known to walk to class with one eye on the front range of the Rockies. The first big snow signals an exodus from classes, and a rush of skiers ready to hit the slopes and begin another ski season. Prior to experiencing the adrenaline-pumping excitement of the downhill trails, a savvy skier embarks on a workout program. One of my old buddies always said you can't just walk out of a dark bar and start skiing; you need to pump some iron and stretch out those muscles. So make your choice, snow boards or skis. Challenge yourself to the daunting slopes by day and the cozy atmosphere of a resort by night. Imagine sitting around a crackling fire, your honey on one arm, a cast on the other–I tell ya, it doesn't get much better than that.

For expertise on skiiing, I asked for help from Dan Leeth, a prominent free-lance writer who has specialized in ski areas for many years. What follows, he says, is his list of "the West's 10 most outstanding ski areas that offer great skiing for all abilities, an array of distinctive lodging options, tempting restaurants and pleasant après ski bars, pubs and dives."

Outstanding Ski Areas

Western United States–List compiled by Dan Leeth

Aspen/Snowmass, Colorado	Four separate areas under one ticket.
Deer Valley, Utah	Skiing only - no boards, seldom crowded, great service.
Jackson Hole, Wyoming	Better for those who crave tougher terrain and Moose Drool beer on tap.
Heavenly Valley, California/Nevada	Views of Lake Tahoe are as fantastic as the nightlife.
Snowbird, Utah	Great for the steeps and deeps -- now, if they just sold real beer on draught.
Squaw Valley, California	Enough terrain and variety to appeal to skiers of all abilities
Steamboat Springs, Colorado	Something for everyone, including après ski hot springs for soaking sore muscles.
Sun Valley, Idaho	A classic with some of the swankiest day lodges found anywhere.
Vail/Beaver Creek, Colorado	Fantastic on all fronts, but can be overcrowded on weekends and powder days.
Whistler Blackcomb, BC	When the snow is good, this may be the absolute best.

Other Gems of Special Note

Here are runner-ups that offer great skiing, but are smaller or lack some amenities.

Alta, Utah	A classic, skier's only area that's not a real estate development with ski runs attached.
Big Sky, Montana	Fantastic terrain for all abilities and far from big city crowds.
Crested Butte, Colorado	Small but challenging slopes outside one of Colorado's prettiest historic mining towns.
Northstar-at-Tahoe, California	Fantastic new base area on terrain that's 73% easy or moderate.

Other Gems (Cont.)

Revelstoke, BC	A region that was once the domain of heli-skiers only and a downtown whose upscale hotel features a strip club.
Sunshine/Lake Louise, Alberta	The skiing is great and the views breathtaking, but towns lie a few miles away.
Taos Ski Valley, New Mexico	Tougher terrain, but hey, the tacos make up for it.
Telluride, Colorado	Only its size keeps this from being a world-class ski destination.

Fast forward to New England, where ski runs like Killington and Stowe, to name a couple—quickly fill the lifts with day-trippers and weekend enthusiasts. Hilary Nangle has been writing about Eastern ski haunts for many years and adds her outstanding lists for your review:

New England—List compiled by Hilary Nangle

Killington, Vermont	Huge ski area, very popular, can be crowded
Smugglers Notch, Vermont	Maybe the best family resort on the East Coast
Stowe, Vermont	Lovely town, classic New England ski area
Okemo, Vermont	Fabulous cruising and family oriented
Lake Placid, New York	Olympic games, great history and tradition
Sugar Loaf/USA, Maine	Snow fields above the tree-line,
Sunday River, Maine	7 peaks, well-groomed, big area
Bretton Woods, New Hampshire	Great View, Mt. Washington Hotel
Mt. Washington Valley, New Hampshire	Three resorts, little towns and many choices

Other Gems of Special Note

Mad River Glen, Vermont	Narly, "Ski it if you can."
Tuckerman Ravine, New Hampshire	Spring only, for experts, hike to the top, no lifts

The Balsams, New Hampshire	Classic ski area, with grand old hotel

Canada

Mont Tremblant, Quebec Province	Fancy European town
Mount St. Anne, Quebec Province	Full resort on the St. Lawrence River
Le Massif, Quebec Province	Lodge at the top, ski to the river

Another Gem of Special Note

Marble Mountain, Newfoundland Province	Next to Humber River (full of Salmon), small resort with view to the sea

Europe

Zermatt, Switzerland	Kitzbuhel, Austria
Jungfrau, Switzerland	Seefeld, Austria
Verbier, Switzerland	Lech, Austria
Portes du Soleil, Switzerland/France	Chamonix (Monte Blanc), France
St. Moritz, Switzerland	Les Trois Vallées, France
Gstaad, Switzerland	Val-d'Isère, France
Grindelwald, Switzerland	Cortina d'Ampezzo, Italy
Davos, Switzerland	Garmisch Partenkirchen, Germany
Arlberg (St. Anton), Austria	Lillehammer, Norway
Innsbruck, Austria	

Other Parts of the World

Portillo, Chile	Queenstown South Island, New Zealand
Bariloche, Argentina	Coronet Peak South Island, New Zealand
Sapporo, Japan	

Bungee Jumping: A short list of land adventures includes everything from a light walk in the park to a bungee jump at Victoria Falls down to within a foot of the hippo- and crocodile-infested Zambezi River. My youngest son Todd made such a leap of faith, as his nervous parents took ceremonial pictures –but this was not our first experience. Earlier, our oldest son Aaron took the plunge at the Shotover River near Queenstown, New Zealand. For a young man, this is a rite of passage. We shall put bungee jumping in the vigorous category.

If high adventure is your desire, sign up for a bungee jump. You are guaranteed an adrenaline rush and an activity that looks life-threatening but has a good safety record. Bungee jumping attracts the younger set where both guys and gals can take jumps at commercial sites throughout the world, from Korea and Japan to Bali, South Africa and Australia. The US, Canada and the UK have well-developed jump locations, but remember, it is a seasonal activity. Here is a brief look at some highlight jump locations.

North America

Blue Thunder Bungee–Alberta, Canada

Great Canadian Sheer Cliff Jump–Wakefield, Quebec Canada (200 ft)

Angel National Forest–Los Angeles, California

Over-the-Edge Bungee–Twin Falls, Idaho–Perrine Bridge over the Snake River (487 ft)

Central America

Colorado River Bridge–Costa Rica, above the tropical forest (265 ft)

Europe

Fairlop Waters–London

Bungee Jumping Center–Ticino, Switzerland –Verzasca Dam (highest in the world 722 ft)

Africa

African Extreme - Zimbabwe/Zambia border Victoria Falls Bridge (341 ft)

Asia

Ultimate Bungy - Nepal–tropical gorge in the Himalayas along the Tibetan border (500 ft)

Pacific

Bungy Bullet - Sunshine Coast Queensland, Australia–slingshot 164 ft into the air

AJ Hackett–Queenstown, NZ–the world's first bungee jump. Kawarau Bridge (141 ft)

Air Adventures: Ballooning, Glider Rides, Tandem Paragliding

Up, up and away ... my beautiful balloon
The world's a nicer place in my beautiful balloon.

−5th Dimension

Ballooning—This light adventure has so much to offer, ballooning gently frees you from earth's gravity. One of the major events occurs in September when balloon enthusiasts head for the Albuquerque Balloon Fiesta, a great pow-wow of balloonists who come together under the warm New Mexico sun. Early in the morning, as the dawn broke on my first visit there as a travel writer, I walked through rows and rows of inflating balloons. They were all controlled by starters wearing black- and white-striped jerseys resembling football referee uniforms.

Once the dawn patrol gave the "good to go," referees released balloons row by row, and a mass ascension of 500 filled the air with a kaleidoscope of colors. My first impression was the peaceful feeling of flight being only occasionally interrupted by blasts of gas. My second impression was the discovery that, looking straight down, there is absolutely nothing under the passenger basket. Final observation—be sure to secure the strap on your camera—no recovery is possible. The sky is reserved only for balloonists and soaring birds, and the ride is a peaceful voyage in meditation. The vista is so heavenly you feel as if you can reach out and touch the face of God. Visit: www.hotairballoon.com

Glider Rides — Fly like a bird and enjoy the thrill of silent flight! What's needed for a glider ride? Mountains for updraft are important, good weather and then a pilot and his tow-plane, and you and your pilot in the glider. I've enjoyed this agile soaring experience in Scottsdale, Arizona and Durango, Colorado. Both locations have dependable lift, but Durango has the bonus of the San Juan Mountains, providing a scenic backdrop. Attach the rope and off you go. Before the tow-plane lifts off the runway, the lighter glider is already airborne. Once we reached proper altitude, my pilot released the rope and we floated over mountain peaks and deep valleys and winding rivers. The yellow aspen of September added a brilliant spectrum of color. After some flight-seeing, my pilot asked if some acrobatics were in order. I readily gave the thumbs-up, so he dipped the wings right and left, then pulled the nose up for a weightless stall. We circled for approach and landed back at the glider port. Landing is a strange experience of the glider flight — the singular wheel sits less than a foot off of the ground; as we landed I pictured my rear scraping the runway. Those who enjoy air activities should hunt down the nearest glider airport and sign up for this light adventure. Modest cost, safe, thrilling and memorable.

For more information on gliders and sail plane rides, visit the national directory website: www.glidersailplanerides.com

Tandem Paragliding — Want to go airborne? You need not enlist with the 101st Screaming Eagles — we'll leave that to the Army. But you can take lessons and skydive from a plane or float in a

very quiet glider. This young sport has developed primarily in the western states and the California coast. My experience began near the Grand Teton. After watching paragliders circle my resort in Teton Village, I signed up and took the aerial tram towards the top of the Grand Teton near Jackson Hole, Wyoming. The event takes little training, because you are strapped to a guide and you both run in tandem down the hill. Just short of a 4,000-foot cliff, the updraft pulls both of you into the sky for a breathtaking ride, slowly circling the valley below. The view of the Grand Teton seems never-ending, but my unceremonious landing put us tumbling ass-over-tea kettle onto the prairie. Nothing like the fresh scent of sage brush lodged in your nose.

Water Adventures: Lakes, Rafting, Snorkeling, Scuba

Water activities allow you to break away from the routine of life, so turn off that precious plasma TV and tighten the straps on your life preserver. Fortunately, state and national parks have your water needs in mind. They protect lakes, rivers and bays for the adventure seeker. If you're in New England, boat or stroll the shores of scenic Lake George, New York–maybe during fall foliage. Crater Lake National Park in Oregon provides summer cruises across the sapphire blue crater and around little Wizard Island. Not far away, jet boat excursions depart daily on the olive green Rogue River. You are guaranteed a scenic ride with safe but exhilarating donut spins and plenty of spray to keep you cool.

Every state in the union has public lakes that have been developed for water adventures. The most well-known are the five Great Lakes, which flow from the upper Midwest to the Atlantic. These lakes represent 20 percent of the world's fresh water and include 35,000 islands. Of interest to vacation travelers, the Straits of Lake Mackinac connect Lake Michigan to Lake Huron. Here you can find Mackinac Island and the famous balcony at the Grand Hotel. No cars are allowed on the island, lending a charming atmosphere and a wonderful venue for lake activities. The Niagara River flows from Lake Erie to Lake Ontario and creates one of the three greatest waterfalls in the world. I've listed some of the scenic recreational lakes in the United States that are popular with tourists. As with all lists, I cannot include every recreational lake; nevertheless, this is a good sampling.

Recreational Lakes in the United States

State	Lake	State	Lake
AR	Beaver Lake & Lake Ouachita	KY	Kentucky Lakes & Lake Barkley
AZ/NV	Lake Mead		
AZ/UT	Lake Powell	**State**	**Lake**
CA	Lake Shasta	LA	Lake Pontchartrain
CA/NV	Lake Tahoe	ME	Moosehead Lake & Sebago Lake
GA	Lake Sidney Lanier		
ID	Lake Coeur D'Alene	MI	Lake Charlevoix, Houghton & Torch
IL	Carlyle Lake	MN	Mille Lacs (much of state is recreational lakes)
IN	Monroe Lake		

State	Lake	State	Lake
MN/ON	Rainy Lake	OK	Lake O' the Cherokees & Eufaula Lake
MO	Lake of the Ozarks & Table Rock Lake	SC	Lake Marion & Lake Murray
MT	Flathead & Fort Peck Lake NC Lake Norman	SD	Lake Oahe
ND	Lake Sakakawea	TX	Lake Meredith & Lake Travis
NH	Lake Winnipesaukee	TX	Grapevine Lake
NY	The Finger Lakes, Lake George & Oneida	WA	Lake Chelan & Lake Roosevelt
NY/VT	Lake Champlain	WI	Lake Winnebago
		WY	Flaming Gorge Reservoir & Yellowstone

Special thanks to Bob Hoelscher for his review of and additions to this list.

Rafting — Let's kick it up a notch with river rafting. This is an adventure activity most people can do, and if training is needed, it lasts only a short time before the trip begins. In the world of rafting, the rivers are rated using a numerical system according to the difficulty of the river, from Class I (easiest) to Class VI. Also, the river level affects the overall rafting experience. Best of all, in-season rafting can be enjoyed in most states, Canada and world-wide rafting areas.

In the first year of my travel agency, I invited my employees on a Western dude ranch adventure, highlighted by a full day of Class III Colorado River rafting. It was a not-to-be-forgotten adventure, as we flipped both rafts on a particularly nasty rapid. Forever imbedded in my mind is the image of my employees bobbing down the Colorado River like loose tree limbs. Next year, I opted for a laid-back beach resort with culinary classes.

Scenic Rafting

Here is a very brief list of scenic rafting or you can refer to www.RaftingAmerica.com:

North America
Canada British Columbia
Golden BC–Kicking Horse River
Lytton BC–Fraser River

Western United States
Alaska
Arizona–Colorado River through the Grand Canyon, allowing for rarely seen side canyons and waterfalls
Colorado–near ski resorts, including Aspen, Vail, Breckenridge, and Steamboat Springs, plus Royal Gorge, Estes Park, Durango, Black Canyon of the Gunnison National Park, Colorado Springs
Idaho–Salmon River
Montana–Flathead River near Glacier National Park
New Mexico–Rio Grande near Taos
Oregon–Rogue River near Grant's Pass
Utah–Near Arches National Park and Moah
Wyoming–Jackson Hole and Grand Teton, half day Snake River

Eastern United States
Connecticut–Housatonic River
Maine–Kennebec River
Massachusetts–Deerfield River
North Carolina–Nantahala River
North Carolina/Georgia–Chattooga River
Pennsylvania–Lehigh River
Pennsylvania/New York–Delaware River

Eastern United States (Cont.)
West Virginia–Gauley River
Vermont–West River

Mexico

Central America
Costa Rica

South America
Ecuador
Chile
Brazil
Argentina

Europe
Slovenia
Croatia

Africa
Zimbabwe/Zambia–Zambezi River

Middle East
Turkey

Asia
Nepal
India–Ganges River
Malaysia
Japan

Pacific
Indonesia/Bali
Australia

Snorkeling—As I stood at the edge of the beach, toes sunk in sugar-like sand, waves gently lapping, shore birds prancing across the foam and with a view out to eternity, I asked myself what could possibly be more alluring. Well, just under the waves, a wonderful subterranean land awaits, a silent world filled to the hilt with multicolored schools of fish, coral of every shape and size, clams, crabs and crayfish. You say you've never put on the mask tube and fins? Not a problem. It's a treat with few prerequisites. Number one—can you swim? Number two—do you enjoy the water? Number three—will you invest in sunblock?

If you're a fan of snorkeling and love to float across the water viewing the underwater creations, you're not alone. It's an easy adventure popular with many vacationers. I take every opportunity to enter the technicolor world of snorkeling. I recall looking down on spiny lobsters crawling across the sea floor in Martinique, swimming between stingrays and Blacktip sharks in Moorea, Tahiti, and giving way to agile green turtles off the Island of Isabela, Galapagos. The view through my mask captivated me for hours. I asked my wife what she recalled about snorkeling at Xel-Ha Mexican Riviera. After a poignant pause, she mentioned the sunburn across her back and my constant yelling "clear your mask." Not absolutely everyone gets a snorkeling high.

SCUBA (Self Contained Underwater Breathing Apparatus)– Scuba is the next step up from snorkeling; people say one leads to the other. Remember, in your youth, the rumor that dancing leads to…love making? And pot leads to…heroin? Maybe those were spoofs, but snorkeling has been proven to pull innocent people toward scuba certification classes. Once they earn their "C" card, there is no hope; the addiction to strap on the tanks and go deep is uncontrollable. There is a difference. Snorkeling is a surface view; with scuba you plunge deep, generally down a reef or wall into a mystical place where bigger is better. Divers hope to find super-sized fish, sharks, eel and coral formations. Sightings of mermaids are as yet unconfirmed.

My first scuba dive came as a surprise during a daylong catamaran excursion to the Great Barrier Reef. The large passenger hydrofoil seemed to float on the waves as we sped toward our underwater destination; the trip out takes an hour and a half from Douglas, Australia, to the world's largest reef. Once out of port, the tour director announced that a resort scuba dive was available at a modest cost. I had some reservations about going down into the ocean, because I had never had the opportunity to scuba. On board, a class taught basic dive technique; the 30-foot dive was accompanied by an instructor. Quick as a flash, my teenage boys groveled and begged to let them strap on the tanks. "Sure," I said, "sure, great learning adventure — go for it." This might not have been a white-knuckle experience, but there was a degree of risk. My wife took it for granted that I was joining in the dive, and when I balked, she insisted I go down to help take care of the boys. "Who's caring for whom?" I responded, "I've never dived before … my deepest plunge was a flop off the high dive at a public swimming pool."

This, then, became an epic trip. The instructor, who had a faint resemblance to Crocodile Dundee, went through the basics. Once we entered the water, I observed a vast display of coral passing by my mask as we sank to the bottom. Escorting our group were two huge green fish that were probably familiar with divers and looking for handouts of food. They were so large I fed them more from fear than curiosity. Standing on the ocean floor, my boys and I had a ringside seat to the wonders of the sea. The clear azure water was bountiful with schools of fish of every possible shape and size. The memorable, 30-minute experience was a triumph over ignorance — after, of course, I fought off the forces of fear. So in retrospect, the dive was an introduction into a realm of unique beauty. I have a suggestion for anyone who yearns for adventure. Get your "C" card and dive into paradise.

Popular Dive Sites Around the World

North America
  Florida Keys
  Santa Catalina Island, CA
  Florida Springs (freshwater)
Caribbean
  Cayman Island
  Belize (Blue Hole)
  Bonaire
  Dominica
  Bahamas
  Cuba
  British Virgin Islands
  St. Lucia
  Turks & Caicos
Central America
  Honduras
  Mexico
South America
  Fernanco de Noronha
  Venezuela
Europe
  Ireland (wreck Dive)
  Cyprus
  Isle of Man
  Malta
  Greece
  Spain
Africa
  Egypt
  South Africa

Africa (Cont.)
  Sudan
  Tanzania
  Mozambique
Middle East
  Jordan
  Israel
Indian Ocean
  Maldives
  Sri Lanka
  Mauritius
  Seychelles
Asia
  Malaysia
  Thailand
  Philippines
  Indonesia
  Taiwan
Pacific Ocean
  Australia (Great Barrier Reef)
  Palau
  Hawaii
  Vanuatu
  Solomon
  Galapagos
  Fiji
  New Zealand
  Truk (wreck dive)
  Tahiti
  Papa New Guinea

Special Interests - Sports Events, Festivals and Fairs

The show is not the show, but they that go.
–Emily Dickinson

Do you have friends, as I do, who love special interest travel, people who fly or drive almost anywhere just to be a part of their special event? Maybe you're that passionate person, maybe you're a theater patron who makes a yearly trip for live performances on Broadway or in Toronto or London. Possibly you're a food and wine connoisseur always on the lookout for tours that feature renowned chefs or exotic dishes with regional wines of France; then très bien. The welcome sign is always out at our travel agency for people on a mission to reach their goals or learn a bit more about their passions. Let's start with collectors—what kind? All kinds…collectors of beer cans, gadgets, baseball cards, memorabilia, plates and porcelain, automobiles, books on everything from horses to birds of the world. I even know someone who collects miniature rhinoceroses; how bizarre (I now have 185).

Pilgrimages—One of the foremost pursuits of special interest travel is religious pilgrimages. This is huge; there are dedicated agencies of the travel industry that serve only pilgrims and their special needs. I remember my wife, Terrie, and I stood in the main square of Santiago de Compostela, Spain, as European pilgrims entered this main plaza. Some may have hiked for weeks to reach the Romanesque cathedral that protects the re-

mains of St. James. The pilgrims attach a seashell to their backpack, which signifies that they are on a holy journey. In another part of the world—Saudi Arabia—the faithful are called for a Hajj, a trip of faith to the holy city of Mecca. Thousands of visitors arrive daily in Jeddah during the month-long Hajj—the volume is so great that there is a dedicated terminal at the airport. From Jerusalem to Canterbury to Mexico City, pilgrims from around the world travel to renew their faith.

Sports Events

This nation loves sports events, in many cases the creation of the sport originated in America. Baseball, football and basketball are homegrown sports that call loyal fans, to travel around the country to support their team or go to major events. The World Series, Super Bowl, Stanley Cup, NBA Finals, and Indianapolis 500 are high-ticket items—not for the thrifty sportsman; but college and pro games are affordable for most fans. A truly memorable sports event is the Hall of Fame ceremonies at Cooperstown in upstate New York. Fans can sit on the lawn for the speeches and then stroll the quaint sidewalks, collecting autographs from Hall of Famers, or enjoy lake activities.

Soccer — Because soccer requires only a flat field, goals, and the ball, the game is widely played around the world and provides endless entertainment to both players and spectators. An avid sports fan can live and breathe every game from opening day through the playoffs. Talk to an Englishman concerning world peace and you get a calm, unemotional response; mention the Manchester United soccer team and he turns into a frothing werewolf. Soccer or "football" rules worldwide — I always suggest taking in a game when you're overseas. You can observe at close hand the natives in their most primeval setting — the soccer game. For a real eye-opener, try a Sunday game at Maracanã Stadium in Rio de Janeiro, Brazil. As neutral fans, we were placed in a protected area between the rival fans of Botafogo and Flamingo. The flags waved and the fans chanted while 30-foot fences prevented mortal combat.

NASCAR — In the United States, NASCAR draws millions to famous tracks such as Daytona, Talladega and Bristol. Throughout the years, the number of fans attending NASCAR continues to thrive. The schedule begins with the Daytona 500 and continues for most of the year at large and small speedways alike. You might find yourself enjoying a race in Las Vegas, Indianapolis, Phoenix or Charlotte, but for this sport, smaller towns and cities can be just as important and enjoyable. Along with the bigger cities, you may enjoy races in Martinsville, VA; Dover, DE; Pocono, PA; or Darlington, SC.

Go to any NASCAR race and be assured that there is no shortage of trucks and vans, barbecue and beer. The races are always held on the weekends unless postponed by rain; it's an American social event like no other. Stock cars accelerate around the racetrack at dizzying speeds, pit stops are measured in seconds, and the lead might change on the skill of one pit crew over another. In this sport, sponsors are the core, and every car displays multiple corporate logos and aligns with car manufacturers. Drivers have their own fans to cheer them on, and loyalty is over the top. Drivers are idolized, and their names have marquee value for products and sponsorship. On the track, Dale Earnhardt Jr. might go bumper to bumper with Jeff Gordon. Nicknames are well-known by loyal fans — particularly if "Jr." is up against the "Rainbow Warrior."

While many people go only for the race itself (like going to a football or baseball game), many die-hard fans make it a family vacation for the whole weekend. They enjoy seeing the cars qualify (each one going around the track individually to set a lap speed that is used to determine the starting positions), which usually happens on either Friday or Saturday, and they also attend the supporting race, on Saturday, which is like AAA baseball, except that many of the top-tier drivers also drive in that series (right now it's called the Nationwide series, named for its sponsor), some to get a feel for the track, some out of loyalty to sponsors who backed them before they made it big, and some just because they love to drive in two races. The top NASCAR series is called Sprint Cup, and those races are mostly held on Sunday afternoon, although with NASCAR's stronger TV ratings some are run on Saturday night.

NASCAR traces its roots to bootleggers in the South who would modify their cars to outrun the law. Drivers prided themselves in developing super fast cars and would race each other for fun on the beaches of Daytona. In 1949, the sport was legitimized and fans started lining up at entrance gates for a 400 or 500 mile race filled with skilled driving, drafting and sometimes pile-ups. If you're a fan and have attended the race tracks, you know there is no shortage of sound and racing excitement. Here are the major race tracks throughout the United States. Because of the early popularity in the Carolinas, many of the important tracks are in the South.

South	East	Midwest	West
Talladega, AL	Dover, DE	Brooklyn, MI	Ft. Worth, TX
Richmond, VA	Long Pond (Pocono), PA	Joliet, IL	Phoenix, AZ
Darlington, SC	Loudon, NH	Indianapolis, IN	Las Vegas, NV
Charlotte, NC	Watkins Glen, NY		Sonoma, CA
Daytona Beach, FL			Fontana, CA
Bristol, TN			
Atlanta, GA			
Martinsville, VA			
Miami, FL			

Special thanks to Brendan Bowers and Brooks E. Bowers for their review of this list.

Horse Racing – The sport of kings gives patrons the double value of gambling and the thrill of the race. A day at the track can serve varied pleasures. First, it may be a social event with the opportunity for ladies to sport their chic outfits as they mingle with the who's-who. Who could forget Eliza Doolittle in "My Fair Lady" with her fashionable ensemble, parasol and champagne? The grand tradition of the Kentucky Derby heralds the beginning of the Triple Crown season. Ladies display fanciful hats - many in full plumage, as the rich and very rich enter their horses in expectation of winning "the run for the roses." Fans are known to get teary-eyed as the band plays the traditional "My Old Kentucky Home," and excitement then builds as the

horses enter the gate. First there's a hush and a pause, then they're off.

The Preakness at Pimlico in Baltimore and the Belmont Stakes at Belmont Park in Elmont, N.Y., complete the Triple Crown, but racing goes on year-round. The parimutuel gamblers support the cost and operation of the tracks. If you really like to watch the ponies run, try a little overseas action—you can find horse tracks in many parts of the world. In Argentina, the whole country is wrapped up in horse racing and horse breeding. The historic Jockey Club in Buenos Aires is a show place for the city. In Great Britain, the Royal Ascot is one of the world's famous races. Also, racing in France and Spain has been a tradition for many, many years. In Asia, Singapore, Malaysia and Japan have a long history of horse racing, and the Royal Hong Kong Jockey Club began horse racing in 1884. Thoroughbred horse racing started originally with chariot races in Rome, but today this equestrian sport is popular from Dover to Dubai. Here is a list of some major horse race tracks in the United States:

Belmont Park, Elmont, New York—on Long Island (1905)
Churchill Downs, Louisville, Kentucky (1875)
Fairmount Park Racetrack, Collinsville, Illinois (1925)
Hialeah Park Race Track, Hialeah, Florida (1925)
Keeneland Race Course, Lexington, Kentucky (1936)
Pimlico Race Course, Baltimore, Maryland (1870)
Santa Anita Park, in the San Gabriel Valley, California, near Los Angeles (1934)
Saratoga Race Course, Saratoga Springs, New York (opened in 1863)

Golf — While NASCAR has its thundering noise, golf has just the opposite — patrons standing motionless as the pros putt for PGA Tour money. At Augusta National Golf Club, I watched respectfully as Arnold Palmer finished a practice round one day before the start of the Masters. It was his retirement swan song, and he was flanked by Jack Nicklaus and Tiger Woods. I also admired the grounds that are perfectly groomed.

My friend Ron Cobb lives and breathes the sport of golf. As a former travel editor for the *St. Louis Post-Dispatch*, he has written about courses throughout North America and the British Isles. We have long talks sharing the latest news in golf or debating some golf trivia — he always wins. Once I told him that playing golf in Japan was a very expensive activity and that many Japanese practice their swings in multi-tiered practice cages. With land being at a premium, they almost never get a chance to play in their own country. So when you see Japanese golfers in Hawaii, you know it's their dream to get onto a real golf course. Ron agreed, noting that Japanese golfers have a passion for the game like no other. So I ask myself, who really has the greater passion, Japanese golfers or Ron Cobb?

I can't think of a better person to write this section on the beauty of golf. Ron carries a 10 handicap, which is superseded only by his ability to visualize a course and put it on paper. To get him to write this article has cost me at least four rounds of golf, but payback is so much fun. Please enjoy this in-depth look at golf travel.

The Beauty of Golf
by Ron Cobb

In 25 years of playing golf, I've played hundreds of rounds in my hometown, and all but a handful have faded from memory. So if you ask me for my fondest golf memories, nearly all of them would involve rounds that I played as a traveler. I have vivid memories of playing golf at Pebble Beach in California, at Pinehurst in North Carolina, at El Dorado in Cabo San Lucas, at Ballybunion in Ireland, at Royal Lytham in England, at St. Andrews, Turnberry and Carnoustie in Scotland and at other renowned and scenic golf courses wherever my travels took me.

That's the beauty of golf. A traveler can go virtually anywhere in the world and find a golf course to play. A devoted tennis player can't go to England and play Wimbledon, but a golfer can visit the UK and play St. Andrews. A basketball player can't travel to New York and play Madison Square Garden, but a golfer can go to Long Island and play Bethpage Black, the site of two U.S. Opens. A baseball devotee can't go to Milwaukee and play Miller Park, but a golfer can travel just up the road in Wisconsin and play Whistling Straits, site of two PGA Championships.

Golf and travel accommodate each other in incredible ways. No one knows better than the author of this book, Gig Gwin, that if you're traveling and you get the urge to play golf, you can do it. One of Gig's adventures took him to the south Atlantic island of Tristan da Cunha, and he played golf on a course where cows grazed. He actually putted through the legs of a cow that was standing on the green. That golf course would be at one end of the spectrum and St. Andrews and Pebble Beach at the other, and in between are thousands of golf courses around the world of all pedigrees, open to the traveling golfer.

While it's true that many of the world's most famous golf courses are accessible to visitors, many others aren't. That's especially so in the United States. All but four of the golf clubs that have hosted U.S. Opens are private, and so is the home of the Masters, Augusta National, as well as the highly acclaimed Cypress Point Club, just up the road from Pebble Beach on the Monterey Peninsula.

Still, it's possible for the ambitious golf traveler to play courses on which the game's best have played, including some of the courses on the current PGA Tour schedule. In the United Kingdom, all of the courses that host the British Open on a rotating basis are accessible to visitors. Some are more accommodating than others, while one or two require some effort. But it can be done.

If following in the footsteps of the greats isn't a priority, golf travelers can opt for scenery over tradition and play any of the abundance of courses that sit alongside oceans or in the shadows of mountain ranges — or sometimes up in the mountains themselves.

It would be impossible to list or describe all of the world's great golf courses, but I'll discuss some of the best destinations for golf travelers while hoping that my omissions aren't too egregious.

Ireland & Great Britain

Going overseas to play a true links course in Ireland or Great Britain is an experience that every avid golfer should have. Whether it's Ireland, Northern Ireland, Scotland, England or Wales, there are links courses one after the other along the coastline, all willing to accept foreign visitors.

By definition, a links course is situated on sand-based land that "links" the sea and the fertile land farther inland. Not much good for growing anything but grass, the links land is ideal for only two things: grazing and golf. Links courses are devoid of trees, and they appear to the eye to be wide open, but the challenge comes in the form of numerous bunkers, dunes, gnarly rough and scrubby vegetation that swallows up errant shots. The weather on links courses in the British Isles is sometimes wet and often windy, adding to the challenge.

Although Scotland and, to a lesser extent, England boast the most world-famous courses, the quality of golf is basically as good in Ireland, Northern Ireland and Wales. What separates Scotland and England are the nine courses that make up the British Open rotation: St. Andrews, Muirfield, Royal Troon, Turnberry and Carnoustie in Scotland and Royal Lytham and St. Annes, Royal Birkdale, Royal Liverpool and Royal St. George's in England. Unlike the private, inaccessible American courses that have hosted most of the major championships in the United States, all of these British Open courses accept visiting golfers.

Muirfield, by reputation, is the hardest to get on, but it can be done.

Visitors pay a premium to play on these hallowed courses, but they provide a rare chance to immerse oneself in the history of the game. On a visit to St. Andrews, I played the Old Course and visited the St. Andrews Cathedral to see the gravesites of two of the biggest names in the early history of golf: Old Tom Morris and his son, Young Tom Morris. But my most magical moment occurred one evening at sunset as I stood alongside the 18th green at the Old Course, watching the final golfers of the day finish their rounds. Just behind me, on the road that lines the 18th fairway, was the small, modest Tom Morris Golf Shop. Old Tom Morris, who won four of the first eight British Opens in the middle of the 19th century (Young Tom also won four), was a clubmaker and greenskeeper at the Old Course. I had read that Old Tom lived in one of the buildings alongside the 18th hole.

As I glanced behind me, I noticed an older woman looking out of an open window in the apartment above the Tom Morris Golf Shop. "Is this the house where Old Tom lived?" I asked her." "Yes it is," she said. "I'm his great-great-granddaughter. The shop below is where he worked. This house has stayed in the family all these years."

Travelers often go in search of those "I can't believe I'm here doing this" moments, and this was one of the greatest for me — standing alongside the 18th green at St. Andrews, with the iconic Royal & Ancient clubhouse just a couple hundred feet away, chatting with a relative of Old Tom Morris ... I'm not sure I could have asked for a better British golf experience than that.

Besides the historic (and expensive) British Open venues, there are plenty of other exceptional golf courses throughout Great Britain and Ireland. Two of the best in the world are in Northern Ireland: Royal County Down and Royal Portrush. Wales is stepping up as a golf destination, with scenic links courses such

as Royal Porthcawl, Newport Links and Nefyn & District. The five-star Celtic Manor resort in southeast Wales built the Twenty-Ten Course just to host the 2010 Ryder Cup.

Ireland has renowned courses all along its coastline, from Portmarnock in Dublin to the K Club, the European Club, Mount Juliet, Waterville, Old Head, Tralee, Ballybunion, Doonbeg, Lahinch and Ballyliffin. Most Americans are drawn to Dublin in the east, or to Waterville, Tralee and Ballybunion on the southwest coast. They tend to ignore the northern coast, where the best bargains are. Two courses in County Sligo are among Ireland's best: Enniscrone and County Sligo Golf Club, also known as Rosses Point. County Sligo is one of the most scenic courses I've ever played, with several holes running along the top of a plateau with panoramic views of mountains and sea. In the next county over, Donegal Golf Club, also known as Murvagh, is excellent as well.

One thing to note about golf in Ireland and the UK: Golfers there rarely ride carts (which they call buggies). They believe golf courses are meant to be walked, not ridden, but most clubs make carts available for those who need them. Also, Brits and the Irish aren't as keen on hitting balls before a round as Americans are, so don't be surprised if the club you visit doesn't have a driving range. A final word to the wise: Don't wear your ballcap inside the clubhouse.

Pebble Beach/Monterey Peninsula

If you're an avid golfer and you can afford to make a pilgrimage to mecca, you travel to one of two places: Pebble Beach or St. Andrews. Pebble Beach has gained so much favorable exposure from its televised tournaments, the course has attained bigger-than-life status. Sitting on the shore of Stillwater Cove, with waves from the Pacific Ocean crashing onto rocks just off the fairway, Pebble Beach is golf's Shangri-La.

Open to the public, Pebble Beach hosts golfers from all over the world. They pay a premium — almost $500 to play 18 holes. Many consider it a once-in-a-lifetime experience. When I visited, I first laid eyes on the 18th hole after I parked at the Lodge at Pebble Beach and walked through the lobby and out onto a balcony overlooking one of the most famous finishing holes in golf. A man standing near me, a doctor from Houston, said he felt as if he'd died and gone to heaven. A restaurateur from Indianapolis who played the course told me he had realized a lifetime dream.

Pebble Beach Golf Links is one of several courses on California's Monterey Peninsula, 125 miles south of San Francisco. The Pebble Beach Company encompasses not only Pebble Beach Golf Links but three other golf courses — Spyglass Hill, the Links at Spanish Bay and Del Monte Golf Course. It also is the parent company of the Lodge at Pebble Beach, the Inn at Spanish Bay, Casa Palmero and the Spa at Pebble Beach. Only guests at these pricey resorts are allowed to make tee times at Pebble Beach Golf Links more than a day in advance. Non-resort guests have two options: call and hope a tee time is open the following day (an iffy proposition) or show up at the pro shop (the earlier the better), get your name on a waiting list and hope something opens up that day. Not many years ago, the golf course was booked for months in advance, but 9/11 and then the recession opened things up just a bit.

More than a dozen other public golf courses not associated with Pebble Beach Company are available in the Monterey area, including a quirky municipal course called Pacific Grove Golf Links, a.k.a. "the Poor Man's Pebble Beach." The course's back nine is played along the ocean, with waves crashing against rocks just as they do at Pebble Beach, but the greens fee at Pacific Grove is a bargain at less than $50.

Pinehurst

No other destination in the United States captures the history of golf quite so elegantly as Pinehurst, a resort in the central region of golf-rich North Carolina. Pinehurst's allure lies not just in the quality and quantity of golf that it offers, but also in first-rate amenities, historic hotels and the quaint Village of Pinehurst.

The resort, dating to 1895, offers eight 18-holes courses, named simply No. 1, No. 2 and so on. The one course that golfers yearn most to play is Pinehurst No. 2, designed in 1907 by famed

Scottish architect Donald Ross. He created more than 400 golf courses in North America and made Pinehurst his home base for 48 years. No. 2 has hosted two U.S. Opens, most famously in 1999 when Payne Stewart won by sinking the decisive putt on the 18th hole in the final round.

When I played No. 2, I was plenty excited about being there as I warmed up before the round. Then something happened that told me this would be a magical day. Bells from a tiny church just across the road began sounding out "America the Beautiful," and some four hours later, as my group was moving up the 18th fairway, the church played an encore: "The Battle Hymn of the Republic."

The goose bumps are free, but the golf is rather pricey, especially on No. 2. Yet Pinehurst is one of those "bucket list" kind of places that need to be experienced regardless of the cost. Golfers who play No. 2 may be surprised—even disappointed—at its simplicity and relatively small number of hazards. Its most memorable characteristics are its deep swales and difficult, crowned greens. I recall my golf partner becoming frustrated as the shots, and even putts, rolled off the slick greens, but he got over it.

Pinehurst No. 2's history and stature, not its design, are its most abiding features. The entirety of the golf experience attracts golfers to Pinehurst.

Bandon Dunes

The closest thing the United States has to the kind of links golf found in the British Isles is Bandon Dunes, a relatively new resort along the southwest coast of Oregon. The resort consists of four golf courses: Bandon Dunes, Pacific Dunes, Bandon Trails and its newest, Old Macdonald, opened in 2010. All but Bandon Trails overlook the Pacific Ocean.

As exceptional as it is, Bandon Dunes may not be for everyone. Everyone must walk the golf course, with caddies optional. Carts are allowed only for those who can produce a doctor's note verifying a permanent disability. "Golf as it was meant to be" is the motto at Bandon Dunes.

The owner, Mike Keiser, co-founder of a greeting card company, veered off into the golf course business, saying he was interested not in commercial golf but dream golf. Bandon Dunes, opened in 1999, was his second venture.

Myrtle Beach

For sheer quantity of golf, nothing can match Myrtle Beach, S.C. This city on the Atlantic Coast is a mecca for buddy golf trips, what with some 102 golf courses in a three-county area, plus the beach, more than 1,000 restaurants and a lively nightlife of music theaters, show palaces and, ahem, gentlemen's clubs.

A half-century ago, Myrtle Beach had only two golf courses. By 1999 there were 100, and a peak of 120 was reached in the early 2000s. The came the downturn in the economy and in the golf industry, and some 20 courses met their demise. The current total of 102 includes only a handful of private courses. The rest are public, making Myrtle Beach truly a golf mecca.

Stay-and-play packages are the way to go when planning a visit to Myrtle Beach, and offseason deals can be very inviting. Visitors often package a deluxe course with others more moderate. Deluxe courses include the Dunes Golf & Beach Club,

Caledonia Golf & Fish Club, Tidewater Golf Club & Plantation, Grande Dunes, and Barefoot Resort & Golf. Barefoot offers four courses designed by Pete Dye, Greg Norman, Davis Love III and Tom Fazio.

Hilton Head/Kiawah Island

Hilton Head Island and Kiawah Island in South Carolina know they can't compete with Myrtle Beach in terms of number of golf courses, but they like to think they offer equal or better quality. These two islands offer a resort feel that may not suit golfers on a budget. The star attraction of Hilton Head is Harbour Town Golf Links, host of a PGA Tour event and known for its light-house on the Atlantic coast. Kiawah's biggest claim to fame is the Ocean Course at Kiawah Island Golf Resort, site of the 1991 "War by the Shore" Ryder Cup and future site of the 2012 PGA Championship.

Reno/Tahoe

Reno/Tahoe is a golf destination that is sometimes overlooked but has everything the golf traveler could want except an ocean. The area offers 40 public-accessible golf courses within about an hour's drive of Reno, stretching south to Carson City, southwest to Lake Tahoe, and west and northwest into Truckee and Grayeagle in California. Part of what makes this an ex-ceptional golf destination is the variety. On one visit, a golfer can play a high desert course one day and a mountain course among ponderosa pines the next. With a wide assortment of quality golf courses, the best include Edgewood Tahoe (a picturesque course along the edge of the lake), Genoa Lakes, Old Greenwood, Coyote Moon and Whitehawk Ranch. At night, casinos and big-name entertainment are available in Reno and south Lake Tahoe.

Phoenix/Scottsdale

While golf in most of the country slows to a trickle in the winter, just the opposite occurs in Arizona. Scottsdale boasts an abundance of first-rate courses, including TPC Scottsdale, home of the annual tournament on the PGA Tour. Troon North is another of Scottsdale's high-end courses, but there are plenty of others to consider. The greater Phoenix area encompasses some 200 golf courses, and there is no shortage of options farther south around Tucson. Golf can be pricey in Arizona in the peak season of January through April, but more reasonable rates can be found at other times of the year.

Las Vegas

Golf in Las Vegas can be as opulent as you want it to be, starting with Shadow Creek, which will send a private limousine to your hotel to take you to the golf course, and Royal Links Golf Club, which simulates famous holes from British Open courses and, instead of regular caddies, offers ParMates, attractive young women who perform caddie duties as well as providing companionship.

Visitors can play golf right on the Strip at Bali Hai Golf Club in the shadow of Mandalay Bay, or they can venture away from the center of town to courses in the mountains and desert. Las Vegas offers budget courses as well as high end, but, regardless, golfers rarely visit just for the golf, not with so much entertainment available on the Strip.

Golfers who want a bit less congestion can travel 80 miles up I-15 to Mesquite, Nevada, or they can continue 40 miles past

Mesquite to St. George, Utah. Both provide exceptional golf courses in desert and mountain settings.

Michigan

This is a popular golf destination in summer because of the long days, temperate climate and vast number of golf courses. Michigan boasts of having the most public courses of any state in the nation—more than 700. The season is relatively short, but during those few months of accommodating weather, the state goes golf crazy. Michigan pops up frequently on lists of America's best public courses, including Arcadia Bluffs, Black Lake, Eagle Eye, Bay Harbor, St. Ives Resort, Forest Dunes and Shepherd's Hollow.

Southern Mississippi

When winter shows signs of ebbing, southern Mississippi enjoys an influx of golfers from colder climates. The locals generally consider late February and March too chilly for golf, but parking lots of southern Mississippi golf courses will be full of cars bearing license plates from Wisconsin, Iowa and Missouri.

High-quality golf at reasonable prices are part of the attraction, particularly at Canebrake and Timberton in Hattiesburg. High-end courses include the Grand Bear in Saucier and Fallen Oak at the Beau Rivage Resort & Casino in Biloxi.

Florida

Golfers rarely need a GPS to find a golf course in Florida. Just drive a few blocks and you'll find one. Some of the best are private, such as Seminole Golf Club in North Palm Beach. The cream of the crop among public-access courses is TPC at Sawgrass in Ponte Vedra Beach, where the Stadium Course is host to The Players Championship every spring. Golfers come from far and wide to try their luck at the par-3 17th hole, the famous island green that sometimes leaves even the pros muttering to themselves.

Heading south, Arnold Palmer's Bay Hill Club in Orlando is highly rated and also home to a PGA Tour event every spring. In south Florida, premium courses include PGA National Resort & Spa in Palm Beach Gardens, and the Blue Monster course at the Doral Resort in Miami.

Courses whose profiles aren't as high but are held in equally high regard include the Copperhead Course at Innisbrook Resort in Palm Harbor, the Ocean Course at Ginn Hammock Beach Resort in Palm Coast, and the Pine Barrens Course at World Woods in Brooksville.

Hawaii

The premium courses in the Hawaiian islands include The Prince Course at the Princeville Resort on Kauai, the Plantation Course at Kapalua Resort on Maui, the Challenge at Manele on Lanai, Poipu Bay on Kauai, and Mauna Kea on the Big Island. But can you really go wrong with any golf in Hawaii?

Southern California

So many of the best courses in Los Angeles and San Diego are private, those cities don't really come to mind when you think of golf destinations. Exceptions would be Torrey Pines, owned and operated by the city of San Diego, and Trump National Golf Club, 30 minutes south of LA. Situated on cliffs overlooking the Pacific Ocean, Torrey Pines offers a similar kind of allure as Pebble Beach. The municipal facility consists of two 18-hole courses — the North and the South. In addition to hosting a PGA Tour event every year, Torrey Pines was the site of the 2008 U.S. Open, won by a hobbling Tiger Woods in a playoff over Rocco Mediate.

Trump National is one of 10 courses that have been opened or are being developed by Donald J. Trump, including one in Puerto Rico and another in Scotland. As you might imagine, the Trump courses are top of the line, both in price and quality.

About 100 miles east of LA, Palm Springs offers upscale golf on exceptional courses in majestic surroundings. When you talk about Palm Springs golf, you're really talking about the cluster of cities in the Coachella Valley, including Palm Springs, Palm Desert, Indio, Indian Wells, La Quinta and Rancho Mirage. Most of Palm Springs' courses are private, but close to 50 others are public-accessible. PGA West and La Quinta have long been the standard bearers, but some of the newer resorts are gaining popularity, such as SilverRock, now home of the Bob Hope Classic, and Indian Wells and Desert Willow. PGA West consists of three courses, including the TPC Stadium Course, the original home of the Skins Game. The La Quinta Resort has the highly rated Mountain Course plus the Dunes Course.

Caribbean & Bahamas

Typically, the attraction of island golf is the scenery rather than the golf course itself. With fresh water being at a premium, island golf courses often aren't as green and manicured as top courses in the United States. But that's not to say there aren't first-rate, even famous, golf courses in the Caribbean.

The Dominican Republic has become a top golf destination. Perhaps the most famous course in the Caribbean is Teeth of the Dog at Casa de Campo resort, where architect Pete Dye set the standard for island courses by carving out seven holes along the ocean. More recently, Punta Cana Resort & Club and

Jack Nicklaus' Cap Cana Resort and Club have upped the ante, pushing Punta Cana to the top of Caribbean golf destinations.

On Jamaica, Half Moon sits at the top of the list of golf courses, along with Tryall. Mahogany Run, the only golf course on St. Thomas in the U.S. Virgin Islands, has long been a favorite.

Donald Trump's golf empire has expanded to Puerto Rico with two courses at Trump International Golf Club. Other highly rated courses in Puerto Rico include the Palm Course at Palmas de Mar Country Club, and Bahia Beach Resort and Golf Club.

The Bahamas offers top-notch golf at the Abaco Club on Winding Bay, Radisson Cable Beach and Golf Resort in Nassau, and the Blue Shark Golf Club, also in Nassau.

Canada

Despite its short season, Canada offers golf in some of the most breathtaking settings you can imagine. Canadians, often adept at swinging a hockey stick, make the transition easily and eagerly to golf. Golf is found all across the country, from Prince Edward Island in the east to British Columbia in the west. Golf in mountain settings is found north of Montreal in French-speaking Quebec, while the Rockies provide stunning backdrops for golfers in British Columbia and Alberta, especially in the Banff and Lake Louise areas.

Robert Trent Jones Golf Trail

The Robert Trent Jones Golf Trail stretches for more than 100 miles and consists of 26 public courses at 11 sites throughout Alabama. Named after the legendary architect who designed most of the courses, the trail might just as well have been called the Dr. David Bronner Golf Trail. It was Bronner who, in the late 1980s, conceived the idea for the trail for the purpose of increasing tourism in Alabama, attracting retirees and strengthening the state's pension fund. Bronner was CEO of the Retirement Systems of Alabama.

The original trail consisted of eight courses and has since added three. Grand National in Opelika, Capitol Hill in Prattville, Ross Bridge in Hoover and Magnolia Grove in Mobile are the most highly rated, but all are quality golf courses. The success of the RTJ Golf Trail spawned numerous other golf trails across the country. Just to name a few: the Tennessee Golf Trail, the Magnolia Golf Trail in Mississippi, the Red Rock Golf Trail in Utah, the Natural State Golf Trail in Arkansas and the Vancouver Island Golf Trail.

Cabo San Lucas

Cabo San Lucas doesn't have an abundance of golf courses, but those it has are exceptional. Think of a premium course in Scottsdale and then transplant it to the southern tip of Baja California. Suddenly you're playing a desert course at the edge of the Sea of Cortez.

Whether it's Cabo del Sol, Cabo Real or Palmilla, you can count on golf in a picture-perfect setting. Expect to pay $200 and up for the experience. While you're there, remember that Cabo offers some of the best sportfishing in the world.

Top 25 Golf Courses in America (private and public)—From Golf Digest

1. Augusta National, Augusta, GA
2. Pine Valley, Pine Valley, NY
3. Shinnecock Hills, Southampton, NY
4. Cypress Point, Pebble Beach, CA
5. Oakmont, Oakmont, PA
6. Pebble Beach Golf Links, Pebble Beach, CA
7. Merion, Ardmore, PA
8. Winged Foot, Mamaroneck, NY
9. Fishers Island, Fishers Island, NY
10. Seminole, Juno Beach, FL
11. Oak Hill, Rochester, NY
12. Chicago Golf Club, Wheaton, IL
13. Sand Hills, Mullen, NE
14. Pacific Dunes, Bandon, OR
15. National Golf Links of America, Southampton, NY
16. Crystal Downs, Frankfort, MI
17. Wade Hampton, Cashiers, NC
18. The Country Club, Brookline, MA
19. Muirfield Village, Dublin, OH
20. Medinah Country Club, Medinah, IL
21. Prairie Dunes, Hutchinson, KS
22. Whistling Straits, Straits Course, Haven, WI
23. Oakland Hills, Bloomfield Hills, MI
24. Victoria National, Newburgh, IN
25. The Ocean Course, Kiawah Island, SC

Top 50 Public Courses in America–From Golf Digest

1. Pebble Beach, Pebble Beach, CA
2. Pacific Dunes, Bandon, OR
3. Whistling Straits, Haven, WI
4. The Ocean Course, Kiawah Isl., SC
5. Bethpage Black, Farmingdale, NY
6. Pinehurst No. 2, Pinehurst, NC
7. Bandon Dunes, Bandon, OR
8. Shadow Creek, N. Las Vegas, NV
9. TPC Sawgrass, Ponte Vedra Beach, FL
10. Arcadia Bluffs, Arcadia, MI
11. Spyglass Hill, Pebble Beach, CA
12. The Prince Course, Princeville, Kauai, HI
13. Harbour Town, Hilton Head Island, SC
14. Bandon Trails, Bandon, OR
15. Tullymore, Stanwood, MI
16. Blackwolf Run, River Course, Kohler, WI
17. Karsten Creek, Stillwater, OK
18. Forest Dunes, Roscommon, MI
19. Fallen Oak, Saucier, MS
20. The Quarry at Giants Ridge, Biwabik, MN
21. Wolf Creek, Mesquite, NV
22. May River at Palmetto Bluff, Bluffton, SC
23. The Broadmoor, East Course, Colorado Springs, CO
24. The Homestead, Cascade Course, Hot Springs, WV
25. Kapalua, Plantation Course, Maui, HI
26. Mauna Kea, Kohala Coast, HI
27. Golf Club at Redlands Mesa, Grand Junction, CO
28. Osprey Meadows at Tamarack Resort, Donnelly, ID
29. Pasatiempo, Santa Cruz, CA
30. Whistling Straits, Irish Course, Haven, WI
31. Sea Island, Seaside Course, St. Simons Island, GA
32. Golden Horseshoe, Williamsburg, VA
33. The Heritage Club, Pawleys Island, SC
34. Black Lake, Onaway, MI
35. The Challenge at Manele, Lanai, HI
36. The Harvester, Rhodes, IA
37. Chambers Bay, University Place, WA
38. The Dunes, Myrtle Beach, SC
39. Golf Club at Cuscowilla, Eatonton, GA
40. The Classic at Madden's Resort, Brainerd, MN
41. Tidewater, North Myrtle Beach, SC
42. Shepherd's Hollow, Clarkston, MI
43. Paa-Ko Ridge, Sandia Park, NM
44. Ocean Course at Ginn Hammock Resort, Palm Coast, FL
45. Cog Hill, Lemond, IL
46. World Woods, Pine Barren Course, Brooksville, FL
47. Eagle Eye, East Lansing, MI
48. Kiawah Island Resort, Turtle Point Course, Kiawah Island, SC
49. Cascata, Boulder City, NV
50. Barton Creek, Austin, TX

Rodeos

Courage is being scared to death but saddling up anyway.
–John Wayne

The rodeo is a creation of the western United States and western Canada. It offers the spectator a unique sporting event guaranteed to provide action and entertainment. Cheyenne, Wyoming held its first rodeo in 1898, followed by one in Calgary, Alberta, Canada. Today, these two rodeos are still very popular, and seats are hard to come by for the Cheyenne Frontier Days or the Calgary Stampede. The sport of bull riding, bronco busting, roping, along with wild horse riding and barrel races, began as routine training for cowboys. While it developed into a sport, other countries developed their own rodeo style – adding parades and bands, with a fiesta atmosphere. Major rodeo countries around the world include Mexico, Chile, Brazil, Argentina and Australia.

Not being a country boy, I had to learn to like rodeos. During my cowboy education, I discovered there are plenty of rodeos throughout the West. During Cheyenne Frontier Days in Wyoming, I learned the fine points of this rambunctious sport. Little doggies sprint out of the roping chutes, ill-tempered bulls come bucking out of the riding chutes; this rodeo is called the "Daddy of 'em all." It seems everyone wears Western shirts, big buckles, tall hats and expensive boots. You see cowboys, clowns, queens and dandies all performing their rodeo skills. This week-long summer rodeo offers something for everyone, with Western shops, carnival midway, Shoshone dancing and a parade of horse-drawn carriages. Rodeos provide family entertainment at reasonable prices, although the big Houston and Las Vegas events can be a little pricey.

There are seasonal rodeos throughout North America, including Cody, Wyoming, where the rodeo is a nightly or weekly event; and the very popular Calgary Stampede in Alberta, Canada, famous for its chuck-wagon races. I personally like local rodeos where the skill is not so sharp, but local "wanna-be" cowboys compete to win a belt buckle or impress the girls. Although the West was the birthplace of rodeos, today you can find them in most states, with particularly good rodeos in Michigan and North and South Carolina. Here is a list of some of the popular rodeos throughout North America:

Calgary, Alberta, Canada - Calgary Stampede
Cheyenne, WY - Frontier Days Rodeo
Cody, WY - Cody Stampede
Pocatello, ID - Pocatello Frontier
Pendleton, OR - Oregon Stampede
Denver, CO - Stock Show
Reno, NV - Reno Rodeo
Las Vegas, NV - PRCA National Finals
Phoenix, AZ - National Stock Show & Rodeo
Ft. Worth, TX - Stockyards Championship Rodeo
San Antonio, TX - Stock Show & Rodeo
Houston, TX - Houston Rodeo

Special thanks to Randy Wagner for review of this list.

Festivals and Fairs

Are you going to Scarborough Fair?
Parsley, sage, rosemary and thyme.

–Simon & Garfunkel

Spring, summer and fall bring out fairgoers in large numbers; they come from miles around to celebrate events from the Shenandoah Apple Blossom Festival in Winchester, Virginia, to the Newport Jazz Festival in Rhode Island. What fun it is to go to a festival or fair. It seems to show off the town's best colors. Social clubs in New Orleans plan and paint for a year to get ready for Mardi Gras. On the Fourth of July weekend, veteran volunteers—many with protruding bellies—form regiments to re-enact battlefield engagements at Gettysburg, Pennsylvania. In the Deep South, ladies and gentlemen of Natchez, Mississippi, dress in period costumes to welcome visitors to their Antebellum homes during the March pilgrimage.

If you're going abroad, look no further than Bavaria's Oktoberfest, where having a few under your belt is just fine. Is this the year for a World's Fair? I've been to four and hope to go to more, but the world exposition is fading from popularity. Not to worry, there is a fair that pays tribute to beasts of burden. The Pushkar Camel Fair in Rajasthan, India, is one of the largest marketplaces for new and used dromedaries. I bet you're saying to yourself, "I could sure use a couple extra camels this year." OK, then just connect to a flight from Kennedy, and then it's a short hop to New Delhi, an easy full-day bus trip, and then an ever-so-fast cab ride to the fairgrounds. See, in no time at all you're there. If you feel jet lag, don't worry, the aroma will soon wake you up. A couple of words of caution — if you don't speak fluent Hindi, bargaining can be a challenge and shipping is not included.

All 50 states hold state fairs. Many times local and county fairs are held first, with blue ribbon winners continuing on to compete in the state fair. In early times, country fairs were competitive exhibitions of livestock and farm products including baked goods, jellies and jams. Today, most state fairs have added elaborate musical shows, carnival rides and auto or horse racing.

What does a state fair mean to an urbanite like me, for I never milked a cow, collected eggs or harvested any crop. My father, on the other hand, was raised on a farm near Tyrone, Pennsylvania. He left for college and never returned to farming, but he always had a love for the agrarian way of life. So yearly, Pop and I would spend a long day at the state fair. Living in St. Louis gave us a choice of Sedalia, MO, or Springfield, IL. Being a curious soul, I never tired of walking through the barns of cattle, horse, sheep and, of course in Missouri, mules. Stuff on my shoes or the pungent odor was never a problem, and seemed part of the farming atmosphere. Pop would explain the different breeds of cattle and their uses. I remember beef cattle were Black Angus, Herefords and Charlets; milking cattle were Holsteins, Jerseys and Guernseys...maybe...I think?

Once out of the barns and chicken coops, we kicked tires at the tractor display and watched stock car racing. My father was a charismatic conversationalist and taught by example. He spun fascinating stories about rural life, and I never once got bored with his tales of the farm. Now on occasion, I'd take my boys to the state fairs — we were lucky to know one end of an animal from the other, but it's still an entertaining day.

Fairs and festivals are chicken soup for travelers; they uncover hidden delights and add to your travel experiences. Timing is important. You can enjoy a fair only during its set dates, so double-check for the timing of an event. Here is a list of the most popular types:

Music (#1 Festival)	Flower
Arts & Crafts	Food Harvest, Wild Game & Wine
Community	Pagan
Cultural, Heritage & Folk	Seasonal
Fine Arts & Theatre	Storytelling

Zoological Parks

"I went to the animal fair, The birds and the beasts were there,
The big baboon by the light of the moon —
was combing his auburn hair."

–The Animal Fair (Children's song)

In many cities throughout the world, zoos are the pride of the community. Volunteers and benefactors, and especially animal lovers, choose to support their zoos with time and money. This has led to an explosion of outstanding zoos displaying animals in natural environments. Gone, for the most part, are the cramped cages with cement floors and iron bars. Today's modern zoos present their prized animals in sometimes deluxe accommodations. International breeding programs protect endangered species, plus wildlife trips and safaris sponsored by the zoos encourage patrons to explore animals in their natural settings.

Each zoological park offers something different, and since I'm an animal lover, I have taken the time to visit zoos around the world. Here are some I remember:

- Want to take a break from the waves of Waikiki? Then walk down the street and visit the Honolulu Zoo, which features animals of the savannah plains all in one open area. (It might be noted that lions, tigers and bears are restricted from this area due to lack of proper social behavior.)

- Berlin Zoo features 240 acres of landscape guiding visitors through six continents of fauna - from big cats & pachyderm, to their snake farm, and crocodile exhibit.

- When I visited the Bronx Zoo, the newborn baby gorilla was peeking out through its mother's arms. I found the tiger and Madagascar exhibition exceptional.

- The San Diego zoo's newly remodeled Polar Bear Plunge features outdoor and underwater viewing. They also host a live cam for polar bear viewing on line.

- I flew from St. Louis and my sister flew from Washington, DC, to meet at the Cincinnati Zoo. We went to visit the Sumatran Rhinoceros pen, where a very successful breeding program has resulted in a not-so-little, but hairy baby rhino. The grounds are hilly with large trees dividing the different animal areas.

- Many young people get their first experience with wildlife at Disney's Animal Kingdom near Orlando, or Lion Country Safari in West Palm Beach, Florida. These areas are a little commercial, but leave it to Disney in particular to put on a great natural open-air display.

- The National Zoo in Rock Creek Park, Washington, DC, is proud of its panda area; but I also remember the zoo in Beijing, China and its assortment of pandas (all made in China).

The menagerie of animals is not the only point of interest in today's modern zoos. Many offer themed restaurant dining and unique shopping opportunities. The St. Louis Zoo has a Zooline Railroad that meanders through animal exhibitions and twisting tunnels. The San Diego Zoo has a wonderful Old Town Trolley, transporting visitors throughout the grounds.

For a lot of people, a zoo experience is not too far away. Most mid-size and large cities welcome families at modest rates. Do you remember when your parents took you to see the animals? Bet you were excited... so return the favor and take a little one to experience the great variety of wild animals. Here is a short list of cities with well-known zoos worldwide.

United States

Bronx Zoo - New York City, NY

Philadelphia Zoo - PA

National Zoo - Washington, DC

Disney's Animal Kingdom - Orlando, FL

Lion Country Safari - West Palm Beach, FL

Columbus Zoo - OH

Cincinnati Zoo - OH

Lincoln Park Zoo - Chicago, IL

Brookfield Zoo - Chicago, IL

Omaha Zoo - NB

St. Louis Zoo - MO

Audubon Zoo - New Orleans, LA

Fort Worth Zoo - TX

San Antonio Zoo - TX

Houston Zoo - TX

Phoenix Zoo - AZ

Arizona Sonora Desert Museum–Tucson, AZ

San Diego Zoo - CA

San Diego Wild Animal Park - CA

Los Angeles Zoo - CA

San Francisco Zoo - CA

Woodland Park Zoo (Seattle)

Worldwide

Chapultepec Zoo - Mexico City, Mexico.

Berlin Zoo - Germany

Berlin Tier Park - Germany

Leipzig Zoo - Germany

Frankfort Zoo - Germany

Wilhelma Zoo - Germany

Vienna Zoo - Austria

Salzburg Zoo - Austria

Budapest Zoo - Hungary

London Zoo - England

Edinburgh Zoo - Scotland

Artis Zoo - Netherlands

Rotterdam zoo - Netherlands

Zurich Garden - Switzerland

Taronga Zoo - Sydney, Australia

Healesville Sanctuary - near Melbourne Australia

Ocean Park - Hong Kong, China

Special thanks to St. Louis Zoo President Dr. Jeffrey Bonner and Jack Grisham, Vice President of Animal Collections for review of this list.

Botanical Gardens

Oh, tiptoe from the garden, by the garden of the willow tree
And tiptoe through the tulips with me.
−Nick Lucas, American singer (and) Tiny Tim

Many people enjoy gardening and the eye-appeal of flowering plants. The natural progression is a visit to a botanical garden, and stroll among abundant floral displays and stately trees. On your next exploration of education, you might consider a visit to one of the great gardens — you have a choice of thousands around the world. Botanical gardens are well-maintained parks that exhibit ornamental plants of nature. Additionally, they function as botanical research, classification and collection.

Grand gardens have a noble past, starting with the famous Hanging Gardens of Babylon that were included as one of the ancient Seven Wonders of the World. During the renaissance, universities in Northern Italy developed botanical gardens with elaborate fountains and walkways, and that relationship between universities and botanical gardens remain strong to this day. The 18th Century saw the development of greenhouses and conservatories, built primarily to house plants in a protective environment. An outstanding example is Royal Botanic Gardens at Kew near London. The use of structured glass helped create a new architectural art form. If you are in London, you can plan a full-day outing to Kew, allowing time to wander among the countless displays that the garden has to offer. Make sure to leave time for a spot of Earl Grey tea just outside of the arboretum.

Europe has numerous gardens, but winter weather restricts some warm weather plants. Outside of Europe, tropical gardens became fashionable in many areas of the world including Cape Town, South Africa; Rio de Janeiro, Brazil and Singapore. Today many countries have taken garden design to new heights. Here are some of my recollections of unique garden features around the world.

- **The Missouri Botanical Garden** in St. Louis is a national historic landmark and has the world's largest database of plant information. A few years back, it featured "Glass in the Garden" with dramatic glass structures placed creatively throughout the garden. Artist Dale Chihuly, creates intriguing multi-colored glass sculptures that seem to blend perfectly with the botanical displays. The spring and summer show was a sell-out and had to be extended into the fall, to handle the large crowds.

- Nothing tops **Butchart Gardens** on Vancouver Island, Canada. The floral gardens simply can't be beat for a one-day excursion. To do it right, start in Vancouver and take a float plane to Victoria's inner harbour, then for a little variety - return via the regular ferry boat service back to Vancouver. Butchart has an interesting past - the Butchart family, who owned Portland Cement Company, developed the gardens after the rich limestone deposits were depleted. This famous sunken garden was once an ugly quarry, but after extensive work the garden began receiving visitors in 1926. A highlight is to view and photograph this sunken garden from different heights and locations. It is still privately owned and is cared for in detail, which gives Butchart an A+ rating.

- To the Japanese, gardens combine culture and religion rolled into one—true expressions of life. If you're fortunate enough to visit the **Golden Pavilion** in Kyoto, Japan, you will discover a harmony between inspiring temples and graceful gardens. This Zen sanctuary is technically not a botanical garden, though it's pretty close. It overlooks a reflecting pond, flanked by a variety of trees. A small tea garden is the perfect resting place to contemplate the Japanese artistry with plants and nature. The flowers start blooming in spring and go through summer, but color changes in autumn can be spectacular.

- **Terra Nostra Botanical Garden** on San Miguel Island in the Azores, is not the typical garden setting. When I visited this remote sight it was under renovation.

The gigantic trees shade most of the garden and pond, acting as a canopy for flowering bushes. Lily pads and water flowers are part of the very bizarre endemic species that flourish on the island. The town of Furnas has hot bubbling, steaming, springs. There are twin lakes formed by ancient craters, with hiking trails and dramatic look-out points. The awesome lakes and surrounding area is protected and unspoiled. Although very much off the beaten trail, this garden is one of the hidden wonders of the botanical world and little-known tourism treat.

With so many botanical gardens around the world, you are spoiled for choice. **Special Note**: I asked Dr. Peter Raven to review this botanical garden list. Peter is the president of the Missouri Botanical Garden and a world renowned expert on botanical research—he has added some excellent choices of his own. Here is a selected list of for your review:

North America

The Butchart Gardens—Vancouver Island, Canada

Royal Botanical Gardens—Hamilton, Ontario, Canada

Montreal Botanical Garden—Canada

Dominion Arboretum and Botanic Garden—Ottawa, Canada

University of California Botanical Garden at Berkeley, CA

UC Davis Arboretum—Near Sacramento, CA

Denver Botanic Gardens—CO

Missouri Botanical Gardens—St. Louis, MO

Chicago Botanic Garden—Chicago, IL

Memphis Botanic Garden—Memphis, TN

Longwood Gardens—Brandywine Valley, PA

Brooklyn Botanic Garden—NY

The New York Botanical Garden—Bronx, NY

Arnold Arboretum—Boston, MA

The United States Botanic Garden—Washington, DC

Fairchild Tropical Botanic Gardens—Coral Gables, FL

Atlanta Botanical Garden—GA

The Huntington Botanical Garden—Santa Marino, CA

University of British Columbia Botanical Garden—Vancouver Canada

Chanticleer Garden—Wayne, PA

Ganna Walska Lotusland—Santa Barbara, CA

National Tropical Botanical Garden—Kauai, Hawaii

> "Of all these gardens, Butchart is the only one that's not a botanical garden, but just a place for showy plants—no botanical purpose whatever, nor much diversity—but having said that, it is certainly spectacular."
>
> **– Dr. Peter H. Raven,
> President, Missouri Botanical Garden**

Caribbean

St. Vincent Botanical Gardens—St. Vincent, Island

Botanical Gardens (Cont.)

South America
Jardim Botânico–Rio de Janeiro, Brazil
Atlantic Ocean
Terra Nostra Botanical Garden–Azores
Palmetum of Santa Cruz de Tenerife–Canary Islands, Spain

Europe
Royal Botanic Gardens (Kew Gardens)–Kew, England
Royal Botanic Garden Edinburgh–Scotland
National Botanic Gardens–Dublin, Ireland
National Botanic Garden of Belgium–Meise, Belgium
Jardin des Plantes–Paris, France
Jardin botanique de Lyon–Lyon, France
The Botanic Garden Berlin-Dahlem–Germany
Uppsala University Botanical Garden–Sweden
Geneva Botanical Gardens–Switzerland
Botanical Garden and Museum–Copenhagen, Denmark
Botanic Garden Komarov Botanical Institute–St. Petersburg, Russia
Main Moscow Botanical Garden–Russia

Africa
Kirstenbosch National Botanical Garden–Cape Town, South Africa

Asia
Singapore Botanic Gardens–Singapore
Royal Botanic Gardens Melborne–Australia
Wellington Botanic Garden–New Zealand
Christchurch Botanic Gardens–New Zealand
Royal Botanic Garden–Sydney, Australia
South China Botanical Garden–Guangzhou, China
Beijing Botanical Gardens–China
Shanghai Botanic Garden–China
Nanjing Botanical Garden Memorial Sun Yat-Sen–China
Xishuangbanna Tropical Botanical Garden–Yunnan, China
Kunming Botanic Garden–Yunnan, China

I wandered lonely as a cloud
That floats on high o'er vales and hills,
When all at once I saw a crowd,
A host, of golden daffodils.
– William Wordsworth

Special thanks to MO Botanical Garden President Dr. Peter Raven for review of this list.

Performing Arts

Summertime and the livin' is easy,
fish are jumpin' and the cotton is high.

−"Porgy & Bess," George & Ira Gershwin

If you have a particular love for live performances, this section may help you in crafting an extraordinary vacation directed towards the performing arts. Most travel agents at one point or another have organized group trips that centered on music, dance, opera or theatre. A few years ago I had the honor of organizing and escorting a group to Carnegie Hall in New York City for a symphony performance. If you haven't been inside, the next time you're in the Big Apple, treat yourself to a performance and drink in ambiance. We can't leave out the old joke about this historic building — A traveler got lost in Brooklyn... seeing an old man sitting on a stoop, he rolled down the window and asked, "Hey buddy, how can I get to Carnegie Hall?" The man thought a minute and said, "practice my son, practice." I also took groups to London and Toronto for live theatre performances, and additionally, have organized numerous groups to music festivals.

The performing arts have spawned not only music, but great architectural achievements. An outstanding example is the Sydney Opera House completed in 1973, which was voted among the most revolutionary and beautiful architectural structure of the twentieth century. Cities and countries take great pride in building symphony halls and opera houses, theatres and amphitheatres.

Vacation goers might plan an entire travel experience around a special performance in another city. Modern dance and ballet draw from all parts of the country. Many cities that do not have a permanent ballet company can look for touring ballet troupes who may perform in their area. In some large cities, there is a regular season for ballet performances. Theatre, in its many forms, continues to rank high on many trip-goers lists of things to see and do. Broadway and the theatre districts of Toronto, Canada and London, England — are some of the mecca's for drama and musical theatre performances. Jazz, the great American creation, can be enjoyed in small dark jazz houses, or large festivals throughout the world. Jazz started in the south as an African-American musical expression, and today has worldwide appeal. As a matter of fact, when I travel the globe and listen to radio stations or music performances, the most requested music is jazz, rock n' roll and Latin music.

Symphony Music — Go to the symphony and let yourself drift into the splendor of melodic tones. Sit back, take a deep breath and listen to the orchestra perform at the pinnacle of music excellence. The blending of strings, brass, woodwind and percussion, fill the hall with the great joy of music. Whether it's a hometown performance or the Chicago Symphony Orchestra, classical music remains a mainstay of our cultural heritage.

As small cities grow, they begin to support and sponsor orchestras, and find donors who help build concert halls that provide practice and performance facilities. Throughout Europe music fills the air with world class symphony orchestras. You can be assured of outstanding performances in cities like Prague, Amsterdam, Berlin, Vienna or London, Budapest or Dresden. If you are traveling to the US, enjoy outstanding symphony performances in Chicago, Cleveland, Los Angeles, New York City and Washington DC. You can expect to find new composers with varied pieces being played right next to your old favorites — Bach, Beethoven, Brahms or Mozart, Chopin and Tchaikovsky. They are all there waiting to entertain you with great music of the world.

Opera — The wonderful art form of opera, by its nature, demands substantial preparation time and resources. To perform an opera requires skilled singers and musicians combined with a libretto or story-line, and a musical score. The requirements for a traditional opera begin with an opera house, costumes, sets, and orchestra.

Opera can be infectious. A beautiful song or aria can endear you to this wonderful musical experience. I learned opera through my son, who was required to take an opera class in college in his freshman year. He would call home and ask me questions that I was ill-prepared to answer. So I bought a 2-hour tape called "Opera for Dummies," and on one of my long international flights learned the basics of opera. In the middle of his semester, we hopped on a plane to New York, where we both enjoyed our first opera at the Metropolitan Opera — Lincoln Center, New York. This imposing opera house seats 3,800 people, and the performance included a small screen in front of our seats that translated Italian to English. The opera was Giacomo (Antonio Domenico Michele Secondo Maria) Puccini's Madame Butterfly, and seemed to go a little slow until the soprano sang a sad aria and stole my heart away.

I was hooked, and traveling to different continents has afforded me the opportunity to visit a variety of opera houses and enjoy the music and people. In Rome on an off night, I bought a ticket to an opera performance for a very reasonable price. When the cab let me out, I was at the front steps of a local high school auditorium — a long step down from La Scala in Milan. Oh no, I thought, it must be amateur night; but right from the first note, the quality of singing was outstanding, and the performance was one of the highlights of my trip. When young boys and girls grow up in the US, they practice on the ball fields; I guess in Italy, kids are not given a bats and balls but rather singing lessons.

Coming off a touring day in the Vienna Woods, the motorcoach dropped me off in front of the Vienna State Opera. When I got excited, the guide informed me that all tickets for that night's performance of Carmen were sold out months ago. Being the tenacious sort, I asked at the ticket window…and yes, one seat in an upper balcony was available, but with an obstructed view. As I entered the hall, I was treated to a spectacular interior with ornate gold décor and dark red velvet seats. The theatre is built in a classic horseshoe design which provides the audience with high quality sound and nearly unobstructed views. At intermission, the couple in front of me left the theatre, but politely gave me their seats and for the rest of the performance I had the best seats in the house.

Santa Fe was quite a different experience. After a long day of walking, I chose the large Jacuzzi at my resort to relax and unwind. Just as I was turning red in the hot tub, a convention goer offered a ticket to the opera, but it started in less than an hour. In one minute I changed from Clark Kent into Superman — jumped out of the tub, fast change of clothes, keys into the rental car and off I drove. The Santa Fe Opera House is on the outskirts of the city, and is an open-air structure, what a joy to hear Mozart's Marriage of Figaro under a starlit sky.

So if you like the bold sound of Richard Wagner or Verdi's Triumphal March from Aida, or the memorable music of Carmen — opera can be a lifelong indulgence. Some opera houses are so magnificent they are the architectural highlight of city tours, and as the Europeans influence expanded throughout the world, great opera houses were built on every continent, including the jungles of Brazil. Here is a brief list of some well-known opera houses around the world.

North America

The Metropolitan Opera House–New York City

Lyric Opera of Chicago (Civic)

Santa Fe Opera (Crosby)–New Mexico

War Memorial Opera House–San Francisco

Palace of Fine Arts–Mexico City

John F. Kennedy Center for the Performing Arts Opera House–Washington DC

Dorothy Chandler Pavilion Los Angeles Opera–California

McCaw Hall and Seattle Opera House –Washington

South America

Manaus Opera House–Brazil

Teatro Colón–Buenos Aries, Argentina

Europe

Royal Opera House - London

Oslo Opera House - Norway

Copenhagen Opera House - Denmark

Europe (Cont.)

Bolshoi Theatre - Moscow

Mariinsky - St. Petersburg, Russia

Novosibirsk Opera Theatre - Russia

Odessa Opera Theatre - Ukraine

Palais Garnier - Paris, France

Prague Estate Theatre - Czech Republic

Staatsoper unter den linden - Berlin, Germany

Semperoper - Dresden, Germany

Munich Bavarian State Opera - Germany

Vienna State Opera - Austria

Theatre de la Monnaie - Brussels, Belgium

Opéra de Monte-Carlo - Monaco

Gran Theatre del Liceu - Barcelona, Spain

Teatro alla Scala - Milan, Italy

Zurich Opera House - Germany

Africa

Alexandria Opera House - Egypt

Pacific

Sydney Opera House - Australia

Special thanks to Bob Hoelscher for review of this list.

Your Personal Travel-Style Survey

If you're at all confused about choosing your next grand tour, let's check your mindset and see together if we can direct a course for the trip you're planning. Take a few minutes and fill in this travel survey covering the different styles of travel. You can rate your interest in each category from 1 (favorite) up to 5 (less favored); or, simply check what interests you and leave blank what doesn't. No intense math, just a quick assessment.

The focus of this survey begins and ends with your personal travel style. You may find you are breaking out of preconceived travel patterns, or the survey becomes a reconfirmation of your present travel choices. OK, check or number your favorite categories and draw your own conclusions. One last thought: suggest to your spouse or travel partner that they check off their favorite type of travel dreams – and compare your results. This may alter an established orthodox view or conjure up new destinations to discover.

General Activities

There's only a day to plan activities at a new locations; what do you do?

❏ Relax by the pool or beach
❏ City sightseeing tour
❏ Round of golf or tennis
❏ Local shops with specialty items
❏ (Other)

Evening Activities

A half moon shone over the French town of Divonne near the Swiss border. The concierge suggested three tempting venues for the evening; I was spoiled by the choices ... Which would you choose?

❏ Fine dining at my hotel Domaine de Divonne, surrounded with art deco décor
❏ Formal evening at the European casino pretending to be a bit cosmopolitan
❏ A cab ride across the border to Geneva for a lively band with beer and burgers
❏ (Other)

Cruising

With 40 sailings under my belt, I've experienced the gamut of cruising. Of these selections, which do you prefer?

- ❑ Three week Atlantic crossing from the Canary Islands to the Falkland Islands. **Features**: remote island touring and hiking, zodiac rubber boat excursions, arms-length photography of seals, penguins and bigger-than-life whale watching.

- ❑ Week long Caribbean cruise with ports of call including Jamaica, San Juan, St. Thomas. **Features**: beach and pool bathing, steel drum music, nightly stage shows. Tours—Dunns River Falls climb, El Moro Fortress; shop-til-you-drop on a Virgin Island (non-virgins welcome).

- ❑ Danube River Cruise - river ports include Budapest, Vienna and motor coach to Prague. **Features**: gentle waters, lavish dining with complimentary local wines, historic cities and bucolic landscapes, visits to grand castles and spiraled cathedrals, classical music and gypsy violins.

- ❑ Alaskan inside passage cruise boarding in Seward with stops in Sitka, Juneau, Skagway and Ketchikan. **Features**: Large ship amenities with an array of dining rooms, bars and entertainment, with deck viewing of waterfalls, forests and wildlife. Excursions—calving glaciers, totem pole parks, picnic salmon bakes, gold mine train, and swooping over ice fields in a helicopter.

- ❑ (Other)

Family Vacations

It's summer time and the livin' is easy, kids are jumpin' and vacation plans are high. Here are three trips to consider ...

- ❑ Grasp the heritage of Washington, D.C. by visiting the White House, Capitol, Smithsonian, and walk the mall with inspirational war monuments.

- ❑ Wide Wyoming - beginning with Jackson Hole, the Grand Teton, and Yellowstone National Park. You can't bear to miss the wildlife and the very fine on-time Old Faithful Geyser.

- ❑ Riviera Maya is a sun-therapy dream come true with all-inclusive Mexican resorts stretching down the coast. Are there beach activities for the young and old? Sí, señor.

- ❑ (Other)

Romance

For lovers of all ages – unlock the treasures of your heart and discover a getaway to romance.

- ❏ On arrival in Kauai, Hawaii catch the wafting aroma of garland leis, as the long flight from the mainland fades to a distant memory. **Features**: A lush green island blest with free-style resorts and beckoning beaches. Day-trippers usually head for Waimea Canyon, Na Pali Coast or North to Waialua River for a romantic cruise or the best-in-class helicopter ride around the wettest spot on earth, Mt. Waialeale. Did I fail to mention spas, golf, lush gardens and macadamia nuts?

- ❏ For a scenic place in North America try the resort town of Whistler, B.C., Canada. **Features**: In winter, the ski slopes are active and the fireplaces burn with the smell of cedar. Spring, summer and fall are made for festival lovers. Whistler is nestled in coastal mountains, it's a well-planned stylish village. Adventures vary from Ziptrek cable rides to mountain golf courses, opulent spas, trail hikes through virgin forests or gondola rides to panoramic vistas. The drive from Vancouver presents visitors with a world-class scenic transfer passing mirror-like lakes and mountains.

- ❏ Bali is a timeless island of terraced rice-scapes and Hindu faithful who welcome guests and sunsets with equal grace. **Features**: Wander the open-air shrines, offer your shoulders to the playful temple monkeys, or after the torches are lit, feel the rhythm of a hundred villagers swaying to the traditional monkey dance; or retreat to your beach cottage and just monkey around. Reminder, aimlessly walking on sandy beaches without a watch or a care is considered proper behavior.

- ❏ The Simplon Orient Express Train from Venice to London was made legendary by Agatha Christie's mystery novel "Murder on the Orient Express." **Features**: Hire a gondola through the canals of Venice or drink a peach Belini at Harry's Bar before you begin your 2-day historical train trip. Matching romance and glamour for more than a century, guests can gather around the bar car in gowns and tuxedos as the train climbs through the Brenner Pass and into Austria, then Paris, the Chunnel and finishing in Victoria Station London.

Adventure, History, Wildlife

Here are three different directions you as a traveler can experience. Check the one that fits your lifestyle.

- ❏ Glacier National Park, Montana–settle into your cabin at Lake McDonald Lodge. Take a cruise on the lake, toss horseshoes or ride the historic red buses to Logan Pass over Going-to-the-Sun-Road. Now grab your backpack, water bottle and bear bells for your hike to Avalanche Lake. Wildlife alert ... bears have been repeatedly warned not to feed the hikers.

- ❏ Ephesus, Turkey - First the Greeks then the Romans build a magnificent city near the shores of the Mediterranean. It has been carefully dug out of the Turkish soil and restored in part to its grandeur. One of the great ruins of the world, the city is usually reached off the back of a cruise ship; visitors can walk the ancient roads lined with columns, walk by Trajan's Fountain on the way to the 3-story library and Agora Market.

- ❏ Galapagos Islands, Ecuador–Animal lovers need a laundry list to identify all of the varied wildlife living here. Tame and unassuming, animals, birds, reptiles, and tourists mingle in harmony. Extremes are the order– big turtles, very Blue Footed Boobies, small penguins and gray salt spitting iguanas that only a mother could love.

I shall go forward with my history,

describing equally

the greater and lesser cities.

—Herodotus, known as the father of history

Chapter 2:
Tourism Through the Ages

I am a curious person by nature; I want to know what's around the next corner. Why, for example, Tahitians tattoo their bodies; or why Greek philosophy from 2,500 years ago remains part of our time-honored values; or why people get excited over beautiful architecture. Most of us possess, to a degree, an interest in the unknown–a fascination to learn a new bit of knowledge. Curiosity, simply stated, brings out the best in all of us – it's the sparkplug that ignites the brain and promotes inquiries and learning. A new fact is a new enlightenment!

The Golden Age of Greece produced Socrates, a giant of thought who professed the philosophy of curiosity. He might say "Ask questions" or "Learn from others" or "Drink red wine, it's better for your health." With this in mind, I looked down the historical road for why people travel and what drives their destination choices. Since history is the building block of society, I gathered the very compelling stories of the past and side-stepped the standard reference works. To better understand our joy of travel, let us follow the yellow brick road of tourism from starting point to the Emerald City.

The Early Dawn of Tourism

Grand tours in early times were limited to exploration or trade. Tourism was restricted by several forces, including poor roads, difficult sea journeys and lack of safety. There was also limited knowledge of the world outside a person's own city or town. As Greeks started to look past their own city-states, the early building blocks of tourism began to evolve. Tales of seagoing

voyages were embellished with stories of great monuments and greater empires. Although many Greek writers were active during the city-state period, the most notable was Herodotus, recognized as the father of history, and because of his impact on Greek civilization, he might also be described as the father of tourism.

A first attempt at anything requires possession of two good personal traits: curiosity and courage. Tackling the unknown puts one in a problematic state of mind filled with both dilemmas and dreams. Most people, unfortunately, use cautious restraint and choose not to engage in the challenges of a new idea. But, if you are the Greek citizen Herodotus, and fortunate to be living in the time of the Golden Age of Greece, then writing the first history of the world is a noble reward.

Herodotus was, by nature, a seeker of facts and seemed to be a born rover, traveling from one country to another — this is a guy after my own heart. Each new culture brought tales of great heroes and evil tyrants. With probing eyes, he described and recorded the mysteries of antiquity. Once he was satisfied he had captured the essence of a particular culture, he packed his bags and moved on to another — and then still another land. You can almost hear his theme song, "How you gonna keep 'em down on the farm, after they've seen the pyramids." Born in Asia Minor or modern-day Turkey, he traveled throughout Babylonia, Egypt, Greece and Italy. He began writing a digest of the world and, by doing so, recorded a great historical document. Everywhere he went, he studied the customs, manners and religious beliefs of the people. He listened and then recorded historical stories, some of which he did not believe, but which appear in his text as the local lore, reality or myth. He wrote in a lively manner, and his descriptive prose made his books captivating to readers of his time. Herodotus' writings became the travel brochure for seafaring travelers and stimulated a Pan-Hellenic tourist trade.

Early world landmark lists. People seem to like lists; they give value to and organize historical places. The Seven Wonders of the World were a list of art and architecture compiled by Greek and Roman observers. There were actually several lists put together that included many different wonders, primarily in the eastern Mediterranean. It's interesting to note that only man-made architecture was mentioned and did not include natural wonders. These landmarks were highly prized by ship captains who could profit from telling their passengers of grand sights. Ancient sight-seeing promoters, for example, would surely mention the most splendid cities of Asia Minor and Egypt. Here, then, is the most celebrated list of the extraordinary structures of antiquity:

The Seven Wonders of the Ancient World

The Pyramids of Egypt — Built as tombs for the Egyptian Pharaohs in Giza, they are the oldest of the seven wonders and the only structures remaining largely intact today.

The Hanging Gardens of Babylon — Built for one of the wives of King Nebuchadnezzar II, near modern Baghdad, the gardens were lofty terraces set amongst groves of trees, rich vegetation and flowers. No traces of the gardens remain.

The Temple of Artemis at Ephesus — One of the largest temples built in the ancient times was built entirely of marble and dedicated to the Greek Goddess Artemis (Diana). A few columns remain near Ephesus, Turkey.

The Statue of Zeus — Dedicated to the Olympic Games, this was perhaps the most famous statue in the ancient world. Sculpted by Phidias and dedicated to Zeus (Jupiter), the statue was made of gold and ivory, stood 40 feet high, showing Zeus on his throne. The statue is gone but parts of the temple can still be seen in Olympia, Greece.

The Mausoleum at Halicarnassus — Built as a tomb for King Mausolus by his wife, the huge marble building was a stepped pyramid 130 feet high with colonnades and topped by a statue of the king in his chariot. Only small pieces of the building remain in modern Bodrum, Turkey.

The Colossus of Rhodes — This huge bronze statue stood near or over the main harbor of Rhodes, in the Aegean Sea. The statue was in honor of Helios, the sun god and stood 120 feet high. It was destroyed by an earthquake and the metal sold for scrap.

The Lighthouse at Alexandria — Located on the Island of Pharos in the harbor of Alexandria, Egypt, this massive structure stood 440 feet high and was built of enormous stone blocks. Nightly, a fire was lit at the top of the tower to provide light for approaching ships — nothing remains.

New Seven Wonders of the World

In 2001 a Swiss corporation, New Seven Wonders Foundation, initially selected 200 monuments. They then whittled down the list to 21 finalists before opening it up to world-wide email balloting. There was global excitement and when the winners were announced with great fanfare in Lisbon, Portugal on July 7, 2007, the list included:

Great Wall of China

Chichen Itza—Mexico

Petra—Jordan

Coliseum—Rome, Italy

Christ the Redeemer Statue—Rio, Brazil

Taj Mahal, India

Machu Picchu—Peru

Honorary: The Great Pyramids

The voting was unbridled, and it appears that lots of countries stuffed the ballot box for their favorite landmark. So without bias, after visiting all major world landmarks, I would humbly submit my list based on the structure, location, size, beauty and cultural significance:

Great Wall of China
Angkor Wat in Cambodia
Coliseum in Rome, Italy
The Parthenon in Athens, Greece
Taj Mahal in Agra, India
Tikal pyramids in Guatemala
Petra in Jordan

Honorable mentions: The Great Pyramids of Egypt, Machu Picchu in Peru, Mont St. Michel in France

All Roads Lead to Rome

I found Rome brick and left it marble.
–Caesar Augustus, Emperor of Rome

No empire, nation or country built like the Romans. The greatest empire in history put its money where its mouth was and built a massive transportation system that expanded their boundaries, promoted military growth, trade and, for sure, tourism. The Roman Empire at its height encompassed a fourth of Europe, much of the Middle East and the Northern Coast of Africa. To support the expansion, the Romans built roads, aqueducts and bridges so skillfully that many are still in use. Trade was valued and merchants carried food, raw materials and general goods from one end of the empire to the other. Travel became safe both on land and for sailing vessels or galleys that plied the Mediterranean. Their road system linked all parts of the empire and travel became so popular that wealthy patricians hired carriages and drivers; the less fortunate walked or rode their horses. Still seen today, the oldest Roman road–the Appian Way–started in Rome and ended in Taranto, a popular seaport. When the traffic got heavy, slower carts gave way to the swift moving chariots, the Ferrari's of Roman times; even then Italian drivers posed a traffic menace.

The reign of Caesar Augustus marked the beginning of Pax Romana or Roman peace, which lasted 200 years and during that time tourism flourished. Safe roads and reliable sea lanes afforded the well-to-do Roman citizens a travel opportunity to explore cultures in other parts of the empire. Coliseums, many of which stand today, were constructed in major overseas Roman cities. This allowed locals and visitors alike to watch chariot races, gladiators and animal contests. The attendance was so good that a few of the coliseums were flooded for mock naval battles. So if you were a citizen of Rome with those special rights and privileges, you might leave the hustle and bustle of Rome, gather the wife, kids and slaves and off you'd go to Gaul or Egypt, not forgetting the favorite tunica, sandals and a toga or two for those formal nights abroad. Touring the four corners of the empire had never been better.

The Middle Ages and the Crusades

The Templars and the newly arrived Crusaders — this faction was against any truce or co-existence.

–Battle of Hattin by Saladin

The decline and fall of the Roman Empire was a bust for the tourism. No one was swelling up with pride as barbarians ran rampant; roads and bridges deteriorated without the protection of the Roman legions. Gone were the brutal spectacles in the coliseums and the infamous orgies, all a thing of the past. The new agenda — cathedral building, one stone at a time, and Sunday services featuring the latest Gregorian chants. Alas, when things seemed the darkest, in of course the Dark Ages, one had to look for a silver lining. With religion fever reaching a peak, what better way to find divine reward than … a pilgrimage?

Disenchanted with the doldrums of medieval life, thousands of the faithful headed towards Jerusalem only to encounter bandits and the fierce Seljuk Turks who were bound and determined to stop the Christians from visiting the holy places. This was unacceptable to both the European church and state. Councils were convened, arguments made, emotions ran high and soon the crusades began in earnest — Ah, the crusades. These were Christian military expeditions to recapture the Holy Land and they came in four waves, lasting 200 years; this was a noble path to salvation. There was also a less noble path of plunder and land grabbing involved in these military journeys, and many of the Muslim faithful fought to the death to keep the Christian infidels out of the Middle East.

The crusaders needed protection in these strange lands. With cross in one hand and chisel in the other, both soldiers and architects set about constructing powerful fortresses across the Mediterranean and Middle East. Some of the notable strongholds are found today in Malta, Rhodes, Syria, Jordan and present-day Israel. These forts stand as a testament to the crusaders intrepid spirit. A second spin-off of the crusades was the formation of a military and religious order known as the Knights Templar. Formed in Jerusalem, they pledged themselves to protect the Holy Sepulcher and vowed to defend pilgrims visiting the Holy Land. They made quite a fashion statement wearing white robes with full-length bright red crosses. These guardians of tourism fought courageously and their righteous goals are worth repeating — protect both landmarks and tourists. What a noble quest.

The Tales of Marco Polo

If you put together all the Christians in the world, with their Emperors and their Kings, the whole of these Christians — aye and throw in the Saracens to boot — would not have such power, or be able to do so much as the Kublai, who is Lord of all the Tartars in the world.

– Marco Polo

Knowledge of the world was limited in Medieval Europe until Marco Polo, a Viennese trader, became famous for his travel and tales of China. Marco, his father and uncle spent 24 years as traders and diplomats throughout the orient and are probably the most famous voyagers on the historic Silk Road. Marco returned from Cathay (China) in 1295 to his home city of Venice and settled in as a respectable business man. The great wonders of the Far East may not have been told but for a conflict between Venice and Genoa.

Marco Polo was enlisted as a commander of a galley but was captured and imprisoned in Genoa. With time on his hands, he and a fellow prisoner wrote The Description of the World or The Travels of Marco Polo. His account of the great Kublai Khan and the wealth of Cathay soon made his book very popular throughout Europe. Because of a timing problem, he never made the New York Times best-seller list, but he did rock the European establishment by describing the astonishing advancements of the Chinese empire, including a sophisticated multi-tier postal system, the use of paper money — not coins, and the wonders of coal which he described as, "the stones that burn like logs". Many readers had trouble believing that there existed a greater land with greater wealth than that of Europe. The book became know as Il Millone or The Million Lies.

Nevertheless, this fascinating manuscript captured people's interest in travel for centuries to come. It is fair to say, the book has become the most important travel log in history. His admirers included a who's who of exploration. Prince Henry the Navigator of Portugal and Christopher Columbus read his works and subsequently shaped the future of exploration. Marco Polo's accounts of China, the Silk Road, Gobi Desert, Burma, Indochina, the Indonesian Islands, India and Africa, piqued the interest of future travelers and explorers. His writing became the greatest travel brochure of all time.

In Xanadu did Kublai Khan, a stately pleasure-dome decree.
−Samuel Taylor Coleridge, English Poet

The Renaissance and the Age of Discovery

Following the sun, we left the old world.
–Inscription on one of Christopher Columbus' caravel sailing ships

The Renaissance began a period in history when Europeans scrutinized how they viewed themselves and the rest of the known world. Ending the Middle Ages, the renaissance swept across customs and institutions that had dominated Europe for almost a thousand years. The great achievements in art, science and the rebirth of ancient Greek and Roman ideas spawned a new generation of voyagers who explored unknown lands. If you asked the average Renaissance guy on the street about his life, he might nod and suggest there were ample cathedrals to go around and maybe it was time to usher in more earthly projects.

The Age of Exploration reshaped European knowledge of the world! A vibrant new competition developed between Portugal, Spain, Great Britain and France. When the Turks blocked the vital Silk Road to the East, governments looked for new trading lanes to India and beyond. Maybe, in a back-handed way, we can thank the Turks for kick starting the age of exploration. Ship builders learned to construct ships that were fast, seaworthy and had the capacity for large loads. Prince Henry the Navigator established a naval school in Sagres, Portugal. He gathered the best minds, including some from the Middle East, to design the caravel ships that made long sea voyages possible.

The race was on; so raise those sails, boldly cast off, and disregard those nasty rumors that the world is flat and ship-eating sea monsters wait just over the horizon. In short order Diaz discovered the Cape of Good Hope; Columbus sailed west and discovered America. Vasco da Gama sailed to India, John Cabot explored North America; Ponce de León sailed to Florida and Balboa reached the Pacific. During this time, Cortes conquered the Aztec Indians in Mexico, and Pizarro destroyed the Inca Empire in Peru. Magellan, then Drake, capped off the exploration spree by circumnavigating the globe.

When Columbus returned in triumph to Spain, he fired the imagination of Europe saying, "The gate to the gold and pearls is now open." Soon the tales of El Dorado, the city of gold, spread through the European capitals. Oh, that will do it every time! Adventurers rushed to launch ship caravans, and soon exploration expanded at rapid speed. Now there were new adventures–the America's, the Caribbean, Africa and India. So pack your trunk, feel the ocean wind on your face and discover the undiscovered — sail on, sail on.

The Enlightenment—The Origin of the Grand Tour

Traveling is almost like talking with men of other centuries.

–Rene Descartes, French Philosopher

Writers and philosophers set the tone for the Age of Reason – or the Age of Enlightenment. German writer, Emmanuel Kant's motto of "Dare to know," might encapsulate the thinking of the time. Self-confident men viewed reason as the best method of learning truth. The lovers of wisdom of this age were enormously impressed by Sir Isaac Newton's discovery of universal gravity. His famous statement, "If I have seen farther, it is by standing on the shoulders of giants," was a sign of things to come. A great wave of respect for education and research fostered trends for touring as a method of teaching. The proper ladies and gentlemen of Europe, viewed the "grand tour" as necessary for a well-rounded education. Walking through Greek ruins was not enough; now exploration of the non-European world included sailing trips to the colonies. The grand tour became part of a travel curriculum for the well-to-do. If spices and gold ignited the Age of Exploration, then the grand tour for education and worldly knowledge was the driving force in the Age of Enlightenment.

The Golden Age of Travel

The world has become a smaller place thanks to Thomas Cook.

–Andrew Williamson, Writer

In 1841, Thomas Cook, an English innovator of conducted tours, persuaded the Midland County Railroad Company to run a charter train for a special temperance meeting. We must assume there was no 'happy hour' in the dining car that night, but this successful trip was the origin of the travel agency community. It was believed to be the first advertised train excursion and in short order a flourishing symbiotic relationship between railroads and travel agents was established. Ah, from bliss to euphoria, what a marvelous time to be alive!

Thomas Cook was a printer by trade, and he published a wealth of brochures and posters that attracted customers to his travel service. During a Paris exhibition, he conducted an excursion which proved very successful. In following years, he led the first organized grand tours of Europe. He soon became an agent for sale of domestic and overseas travel tickets, including military transportation and postal service; all without the aid of cell phones, fax or email.

From mid-Victorian times, to the start of World War II, steam trains and ocean liners opened up the world to travelers. The glamour of foreign lands could now be properly arranged with a visit to Thomas Cook and Sons Worldwide Travel Agency. Today you may notice Thomas Cook outlets located in many airports, with foreign money exchange services for the traveling public. His spirit lives on.

The Rapid Growth of Tourism in the Twentieth Century

Here is a magic carpet journey to the wonders of the world.
- Lowell Thomas, News Commentator and Author

America took the initiative for tourism in the twentieth century, and no person was more instrumental in romancing world travel than news commentator and author, Lowell Thomas.

Starting in the thirties, his well-known radio broadcasts and motion picture news reels brought travel logs to the world stage. He authored numerous travel books and in the mid-fifties and played a major role in developing three-dimensional Cinerama. Omnimax and Blueray are the latest breakthroughs in viewing, but Cinerama in the fifties and sixties was the bigger than life entertainment experience.

Movie goers flocked to the new state-of-the-art theaters for wrap-around travel films. This distinguished travel reporter, with his debonair moustache, captivated audiences with his realistic style. He flew around the world filming people of other cultures, capturing images of grand architecture and as a result gave millions of people an appreciation of the world's great landmarks.

Specially designed theatres were constructed in major cities throughout the United States. Subsequently, a few theatres were built around the world. Cinerama was a true breakthrough in movie technology. It captured the imagination of the American public and after a full year of media fanfare the splendid three-screen movies made their grand openings.

When I was an impressionable thirteen, my parents announced that on the upcoming Friday night, the family would drive to midtown St. Louis for an evening at the new deluxe Cinerama theatre, located on fashionable Lindell Boulevard. My father told me he had reserved seats to view a new wrap-around three-screen movie Search for Paradise. I recall my father dressed in a handsome navy blue pin-striped suit and my mom dressed to the nines in a lavender outfit which she had specifically bought for this gala evening. When we arrived at the theatre, the well-orchestrated event convinced me that this was the center of the entire universe. Large search lights criss-crossed the sky, flooding the night with white beams. Uniformed policemen directed heavy traffic and swarming movie-goers funneled into the theatres grand entrance. In an alarming move, my father gave the keys to our one and only car to a total stranger who drove off to who-knows-where. That was my first introduction to valet service and by the grace of God, he returned the car after the performance.

My young mind absorbed the memorable events of that evenings performance. I was dazzled with the theatres decorations, which included enormous floor-to-ceiling peach curtains. The peach colored carpet also matched the peach colored oversized seats with cushy arm rests, upholstered in soft velvet. Yes, I was pumped up before the lights ever went down. The panoramic screen was an entertainment thrill; I sat spell-bound as the exotic Islands swept across the screen on an immense scale. Lowell Thomas and the Hollywood movie moguls had planted the seeds of a grandiose travel palace, a place where dreams could be nurtured into future travel explorations. In my young mind, the dye had been cast.

Lowell Thomas would end his broadcasts with his famous saying, "So long until tomorrow." This statesman of travel had a special genius reserved for only a few in the broadcasting business; he presented travel the way a great chef creates a gourmet meal. His descriptions of tours and landmarks presented the palate with a delicious taste of history and a scrumptious serving of peoples and cultures.

Grand tours live on for today's new voyagers. People still yearn to learn about destinations that are mystical or foreign. Although the structure of the grand tour may have changed, brochures from Globus, Trafalgar, Tauck and Abercrombie & Kent echo the original trips that intrigued the travelers in the Age of Enlightenment.

*In traveling, a man must carry
knowledge with him,
if he would bring home knowledge.*

–Samuel Johnson

Chapter 3:
Travel Tips for the Mind & Spirit

Pre-Trip Planning

Pre-trip planning just makes good sense! This section of the book helps travelers organize their needs and lists common-sense requirements for a comfortable journey. It is always time well spent when I outfit my mind and spirit for a trip. First I consider the purpose of the travel and set my goals, then prepare the items that support my needs throughout the trip. So let's begin and organize with the basic essentials.

Passports/Visas/Tourist Cards. If you are going abroad, you'll need a valid U.S. passport, and it takes time for the government to process your request. Basics include an application, normal passport fees and two passport-sized photos that are attainable from a photo shop, or a travel agent with a dual-lens camera. Your local post office can handle your application (some small offices. though, do not have that capability). If you already have a passport, some countries require that it be valid for six months after arrival–so check your expiration date. Depending upon the time of year, the turn-around time for acquiring passports is usually six weeks or less; but, to state this in bold terms–no passport, no trip!

Visas or tourist cards are required for certain countries. They can take some time to acquire, and different countries process at different speeds. Two that come to mind are Australia and India – sometimes their administration takes a little longer and tests your patience. Visas can be obtained through the government of that country's on-line service, a travel agent or a visa service. Again, the same rule applies – no visa, no trip! (Website Resource: http://travel.state.gov/passport/passport_1738.html)

Trip Insurance. A prudent thought for the busy traveler – it's always wise to protect your travel investment and purchase trip insurance, which is readily available through your travel agent. You might think this is an extra or unnecessary cost, but consider the alternative–a personal or family medical issue could force the cancellation of your trip. While tour companies and cruise ships can be understanding six months prior to trip departure, the closer the trip date, the more costly the cancellation. Take stock in your trip, and for a modest price, purchase insurance that will protect your trip investment and give you peace of mind, a worthwhile investment to forgo the possible agony of losing thousands of dollars.

Immunization & Personal Medication. The health of the world has greatly improved over the last 30 years, but today there remain selected areas in the Third World that require hepatitis A & B vaccines, malaria (pills), or typhoid fever shots. To avoid rolling up your sleeve and being vaccinated at the border, check with your government health clinic, travel agent or doctor; however, since shots vary from country to country, most local physicians are not always up-to-date with each country's medical requirement. A rule of thumb, most first world countries don't require shots unless the traveler is coming from an infected area, or there has been a recent outbreak of disease. Website resource: http://wwwnc.cdc.gov/travel/

Many Americans take medication to regulate their well-being. It is best not to rely on an overseas pharmacy that may not stock your particular medication. The savvy traveler stocks up in advance with his local pharmacist and brings a little more medication than he or she might otherwise need. One last rule of thumb: If your particular medical situation is serious, it's best to hand-carry your pills so there is no chance of them winding up in lost luggage. If you're in Tokyo and your pills are in Tangiers, you've probably got a problem.

Recording Your Documents. Once a year, I walk to the copy machine with passport in hand, open my wallet and take out credit cards and IDs, place them on the glass and make two copies. I leave a copy at home or work and carry an extra copy on any trip. For five minutes of work, the reward is well worth the effort. If your original documents get lost on the road, this backup will save you many big hassles. The experienced traveler always has a backup for important documents.

Money. If you are traveling to a remote part of the globe, start your pre-trip with a visit to your local bank and request several smaller U.S. dollar bills—ones, fives, tens and twenty-dollar bills; if you've done it right, you should walk out of the bank with a fist full of dollars and fantasize that you're a billionaire. I go through this procedure every trip, both domestic and international, because I know the correct change can speed up any travel activity. When you arrive in a foreign land, you have the flexibility of small denominations that you are familiar with, even before you have converted in your mind to the local currency, and you'll not over-tip or miscalculate any early purchase.

Foreign Currency. The Euro is well-established, as are several other major countries' currencies; therefore a dollar exchange upon arrival is necessary at the airport or local bank. In some Third World countries where their money lacks stability, dollars are prized. Locals are eager to complete transactions using U.S. dollars, and you can be assured...they've never met a dollar they didn't like.

Spend a little time and learn local money. For example, ask how much in dollars is your local hundred "goobie" bill worth? (I refer to all local currency as goobies, until I've memorized the local name for their money.) Or what do I get with a ten-dollar bill? And quietly remember it's not funny money to them, it's their currency. Here's another "feel good and comfortable" tip: You already know to keep all of your documents in one place, but here's a different safety tip – I separate my money into three places in case my cash and I get separated. For peace of mind, I always know I have funds on me and in other places, like my briefcase or hotel lockbox.

The Black Market. In some countries there is a black market for money exchange; it is a result of weak government control over their own currency. On rare occasions I've used it, but be aware the downside problems are usually greater than the up-side rewards. You are playing with foreign laws that can sting you like a bee.

ATMs. Travelers checks provide security, but I detest standing in line just to cash my own money. ATMs provide a highly efficient way to tap into your own money overseas. Picture yourself entering a provincial shop in rural Cambodia–it looks no better than a rickety shack with a water buffalo grazing near the rice paddies. The shopkeeper probably lives upstairs with his wife and many kids. So after deciding this establishment is not for you, and starting your about-face to exit, you spot a replica bronze statue from the Khmer Dynasty; you examine it with hawk eyes and conclude that it's perfect for your hall niche and would make an interesting conversation piece for years to come. It almost says, "You had me at hello." Then you find you are low on cash, but hope springs eternal; back in the corner of the store, of all things, sits an ATM machine. You ask yourself, "How does this box know who I am?" What a wonderful world; it's connected to the great satellite in the sky … and with the entry of your pin, it spews out money.

Credit cards are great, particularly for purchases of larger items. I use credit cards consistently around the world and have never been cheated or had the amount dramatically altered. Today's modern international banking is in sync with the assistance of satellite communication and large computer systems. Credit cards are convenient and user friendly for overseas travel. So remember to bring that plastic with you – don't leave home without it. One last thought, it's beneficial to let your credit card company know if you are leaving the U.S., so they don't put a "freeze" on your card for suspicious use or high-volume purchases.

Portable Electronics. Let's start with cell phones – every year, expanded services are making international calls easier. If your vacation goals include a relaxing, worry-free experience, leave the cell phone at home. If you're like ET and have to phone home regularly, the international phones are becoming reasonable and their service levels improve yearly. For music buffs, the MP3 player is a traveler's dream come true; no more bulky CD player and case. Now you can fit thousands of songs into your shirt pocket. Laptops, Blackberries, etc., provide a link to home with text messaging and emails, but remember, the smaller the better.

Luggage. Practical and inexpensive luggage is available at most specialty shops and department stores. Two things to consider: 1) Make absolutely, positively sure it has wheels. Dragging an old, heavy bag around the globe won't help your back or your disposition. 2) Buy a color other than black. Most luggage is black and rectangular, so it can be very confusing coming off the baggage carousel. While we know black is beautiful, remember to identify your bags with a bright ribbon or tape, or a large travel sticker that won't peel off. Another bag you might consider is a backpack; I love 'em — light, portable and convenient for hands-free activities, and they're not just for students anymore.

Clothing. Cotton is still king. Comfortable blue jeans or slacks are acceptable for the road. You've also heard "layer up, layer down." This is a great idea — less clothes and more flexibility. I like to start with my favorite go-to clothing. A windbreaker is flexible for both men and women. Slickers or windbreakers are light and practical, come rain or shine; make sure they're water-resistant. Another old adage — bring comfortable shoes. Of course, but better a dark color than high school white. Shoes are bulky in a suitcase, so bring only what you need. One last tip, rubber-soled shoes are the best for a day of touring – they can handle water without soaking through. Also, I bring sandals; they multi-task and can be used for beach & pool side, hiking, casual or in your room. Gentlemen take note—a standard blue blazer with brass buttons is always in style and instantly dresses up any pair of slacks. You are never in doubt, particularly in Europe if you wear a blue blazer to almost any event or meal. It is my favorite item for any trip.

Packing. Don't make the rookie mistake and overpack. Keep in mind that somewhere down the line you've got to carry it, drag it or push it, so let's keep it simple. Here are some must-pack items: compact umbrella, light fold-up bag for those extra going-home gifts, small alarm clock in case you don't get your wake-up call, gloves and caps (which don't take up much space in your suitcase), and always bring Ziploc bags for unexpected dilemmas.

Jewelry. Don't bring the good stuff; it may disappear without a trace. The idea is to buy jewelry there and bring it back as your new trophy. For men, keep this in mind—a watch can slip from your wrist as a seemingly innocent person bumps into you and in a split second that Rolex is gone. Here's my approach—there are times I arrive in an unsavory location, a land void of law and order, a den of thieves; so I invest in an inexpensive plastic watch and say, go ahead make my day—rip me off for $5 bucks and see if I care.

Gift Shopping List. Prior to departure, walk around your house and make a list of household items you may want or need in your home. Maybe it's a new tablecloth, or hardware for that old scratched door handle. I remember writing on my list that I would like a new pair of gloves. So during shopping time I focused on leather goods and found a soft calf-hide pair in Peru—they are still my favorite. The idea behind the list is to set your mind thinking about practical items that will brighten your home. Remember, many foreign products can be found in your own hometown, so your "finds" should include unique items local to that country, which can become cherished mementos in your life.

Beginning Your Trip. On the day of departure, you've looked at some of these travel tips and are ready to go. You start off your trip by dressing up, not down, for your flight. It is the fastest way to get good service throughout your trip. You have avoided overpacking, and all your bags have wheels, including hand-carries. You have remembered luggage tags with extra IDs taped inside the bags, and most important—all your travel documents are in the same place. You and all members of your group know that one and only place where the passport and trip documents are kept. That way no one leaves his/her passport on the lounge seat or loses it in the excitement of the departure.

After check-in at the airport, go through customs and security and directly to your gate to establish a beachhead for your friends or family. Then if you need to shop or eat, you're ready for your departure and not held up by long security lines. Now you are off to a good start because as part of your pre-trip planning, everyone has brought a good book, video game or writing project to pass away those long hours in the sky. Oh yes, someone remembered a good local map, so you can get your bearings in advance for your new destinations. After a meal and a movie, you might want to get 40 winks or a night's sleep. To do this, I carry a small pack that includes airline socks, eye shades and ear plugs, which put me in a cocoon of rest and help ward off evil jet lag. If you're traveling across time zones, your body will need to adjust, so drink plenty of water and get your rest. Here is a tip: Drinking alcohol during long flights can make your jet lag worse; it's more important to keep hydrated with water and save the "happy hour" for your new destination.

Helpful Traveler Websites

Currency Exchange: http://www.xe.com/

Global Electric and Phone Directory: http://www.kropla.com

Language Translation: http://babelfish.yahoo.com

Maps: http://www.multimap.com

Seats: http://www.multimap.com/

Time Zones & Dialing Codes: http://timeanddate.com

Tourism Offices Worldwide: http://www.towd.com

Travelers Health: http://wwwnc.cdc.gov/travel/default.aspx

Traveling with Allergies: https://www.allergytranslation.com/Home/home.php

Traveling with Pets: http://www.petswelcome.com

Weather: http://www.accuweather.com

Traveler's Checklist

Cross through inapplicable items & check-off pertinent items as you pack.

Essentials

- ❏ Travel itinerary/tickets
- ❏ Visa/passport
- ❏ Reservation info
- ❏ Credit card(s)
- ❏ Traveler's checks
- ❏ Emergency Numbers
- ❏ Medications
- ❏ Vaccination info
- ❏ Birth certificate
- ❏ Foreign currency
- ❏ Calculator ($ exchange)
- ❏ Cash ($ bills for tipping)
- ❏ Insurance health/travel
- ❏ Wallet/purse

Traveler's Checklist (Cont.)
Miscellaneous

❑ Glasses/sunglasses	❑ Alarm clock
❑ Contacts/solution	❑ Camera/film/video tape
❑ Batteries	❑ Maps/guidebooks
❑ Umbrella	❑ Elec. converter/adapter
❑ Sport equipment	❑ Games/books/ebooks
❑ Binoculars	❑ Flashlight
❑ Packing tape/string	❑ Resealable plastic bags
❑ Business cards	❑ Postage stamps/addresses
❑ Notebook/pen	❑ Backpack/waist-pack
❑ Laundry bag	❑ Spot remover/laundry soap
❑ Luggage lock(s)	❑ Language translator
❑ Sewing kit	❑ Home key
❑ Music player	❑ Hair Dryer/curling Iron
❑ Beach bag/towel	❑ Iron/steamer

Toiletries

❑ Shampoo/conditioner	❑ Hair spray
❑ Deodorant	❑ Toothbrush/paste/floss
❑ Comb/brush	❑ Razor/shaving items
❑ Cosmetics	❑ Cologne/perfume
❑ Lotion/cream	❑ Powder/foot spray
❑ Soap/moisturizer	❑ Feminine products

Flying Comfort/Carry-On's

❑ Bottled water	❑ Inflatable neck rest
❑ Reading material	❑ Contact lens supplies
❑ Eye drops/ear plugs	❑ Warm socks
❑ Gum/mints/snack	❑ Tylenol/lip balm

Traveler's Checklist (Cont.)
Health/Comfort Aids

- First aid kit
- Vitamins
- Sun screen
- Insect repellent
- Contact lens supplies
- Aspirin/acetaminophen
- Ibuprofen
- Anti-diarrhea
- Birth control
- Eye drops/ear plugs
- Band-Aids
- Lip balm
- Decongestant, non-drowsy
- Analgesic for burns/bites
- Antibiotic ointment
- Constipation aids
- Sweetener substitute
- Gum/mints/hard candies
- Toilet paper (overseas)
- Tissues
- Hand wipes
- Moleskin, inner soles

Clothing

- Underwear/lingerie
- Casual pants/shorts
- Casual shoes/boots
- Dress slacks/belts
- Dress shoes
- Suit/sport coat
- Neckties/scarves
- Cuff links/accessories
- Belts
- T-shirts
- Sandals/water shoes
- Coat/windbreaker
- Pajamas/robe/slippers
- Casual shirts/blouses
- Sport socks
- Dress Shirts/blouses
- Dress socks/hose
- Dresses
- Jewelry/watch
- Purses
- Exercise gear
- Thermal wear
- Swim wear/cover-up
- Hat/gloves

- Minimize colors to mix & match clothing and accessories
- Layer clothing to add or strip as needed
- Tropic/desert: lightweight cotton fabrics
- Cooler climates: woolens and silks

Traveler's Checklist (Cont.)
Kids Extras

❑ Special medications

❑ Pre-packaged snacks

❑ Games/toys

❑ Paper/pens/pencils

❑ Books/magazines

❑ Gum/candy

❑ Crayons/coloring books

Additional for Infants

❑ Folding stroller

❑ Bottles/pacifier

❑ Diaper cream/powder

❑ Plastic disposable bags

❑ Formula/food/juice/snacks

❑ Can opener (hand held)

❑ Disposable diapers

❑ Wet wipes

❑ Bibs

❑ Favorite blanket

Before Leaving Home

❑ Pay bills that will come due

❑ Make arrangements for care of pets & plants

❑ Newspaper and mail arrangements

❑ Make arrangements for watering plants

❑ Arrange for trash cans to be put out and back

❑ Discard food that might spoil

❑ House key, itinerary & contact #'s to someone

❑ Photocopy important document & prescriptions

❑ Set automatic timers for lights, radio, etc.

❑ Lock windows and doors

❑ Turn off faucets and appliances (even unplug)

❑ Take photo of luggage (if lost, it will be helpful)

❑ Strongly consider TRAVEL INSURANCE

Enjoying Every Moment

Our attitude toward life determines life's attitude towards us.

−Earl Nightingale, Speaker and Author

Don't worry, be happy! Set your mind on enjoying the vacation and not complaining about the minutiae of life. Smile inside, smile outside, and greet the world with an "I'm OK, you're OK" attitude. From start to finish, a big smile sets a welcome tone. If you're a first-time traveler to a distant land, things may seem difficult and clumsy. So what if you're a "duck out of water"? Laugh it off and, most important, if you get in a jam, keep your cool. Don't raise your voice, talk in low tones.

What time does the 9 o'clock bus leave? Here are some ways to stay out of that jam. Allow extra time for most everything. Say you're on vacation…if you are on a motorcoach tour−board a little early; on a flight−get to the airport with time to spare; and don't be late for meals. Now you're on the way to becoming a confident, relaxed traveler. A great way to adapt to a new environment is to learn some local phrases, like: "thank you," "please," "hi," "goodbye" and "where is the toilet?"

Now that you are in such a good frame of mind, let me share one of my best travel tips …works every time, can't miss, guaranteed results. If you are a stranger in a strange land and are curious about the sightseeing highlights of an area, find a shop with a postcard rack. Here displayed for your viewing pleasure in bright colors are pictures with short descriptions of the most interesting attractions. This is a rapid way to get oriented to the area, plus a postcard or two might enhance your travel album.

Health Tips. Most people can't enjoy a trip if they come down with an illness. That's no fun, so train yourself to wash your hands possibly more than you would back home. Here is an innocent mistake travelers make, without much thought; you place your hand on a wall, pick up the germs, then sit down to a meal, grab the fresh-smelling bread and transfer the germs right into your mouth. I seldom get sick overseas because I always remember to wash before meals. Not all countries in the world are as health-conscious as the United States. Another sure-fire health tip— if you are in an area where you don't feel comfortable about the local water, make sure you order your beverage in a sealed bottle or can. Those little amoebas can take you down and put a dent in your vacation plans. One last little rule: respect your body—take a nap and try to get eight hours sleep per night.

Traveler's Safety. Safety can be a bigger problem in your mind than in the streets. The concern about safety can gnaw on your emotions and make you a worry-wart. I'm convinced that the majority of the world is safe if you apply basic principles, although realistically, just being alive at all does involve some risk. Here are some rules I abide by overseas. I always repeat this first rule to my clients and usually mention this in my travel speeches.

1) Anywhere in the world, in a bad part of town at night— you're in trouble. I've walked through some pretty seedy slums, been shot at in Vietnam and arrested by countless border guards who wanted my money; but my fortunes were always better by daylight. The sun is your friend; dark streets in poor areas are not. Keep this in mind—desperate people do desperate things. Someone who might pass by you in the daylight, smile and say hi might rob you at night.

I like touring in the morning; bandits are still asleep during most morning sightseeing.

2) If you're in a questionable area, I recommend traveling in groups, the more the merrier. A person walking alone is a more tempting target for a thief or poor person who needs money.

3) Be alert to places where people congregate, such as tourist areas. Be aware of people bumping into you — they could be pick-pockets, or someone asking you a question to divert your attention from an accomplice.

4) One last comment — in all the hotels and all the lodges around the world, I've never been robbed in my room. Your bedroom is a safe-haven, but don't expose cash or jewelry; place them in your bags or safety deposit box.

Great Shopping

We always hold hands. If I let go, she shops.

–Henny Youngman

Looking for that collectable trophy? Can't resist magnificent craftsmanship at very affordable prices? ... Well, you're not alone. Travel magazines publish annual travel surveys of the most popular vacation activities, and hiking, gambling, romancing, great food and relaxation on a beach don't make the top of the list. Without question, sightseeing and shopping rank 1 and 2. Shopping has been high on people's preference lists since Eve set up shop and started selling those apple-shaped necklaces.

Shopping was a centerpiece in the earliest of times. Greek and Roman markets, or agoras, were lined with shops and trading areas, which still survive today in remote areas. When I am counseling with clients and they inquire about different destinations, I always like to explain the shopping options. Some destinations sparkle with their wide array of products. Others may have less than stellar choices for the discerning shopper.

Quality arts and crafts beckon buyers and change a "not for me" shopper into a "spur of the moment" impulse buyer. Most of us want to come home with mementos either great or small. When I was young, smaller trinkets caught my eye. Now being older and more comfortable, my shopping eyes look for items of value to fit a special need in my home.

The array of shopping ranges from local flea markets to posh boutiques. I remember purchasing an expensive inlaid wooden coffee table in Capri, Italy, that is the pride of my living room. Later in St. Petersburg, Russia, my wife and I found a replica of a Fabergé ceramic egg and bargained with the local vendor for a final price of five dollars. The two items blend neatly together — this elegant coffee table and the knock-off Russian egg both bring me joy and stir fond memories.

Let's talk shopping. Sometimes it may begin as your motor coach tour stops at the carpet factory recommended by your local guide. He or she, of course, will quietly receive a commission for bringing you to the owner's shop, but generally the selection is good and the comfortable surroundings allow time to browse through the array of items. Foreign shops and boutiques usually offer a variety of locally produced goods. It is true that you can buy a cashmere sweater in your hometown, having a choice of a dozen or so sweaters, but cashmere shops on High Street in Edinburgh offer endless racks of cashmere in numerous colors and styles. Many of the better shops will ship home your purchases, a convenient and appreciated amenity.

Duty-free shopping has its perks: reduced taxes, airport convenience and a swift way to use leftover currency. Once you get past the duty-free liquor, perfume and cigarettes, it can be time well spent reviewing the variety items – some good, some bad.

If you're a shopper at all, you've got to love the local markets with the noise of bargaining and bickering, and the local smells —some pleasant, some not. Take a look around and you may see grandmother in her local garb selling chickens while doll-like children seem to be running around unattended. Primarily, these are common people scratching out a living, so here are some polite rules. Don't delve into long negotiating unless you intend to buy, and try not to touch the items until they are yours. So how do you bargain? Ask the price and cut it in half in your mind and negotiate middle ground until you're happy. Cash, many times U.S. dollars, works surprisingly well. You might want to flash a twenty to set the stage. Credit cards are not always accepted by smaller shops and seldom at local markets. When time allows, break from your bargaining and take stock of your surroundings; you may observe a rhythm of people engaging in the time-honored activity of local commerce.

Photography—Capturing the Memory

To collect photographs is to collect the world.

–Susan Sontag

A picture truly can be worth a thousand words, and that special captured photo holds a remembrance for another day. Yesterday's odysseys can be rekindled time and again with the help of a travel album. I took this notion to the max. For 40 years, I carefully organized each of my trips into travel albums and included photos, brochures, postcards, business cards and ticket stubs, then added key memory words to help me recall places and events. Granted, using albums to help travelers with their next trip constitutes, in large measure, my everyday job, but blending work with pleasure is not all a bad thing.

There is a more pragmatic side to photo albums. Considering the outlay of money for your trips — travel does have its price. So after investing in a camera, the cost of processing and the album, you now have accumulated a valuable travel estate — a treasure trove of memories frozen in time through the miracle of photography. Here is one other thought. Don't let the album collect dust; six months or so after your trip, pull it out and reminisce with friends and family about the trip.

We are living in the age of a digital revolution. Long live the revolution! Viva the compact flash card, power to the pixels. Much applause to Eastman-Kodak over the last century, for they have served us well. Gone and obsolete is my reliable Kodak gold 200 35mm color-print film with 24 or 36 exposures. Farewell old friend, parting is such sweet sorrow. I recall snapping countless rolls of film loaded in a variety of camera bodies. Some people may remember the old box-shaped Brownie for which you had to look down on the lens and focus from your groin. In my archives rest film cameras of by-gone times; equipment once of great worth now gathers dust in a lonely drawer.

Today as I venture out on my new journeys of discovery, I carry an efficient assortment of lightweight photo equipment. My list includes one digital camera with zoom lens, one small digital pocket camera for use in the evening or at any hands free event. A modest-size camera bag with shoulder strap containing battery charger, lens cleaner, backup battery and compact flash card is necessary, but try to avoid carrying the kitchen sink.

Now let's talk about the shot itself. Here are some helpful suggestions. In Hollywood it's called the golden hour—when the lighting is just right for picture taking. Nothing beats early morning and late afternoon light. Even when the sun has dropped below the horizon, great shots are there for the taking. Try to avoid shots when the sun is bright and high. Another tip from the professionals—stay open to your surroundings and be ready for the unexpected; an unusual subject may be the best photo of your trip. Always remember to try to put people in your landscape shots for depth and contrast.

Let's review some of the basics:

1) Hold your camera very still and frame your shot using your zoom lens to adjust the distance. Sometimes, a closer shot can create a better picture.

2) If you believe you have a great opportunity for a shot, frame the picture from different angles and never stop at one photo. This is always a standard procedure for professionals and it should be for you.

3) If the picture involves people, ask politely if you can take several shots so there is a good chance you can select from a wide variety of photos. 4) Here is another good professional tip; don't let people pose like stone statues. Have them move their arms, try different head angles, maybe have them stand or sit on alternate sites. Better yet, take plenty of candid shots of your family and friends enjoying their vacation. The last thing you want is to get home and discover that all of your photos are the posed, "I was here" kind of shot.

After a day of sight-seeing and camera work, my favorite routine is to find the local watering hole, order a local drink or, as some say, a sundowner. In this end-of-the-day relaxing environment, I carefully delete uneventful shots, keeping the best and clearing the camera for the next day. When the trip is finished and I am back home, I have the pictures developed with a backup CD, buy an album and spread things out on the dining room table. I gather any special brochures and postcards and blend them together with my photography. Additionally, I make time to write a short recap of the trip and insert it on the front page of the album. If you discover you have taken an ideal photo, you may consider having it enlarged and framed. This is a permanent reminder of your trip. One last suggestion: Jot down a reminder in your calendar and revisit the album a year later–anniversaries are always a fitting time to recapture travel memories.

A photograph never grows old.
You and I change, people change all through the months and years,
but a photograph always remains the same.
How nice to look at a photograph of mother or father
taken many years ago. You see them as you remember them.
But as people live on, they change completely.
That is why I think a photograph can be kind.

- Albert Einstein

The world is a book
and those who do not travel
read only one page.

−St. Augustine

Chapter 4:
Grand Tours of the World

S timulated by the 18th-century Age of Enlightenment, the European thirst for knowledge and exploration expanded across areas farther than European boundaries, as far as Egypt, India and the new world. Inn keepers in tourist areas were more than willing to provide a safe room and board, as were local guides happy to inform and embellish the local lore. The expansion of tourism, once ignited, burned brightly, only slightly dimmed by national disasters or the outbreak of war. An enlightened gentleman or lady planned well in advance before venturing on a grand tour. Their expectations were not just to read about, but to visit the grand sights of the world. Touring became an intricate component of the learning experience, and an obligatory part of the modern Renaissance man or woman.

Tours were at first limited to a handful of trusted destinations. In contrast, today's explosion of multi-media travel advertising floods the traveler's senses, sometimes to the point of overload. So let's change the rules of engagement and concentrate on only the finest vacation experiences without persuasion from the outside. Tourist boards and hotel chains have deep pockets ready to sway you toward their particular destinations. They paint a rose-colored picture to win your heart, mind and dollars — but that may or may not satisfy your travel dreams.

I organized "The Grand Tours" using the Travelers' Century Club's 12 geographic regions. In preparing the "best of the best" list, I took into consideration travelers' opinions over many years, as they shared their favorite stories. I was tolerant toward primitive lands with limited facilities that might not always be able to display their cultural icons. I discovered a consistent pattern of client response that led me to start assigning a number rating to the many locations. My field explorations were the heart and soul of the Grand Tour list; I originally identified 186 Grand Tours, then condensed them to fewer than 80. I took key elements of each location and found a template, which, with experimentation, proved reliable. I was bemused at times by the enormity of it all. After some trial and error, a workable pattern emerged, which included the seven most important categories of a trip experience.

This academic exercise was usually performed in the "comfort" of an airline seat as I flew across the globe. Hanging in the air for long periods of time has its advantages; there are no interruptions, allowing time to craft ideas. I had mood swings, sometimes analyzing the list like an accountant with a button-down mind and little emotion. Other times, I found myself swept away by the romance of a destination. If I heard the pealing of bells as I walked down a tree-laden street or caught the scent of a flowering bush wafting through a city park, I fell victim to my own emotions. What does your heart say? Sounds quite noble, but when putting the numbers together, some dreamy locations may not stack up. Here is a good example – during speaking engagements, I gloated over Antarctica. I have cruised these icy waters on three separate trips—observing white and black colonies of penguins, spouting whales and mighty icebergs … a never-to-be-forgotten experience. Then I put the numbers together and looked at the big picture:

- **Activities & Sites** plus **Landmarks & Natural Wonders** rated a 5 out of 5 – an almost overload of pristine nature.

- The next category is **Cultures & People**… no points, no people … an uninhabited continent – rating 0.

- **Food & Beverage** is the next column & I gave the cruise ships a 4 considering you're well-nourished on board. Please note that almost all touring of Antarctica is via a cruise ship.

- **Local Shopping** was again very low as limited shopping can only be found in the gateway port cities of Punta Arenas Chile and Ushuaia Argentina, therefore rating 2.

- **Entertainment, Music & Sports** are not a specialty of adventure sailing. The traditional Salute to Broadway review is replaced by 'early to bed – early to rise', so a slightly generous 2 was given.

- **Accommodations** received a 4 in that today Antarctica's double-hulled ships are usually well-appointed which goes hand-in-hand with their premium cruise costs.

When you add the numbers, the overall rating of 22 is on the lower end of the Grand Tours. Prior to giving a rating, I viewed Antarctica as one of the greatest trips, but under harsher scrutiny, the lack of any substantial culture, shopping or entertainment detracted from this natural wonder experience.

Now let's look at Italy, a splendid Grand Tour. Italy has seen three great historic benchmarks: the Roman Empire–maybe the greatest era of all time; the development of the Christian Church; and the Renaissance, which gave the world a rebirth of art and philosophy–a bounty of sites and landmarks. Add to that the effervescent people, mouth-watering pastas and wine, opera and grand hotels. The numbers speak for themselves, an impressive 33 rating.

So, use the Grand Tours section as a guide toward your next vacation and blend in your personal travel traits. Keep in mind this is my unbiased list—no tourist board or hotel chain paid to get special treatment. The list was developed through years of on-site observations. It is subjective, yet the purpose is to hopefully clean up the confusion in travel advertising.

Your personal travel destination list now awaits you.

Grand Tours (by 12 Regions)

Activities & Events Landmarks	Natural & Manmade	Culture & People	Food & Beverage	Local Shopping	Entertainment Music, Dance & Sports	Unique Lodging	Incl. Ships
North America							
Alaska Cruise: 29 Total							
5	5	4	4	4	3	4	Y
Canadian Rockies: 30 Total							
5	5	4	4	3	4	5	
Vancouver & Whistler: 29 Total							
5	5	4	4	3	3	5	
N. California, Oregon & Washington: 26 Total							
4	5	4	3	3	3	4	
San Francisco: 29 Total							
5	4	4	4	4	4	4	
Yosemite & Sequoia: 23 Total							
4	5	3	3	2	2	4	
Hollywood & S. California: 30 Total							
5	5	4	4	4	4	4	
Las Vegas: 29 Total							
5	3	3	4	4	5	5	
Canyon Country: 27 Total							
5	5	4	3	3	3	4	
New Mexico: 28 Total							
5	5	4	4	3	3	4	
Colorado: 26 Total							
5	5	3	3	3	3	4	
Western So. Dakota: 25 Total							
5	5	4	3	2	3	3	
Churchill, Canada: 20 Total							
3	5	4	3	2	1	2	
Canadian Capitals: 29 Total							
5	5	4	4	3	4	4	
New York City: 32 Total							
5	5	4	4	4	5	5	
Boston / Cape Cod: 28 Total							
5	5	4	4	3	3	4	

Activities & Events Landmarks	Natural & Manmade	Culture & People	Food & Beverage	Local Shopping	Entertainment Music, Dance & Sports	Unique Lodging	Incl. Ships
New England: 28 Total							
5	5	4	4	3	3	4	
Canadian Maritimes: 27 Total							
5	4	4	5	3	3	3	
New Orleans & Natchez: 31 Total							
5	5	4	5	3	5	4	
Washington, DC: 31 Total							
5	5	3	4	3	3	4	
Virginia: 27 Total							
5	4	4	4	3	3	4	
Savannah / Charleston : 29 Total							
5	5	4	4	3	4	4	
Florida: 31 Total							
5	5	3	4	4	4	4	
Mexico's Western Resorts: 27 Total							
4	3	4	4	4	4	4	
Mexican Riviera Maya: 29 Total							
4	4	4	4	4	4	5	

Caribbean

Activities & Events Landmarks	Natural & Manmade	Culture & People	Food & Beverage	Local Shopping	Entertainment Music, Dance & Sports	Unique Lodging	Incl. Ships
North Caribbean Cruise: 26 Total							
4	3	3	4	4	4	4	Y
South Caribbean Cruise: 26 Total							
4	4	3	4	3	4	4	Y
Cuba: 26 Total							
4	4	4	3	2	5	4	

Central America

Activities & Events Landmarks	Natural & Manmade	Culture & People	Food & Beverage	Local Shopping	Entertainment Music, Dance & Sports	Unique Lodging	Incl. Ships
Guatemala: 28 Total							
5	5	4	3	3	3	5	
Costa Rica: 26 Total							
4	4	4	3	4	3	4	

Activities & Events Landmarks	Natural & Manmade	Culture & People	Food & Beverage	Local Shopping	Entertainment Music, Dance & Sports	Unique Lodging	Incl. Ships
South America							
Brazilian Amazon: 23 Total							
3	3	3	3	3	4	4	Y
Machu Picchu Peru: 28 Total							
5	5	4	3	4	3	4	
Rio de Janeiro & Iguasu: 31 Total							
5	5	5	4	4	4	4	
Argentina: 23 Total							
3	3	4	4	3	3	3	
Antarctica							
Antarctic Cruise: 22 Total							
5	5	0	4	2	2	4	Y
Atlantic Ocean							
Bermuda: 25 Total							
4	3	4	4	3	3	4	
Iceland: 26 Total							
4	5	4	4	3	3	3	
Europe							
Scotland: 30 Total							
5	5	5	4	4	3	4	
England: 31 Total							
5	5	5	3	4	4	5	
Ireland: 32 Total							
5	5	5	4	4	5	4	
Northern France: 33 Total							
5	5	5	5	4	4	5	
Southern France: 32 Total							
5	5	5	5	4	3	5	
Northern Italy: 33 Total							
5	5	5	5	4	4	5	
Southern Italy: 32 Total							
5	5	5	5	4	3	5	

	Activities & Events Landmarks	Natural & Manmade	Culture & People	Food & Beverage	Local Shopping	Entertainment Music, Dance & Sports	Unique Lodging	Incl. Ships
Switzerland: 30 Total	5	5	4	4	4	3	5	
Spain: 31 Total	5	5	4	4	4	4	5	
Germany: 29 Total	5	5	4	3	4	4	4	
Danube Cruise: 31 Total	5	5	4	5	4	3	5	Y
Greece: 29 Total	5	5	4	4	4	3	4	
Aegean Cruise: 29 Total	5	4	4	4	4	4	4	Y
Russia: 26 Total	5	5	3	3	3	3	4	
Scandinavian Cruise: 29 Total	5	5	4	4	4	3	4	Y
Orient Express: 31 Total	5	5	4	5	4	3	5	(train)
Western Med. Cruise: 31 Total	5	5	5	4	4	4	4	Y

Africa

	Activities & Events Landmarks	Natural & Manmade	Culture & People	Food & Beverage	Local Shopping	Entertainment Music, Dance & Sports	Unique Lodging	Incl. Ships
Egypt: 28 Total	5	5	4	3	4	3	4	
Morocco: 29 Total	5	5	4	4	4	3	4	
Kenya: 27 Total	5	5	3	4	3	3	4	
Tanzania: 27 Total	5	5	3	4	3	3	4	
South Africa, Botswana & Victoria Falls: 29 Total	5	5	4	4	4	3	4	

Activities & Events Landmarks	Natural & Manmade	Culture & People	Food & Beverage	Local Shopping	Entertainment Music, Dance & Sports	Unique Lodging	Incl. Ships
Middle East							
Turkey: 30 Total							
5	5	4	4	4	4	4	
Israel / Jordan: 27 Total							
5	5	4	3	3	3	4	
Arabian Peninsula: 25 Total							
4	4	3	3	3	3	5	
Asia							
Five Stans: 22 Total							
4	4	3	3	2	3	3	
Iran: 20 Total							
4	4	3	1	3	2	3	
India: 28 Total							
5	5	4	3	4	3	4	
Southeast Asia: 30 Total							
5	5	4	4	4	3	5	
China: 28 Total							
5	5	4	3	4	2	5	
Himalaya Kingdoms: 24 Total							
5	4	4	3	3	2	3	
Indonesia: 30 Total							
5	4	4	4	5	4	4	
Japan: 29 Total							
5	4	4	3	5	3	5	
Pacific Ocean							
Australia: 30 Total							
5	5	5	4	4	3	4	
New Zealand: 29 Total							
5	5	4	4	4	3	4	
Tahiti: 31 Total							
5	5	4	4	4	4	5	
Hawaii: 30 Total							
5	5	4	4	3	4	5	
Galapagos Islands: 28 Total							
5	5	4	4	3	2	5	Y

North America

Alaskan & Cruise   Rating: 29   Best Touring Season: Summer

North to Alaska, go north the rush is on. – Johnny Horton

Highlights: In the summer months, cruise ships begin scenic sailings on the Inside Passage of Alaska and Canada. The history in Alaska has been shaped by fur trading, gold mining, commercial fishing, native people and sourdoughs, or settlers. Add a land tour from Anchorage to Denali National Park and experience Alaska's wilderness. Cruise the Inside Passage–totem poles in Ketchikan; eagles, fur seals and St. Michael's Cathedral in Sitka; White Pass & Yukon Railroad in Skagway; Red Dog Saloon in the capital, Juneau; Mendenhall Glacier and view calving mighty Hubbard Glacier. After the cruise, Glacier Bay National Park; Kenai Fjords National Park; Anchorage to Denali via Alaska Railroad; wildlife in Denali and a view of Mt. McKinley; on a clear day, fly from Fairbanks to Point Barrow, North Slope for an Inupiat artic experience at the top of the world.

My Favorite Encounter: With snow-capped Mt. McKinley in the background and moose grazing in the streams, I walked the spongy tundra of Denali.

Canadian Rockies   Rating: 30   Best Touring Season: Late spring, Summer, early Fall, Winter skiing

When I'm calling you ... you belong to me, I belong to you.
–Jeanette MacDonald & Nelson Eddie

Highlights: The Canadian Rockies are a natural masterpiece. Pine-covered mountains with rapid-flowing rivers and turquoise lakes. Banff - hiking, skiing, mountain golf; gondola up Sulphur Mountain to see mountain goats and bighorn sheep, plus shopping & dine-a-rounds at Banff Springs Resort. Drive north to Lake Louise for boating; hiking around Turquoise Lake; Chateau Lake Louise; Peyto Lake & Hoodoo pinnacles; Columbia Ice Fields with Athabasca Glacier on snowcoaches and Sunwapta Falls; also Yoho and Kootneay National Parks. Plenty of wildlife roam Jasper National Park. Ride the Rocky Mountaineer train to Vancouver.

My Favorite Encounter: Toward dusk a single bagpiper in full regalia began playing outside the Banff Springs Hotel.

Vancouver & Whistler   Rating: 29   Best Touring Season: Late Spring, Summer, early Fall, Winter skiing

I have always thought of Canada as God's country.- Jack Granatstein

Highlights: Strikingly beautiful Vancouver is a port city with inlets and hidden harbors. Its diverse population adds to the city's charm. Whistler is a planned ski resort created with such care, it won the rights for the Winter Olympics. Vancouver–Stanley Park with the Thunderbird Totem Pole, Gastown's steam clock, China Town, Granville Island Market, Grouse Mt. gondola, historic Hotel Vancouver, float planes to Victoria on Vancouver Island, Empress Hotel with an English atmosphere located on Victoria Harbor, spectacular Butchart Gardens, Vancouver to Whistler with breathtaking mountain lakes, and Blackcomb & Whistler ski runs. Scenic mountain golf courses, ATV tour, Ziptrek, village dining & shopping.

My Favorite Encounter: Invited with my wife on a corporate jet; played golf on beautiful mountain courses near Whistler.

N. California/Oregon/Washington Rating: 26   Best Touring Season: Year-round (cold in winter)

This land is your land, this land is my land, from California to the New York Island; from the red wood forest to the Gulf Stream waters, this land was made for you and me. - Woody Guthrie

Highlights: Take the Pacific Coast Highway north from San Francisco, through the wine country, to the world's tallest trees, lake-filled craters, sand dunes and spectacular coastline. Drive through the Avenue of the Giants, coastal redwood & stop in Eureka to visit Victorian mansions. Continue into Oregon and visit Crater Lake National Park & boat around Wizard Island, jet boat the olive green Rogue River, Oregon Dunes National Recreation Area, Newport Aquarium, Three Capes Scenic Drive with lighthouses, seabirds & islands. Stop at Tillamook for a look at the cheese factory, Portland city of roses and the 620-foot Multnomah Falls, on the Columbia River Gorge near Mt. Hood. Washington–visit Mt. St. Helen's National Monument for a view or climb, Olympic National Park, Quinalt Lake & Lodge, La Push Indian Reservation, Hoh Rain Forest, Mt. Olympus, lavender farms near Sequim, Seattle with Boeing Museum, Space Needle, Mt. Rainier National Park, Puget Sound and San Juan Islands.

My Favorite Encounter: The jet boat ride on the Rogue River is an experience for people of all ages; spin & turn, and see natural forests and wildlife.

San Francisco, CA   Rating: 29   Best Touring Season: Year-round
                                                   (cold in the summer)

I left my heart in San Francisco, high on a hill it calls to me.- Tony Bennett

Highlights: Start by hopping on a cable car that slowly climbs up & down the hills of the city, view Victorian mansions, boat to Alcatraz Island, take time to appreciate the Golden Gate Bridge, Lombard switch-back street, bustling Fisherman's Wharf, Chinatown, the food & shops of the Embarcadero & stop at a bakery for famous sourdough bread. Day trips - Monterey Peninsula & 17-Mile Drive, Pebble Beach Golf Links, the village of Carmel-by-the-Sea, Big Sur on Highway 1, the semi-circular Bixby Bridge & McWay Falls, Muir Woods National Monument for redwood groves or Napa Valley & Sonoma Valley for lunch at a vineyard.

My Favorite Encounter: Flew in on the Rams football charter, then was escorted by California Highway Patrol motorcycles to Candlestick Park.

Yosemite & Sequoia Natl Parks, CA Rating: 23   Best Touring Season: Spring,
                                                   Summer, Fall

In every walk with nature, one receives far more than he seeks. –John Muir

Highlights: This wonderful gift of nature was protected as a national park at the end of the 19th century. Naturalist John Muir helped to save the valley for future generations. Yosemite Valley with the granite cliff El Capitan, Half Dome, Yosemite Falls with a height of 2,425 feet, picturesque Bridal Veil Falls. Have a meal at the rustic but elegant Ahwahnee Hotel, drive to Mariposa Grove with large Sequoia trees. A lovely drive is Tioga Pass Road, and in the same area is California gold country and plenty of opportunities to go river rafting. Drive south to Kings Canyon National Park, Scenic Byway, John Muir Lodge, and Sequoia National Park in the Sierra Nevadas. Visit General Sherman Tree (world's largest), hike Morro Rock, wander around Crescent Meadow and stay at Wuksachi Village Lodge. The gateway city Fresno is in the San Joaquin Valley, the breadbasket of California.

My Favorite Encounter: Climbed Morro Rock three times in Sequoia National Park just to get a clear photo for a newspaper article.

Los Angeles, Hollywood & Southern CA Rating: 30   Best Touring Season: Year-round

Hooray for Hollywood. –Johnny Mercer

Highlights: The center of movie making has always been under the bright lights of Hollywood, and Walt Disney created the first modern theme park for kids of all ages. Universal Studios tour, Hollywood & Vine with Grauman's Chinese Theater & the Walk of Fame. Stars homes on the Beverly Hills tour, Malibu, Huntington, & other famous beaches. Don't miss some great museums including Getty, Huntington, Los Angeles County Museum of Art. The first of the great theme parks, wonderful Disneyland, plus Knott's Berry Farm. Fly by pontoon plane to Catalina Island or take a ferry, San Diego with Balboa Park & a world class zoo, harbor cruise, Coronado Island, Gaslamp Quarter historical neighborhood, Sea World, Seaport Village & San Diego Wild Animal Park.

My Favorite Encounter: Took in a first-run movie at Grauman's Chinese Theatre.

Las Vegas, Nevada   Rating: 29   Best Touring Season: Year-round
(hot in the summer)

If you aim to leave Las Vegas with a small fortune, go there with a large one.
–Anonymous

Highlights: The great mecca for gambling with creative casinos, elaborate shows, and expansive shopping. Walk the Strip & downtown, see the dancing fountains in front of Bellagio, special effects at Luxor, MGM Grand, Wynn & many more. Don't miss the Freemont Street Experience and the City Center Complex. Day trips to Hoover Dam and the Grand Canyon.

My Favorite Encounter: Hit the jackpot, but not for money -- flight-seeing of the Grand Canyon, then a front-row seat for Elvis on stage.

Canyon Country, USA   Rating: 28   Best Touring Season: Spring,
Summer, Fall

It's awesomely beautiful ... I gaze about me,
it must take courage to live in such beauty.
–Pearl S. Buck

Highlights: The Grand Canyon is the world's greatest natural wonder and seen by millions of visitors every year. The surrounding land areas encompass both manmade and natural beauty worth your time and exploration. From the North and South rims of the Grand Canyon, hike or ride by mule or horse into the mile-deep canyon floor, great rafting through canyon areas. Take in Zion National Park, Checkerboard Mesa, Weeping Rock Trail, and Angels Landing, Cedar Breaks National Monument, spectacular Bryce Canyon Natural Park with reddish-orange hoodoo peaks, Lake Powell & Rainbow Bridge National Monument. Navaho Monument Valley & Mesa Verde with cliff balcony built by the Anasazi people and protected by Teddy Roosevelt. Other great national parks include Canyonlands, Arches and Capitol Reef, plus Natural Bridges National Monument and Dead Horse Point State Park.

My Favorite Encounter: Bryce Canyon trails for hiking–I spent hours with my three boys hiking through the hoodoos.

New Mexico   Rating: 28   Best Touring Season: Spring,
Summer, Fall

The land of enchantment. – Motto for the state

Highlights: With so many diverse things to see, give this state plenty of time and you will truly discover a land of enchantment. In the north part of the state, Chaco Culture National Park, Shiprock rock formation, the High Road to Taos with Pueblo village, Kit Carson's home, ski lodge, deep Rio Grand Gorge. Visit fashionable Santa Fe with adobe architecture, Canyon Road art galleries, the Plaza and the Palace of the Governors. On to Albuquerque with international Balloon Fiesta; Atomic, Rattlesnake & Turquoise Museums; Acoma Pueblo (sky city), Carlsbad Caverns with the Big Room, Cloudcroft western town, White Sands National Monument & Missile Park & El Paso, Texas on the border.

My Favorite Encounter: I joined a mass ascension of 500 balloons in Albuquerque, an hour of multi-colored photos.

| **Colorado** | Rating: 26 | Best Touring Season: Spring, Summer, Fall & Winter Skiing |

It's a Colorado Rocky Mountain high; I've seen it raining fire in the sky.
–John Denver

Highlights: Where the plains meet the Rockies, a state that grew from silver mining and developed world-class ski resorts. Denver has a great art museum and botanical garden. Colorado Railroad Museum in Golden, Rocky Mountain National Park (Estes Park), Colorado Springs with the Garden of the Gods, Air Force Academy, Pikes Peak Cog Railway, Cumbres and Toltec Scenic Railroad, Royal Gorge, Durango & Silverton Narrow Gauge Railroad, Mesa Verde National Park, little-known Black Canyon of the Gunnison National Park, stately Mt. Wilson, Great Sand Dunes National Park. Ski resorts include: well-heeled Telluride with its dramatic box canyon, Snowmass, Crested Butte, Aspen, Breckenridge, Vail and many more.

My Favorite Encounter: Boarded the Big Boy Steam Locomotive in Denver and rode north to Cheyenne's Summer Rodeo.

| **Western South Dakota** | Rating: 25 | Best Touring Season: Spring, Summer, Fall |

*Carved upon the mighty mountain, the hero's faces pale
in the misty moonlight.*
–Emiko Matsumoto

Highlights: Almost an overload of monuments, wild-life and natural wonders in a relatively compact space. Pastel-colored Badlands National Park and Wall Drug Store, Rapid City, Black Hills, and Custer State Park with abundant animals, Wind & Jewel Caves, Mammoth Hot Springs and excavation site, the four faces of Mount Rushmore, enormous Crazy Horse Memorial, Devil's Tower (Wyoming), Deadwood gold mining town, and Sturgis for Harley Davidson bikers.

My Favorite Encounter: Invited the extended family to a gathering in the Black Hills, 17 members plus a stray buffalo.

Churchill & Hudson Bay, Canada Rating: 20 Best Touring Season: Bear sightings late Oct.

The landscape is bleak but dramatic … the world as it was in the beginning.
–The Honorable James L. Buckley

Highlights: The one place in the world to see astonishing numbers of polar bears without being eaten. Watch the bears wait for the Hudson Bay to freeze so they can go out on the ice and munch on ringed seals. In late October/early November fly or train from Winnipeg, board tall tundra buggies to photograph polar bears, view Arctic fox & hares, owls & white Ptarmigan birds. Dog sled ride near the bay or go helicopter sightseeing, and dine on caribou stew & Arctic char.

My Favorite Encounter: Perched on a high tundra buggy, watched safely as bears swiped at our cameras.

Canadian Capitals Rating: 29 Best Touring Season: Late Spring, Summer, Fall, Winter skiing

I saw a great and wonderful country … a proper land.
–Field Marshal Bernard Montgomery

Highlights: The French-speaking Canadians have an expression, "joie de vivre" or "the joy of life." Begin with Niagara Falls and the Maid of the Mist boat for a good soaking. Visit the orchard & wineries near Niagara-on-the-Lake and enjoy the Shaw Festival & local ice wine. Visit Toronto & the CN Tower, live theater, Ottawa with Parliament Hill and river cruise, Montreal jet boat ride, Old Town & the blue interior of Notre-Dame Basilica - there are great museums in all three cities. Visit Mt. Tremblant ski resort in the Laurentian Mts., great dining, fall foliage, charming Quebec City & Chateau Frontenac Hotel, the only walled city in North America. Plus the 1,000 Islands of the St. Lawrence River and captivating St. Anne de Beaupré Basilica.

My Favorite Encounter: Family jet boat ride down Niagara River toward the falls, spinning donuts turns & having fun & getting very wet.

New York City   Rating: 32   Best Touring Season: Year-Round
                                                    (cold in the winter)

Give me your tired, your poor, your huddled masses yearning to breathe free.
                    –Plaque on the Statue of Liberty.

Highlights: Take a bite out of the Big Apple, tour the town from Broadway to the Bronx, with an incredible selection of restaurants, Rockefeller Center and Carnegie Hall. The list of great activities and landmarks is endless: great theater, museums, sports, zoos, buildings, bridges, it's all there in NYC. View the city from the top of the Empire State Building, visit the United Nations Building or take a carriage ride in Central Park. Visit great museums like Metropolitan, Natural History, Guggenheim and many more; also the Bronx Zoo, Statue of Liberty & Ellis Island; walk the Brooklyn Bridge, enjoy the Lincoln Center for the Performing Arts or live theater on Broadway and Times Square. Don't miss Ground Zero - former site of the World Trade Center, South Street Seaport, Wall Street, and many outstanding churches and cathedrals. Order a Manhattan at the Plaza Hotel or a salad at the Waldorf Astoria, take the Circle Line cruise around Manhattan or go to a Yankees game.

My Favorite Encounter: For a large group, I hired 45 horse carriages—they lined up in front of the Plaza Hotel & left a big mess.

Boston & Cape Cod   Rating: 28   Best Touring Season: Spring,
                                                    Summer, Fall

Listen my children and you shall hear, of the midnight ride of Paul Revere.
                    –Henry Wadsworth Longfellow

Highlights: Proper Boston and Cambridge are big university towns with Harvard, MIT and many more. It has a big history from the Revolutionary War, a big immigration culture and a big dig for its new tunnels and transportation. Visit Freedom Trail with Faneuil Hall, Old North Church, Quincy Market, Old Iron Sides, Boston Common and Public Garden. Outside of Boston, don't miss Harvard Yard, historic Concord & Lexington. Drive from Cape Cod to Provincetown for lobster & shopping; take the ferry to Martha's Vineyard or to Nantucket Island for a relaxing vacation. In Connecticut, tour Mystic Seaport's museum and aquarium. In Newport, R.I., visit the grand mansions & jazz festival.

My Favorite Encounter: In my youth, driving up the Cape Cod coast, a dead whale was a great trampoline for my sister and me.

New England   Rating: 28   Best Touring Season: Spring,
                                             Summer, Fall foliage, Winter skiing

I think that I shall never see a poem lovely as a tree
... poems are made by fools like me, but only God can make a tree.
–Joyce Kilmer

Highlights: Any time is a good season for New England, but in the fall when the sugar maples and other broad-leaf trees turn color, spend time and enjoy a colorful New England holiday. Visit Plymouth & the Pilgrim heritage, White Mountains of New Hampshire, Green Mountains in Vermont, Lake Winnipesaukee, Mount Washington Cog Railway, Franconia Notch, Stowe, Killington, Shelburne Museum, North Conway, Fort Ticonderoga on Lake Champlain in New York, Acadia National Park with Cadillac Mountain and the rugged Maine coast line.

My Favorite Encounter: One little gem is the Grafton Inn in Vermont, with fireplace, blueberry pancakes & maple syrup or sharp cheddar cheese.

Canadian Maritimes   Rating: 27   Best Touring Season: Spring,
                                               Summer, Fall

This is the forest primeval; the murmuring pines and the hemlock.
–Henry Wadsworth Longfellow

Highlights: It's a seafood fest, a golfer's dream and a touring delight. You'll fall in love with Nova Scotia, New Brunswick and Prince Edward Island. Nova Scotia with Cape Breton Highlands National Park & the Cabot Trail, and Halifax, a port town with the noon canon firing at the Citadel. Take a day trip to the churches of Mahone Bay; Mansard Academy in Lunenburg; picturesque fishing village of Peggy's Cove; try whale watching at Digby or eat the delicious scallops. Drive to New Brunswick & Hopewell Rocks for the world's highest tides at the Bay of Fundy. Dine on lobster or seafood chowder on Prince Edward Island in Charlottetown, play golf on green rolling hills, visit Anne of Green Gables Museum, P.E.I. National Park and the not-so-famous Potato Museum.

My Favorite Encounter: My wife and I went twice to Hopewell Rocks, high & low tide, 37-foot difference; walked on the flats around curious high rock formations.

New Orleans, LA & Natchez   Rating: 31   Best Touring Season: Year-round,
                                                 Mardi Gras early Spring, Summer
                                                 humid

Oh when the saints go marching in, Lord I want to be in that number,
when the saints go marching in.
–Louie Armstrong's famous gospel song

Highlights: If you crave great food and music with a soul, New Orleans may be your kind of town. Wander through antebellum mansions in Natchez, Miss. - octagonal Longwood, stately Stanton Hall, Rosalie by the Mississippi River, Monmouth Plantation with lodging and many more. Take the Natchez Trace Parkway to Vicksburg battlefield. Visit the plantations on the Mississippi River between St. Francisville and New Orleans, plus Cajun country near Lafayette, St. Martinsville, Longview Gardens and Lake Ponchartrain. New Orleans is the city of music from jazz to rock. The French Quarter offers great restaurants and dining. Walk to historic Jackson Square for a beignet square doughnut, wrought iron railings, Mississippi River harbor walk, Esplanade Creole mansions, St. Louis Cemetery, Garden District, historic French Cemetery and, of course, Mardi Gras parades & parties.

My Favorite Encounter: Tourism Cares sponsored a clean-up of one of the above-ground cemeteries. I salvaged bricks from inside the tombs.

Washington, DC   Rating: 27   Best Touring Season: Year-round

The capital of Corinthian order, placed upon a noble
and commanding eminence.
–Charles Dickens

Highlights: The nation's capital offers many choices - tour the White House, Capitol, House & Senate by invite, the National Mall, climb the stairs of the Washington Monument, visit war memorials of WWII, Korea & Vietnam, plus the Lincoln & Jefferson Memorials, Smithsonian museums, historic Georgetown, National Zoo, Pentagon, Arlington Cemetery, Alexandria's historic Old Town & waterfront, or cruise the Potomac River.

My Favorite Encounter: When I was 9, my father took me to Eisenhower's inaugural parade; later in life I put my father to rest in Arlington National Cemetery.

Virginia   Rating: 27   Best Touring Season: Spring,
                                            Summer, Fall

*Carry me back to old Virginny, there's where the cotton
and the corn and taters grow.*
–James Bland

Highlights: Virginia is blessed with rich farmland and orchards; house tours of George Washington's Mount Vernon; Thomas Jefferson's Monticello; James Madison's Montpelier & Fredericksburg; Colonial Williamsburg, Revolutionary War Yorktown, English settlement – Jamestown; Shenandoah National Park & Skyline Drive, and Charlottesville & Jefferson's Rotunda at the University of Virginia; Richmond and many Civil War battlefields; also Virginia Beach, Norfolk, Newport and Hampton Roads area.

My Favorite Encounter: After a scenic Skyline Drive, was very impressed by the stalactites and stalagmites of Luray Caverns.

Savannah & Charleston   Rating: 29   Best Touring Season: Year-round

Savannah sleeps among baskets of Azaleas.
–Simone de Beauvoir

Highlights: Savannah, elegant Southern Belle, a port city for cruises on the Savannah River; historic squares – the jewels of the city with mansions, live oaks & Spanish moss; carriage rides and night life on River Street. Vacation on St. Simons Island (Ga.), or visit historic Beaufort for a touch of the Old South. Low Country in Charleston, S.C., with its historic port city with harbor walk and fountains, city market & grand houses; Patriots Point with Yorktown aircraft carrier; Ft. Sumter cruise; plantation tours, including the great gardens of Middleton Place; relaxing Kiawah Island, & Hilton Head Island – with outstanding beaches, golf and kayaking.

My Favorite Encounter: A leisurely carriage ride by the mansions in Charleston, then dining on Low Country She-Crab soup plus shrimp and grits.

Florida   Rating: 29   Best Touring Season: Year-round

It's kind of fun to do the impossible.
–Walt Disney

Highlights: A state blessed with beaches and sun. Visit the National Naval Aviation Museum in Pensacola; historic buildings in St. Augustine, the oldest city in the U.S., and Castillo de San Marcos Spanish fort and a large alligator farm. Go south to Daytona for a beach you can drive on and the Daytona International Speedway; Cape Kennedy rocket launching site. Orlando includes Disney World, MGM & Universal Studios, Sea World and resorts on the gulf, including Tampa Bay, Clearwater, St. Petersburg, Sarasota, Naples, Ft. Myers; Everglades National Park; West Palm Beach; Ft. Lauderdale; Miami Beach, including South Beach art deco area; Florida Keys; Key West & Fort Jefferson, Dry Tortugas Islands. Recreational sports include golf, deep sea fishing and baseball spring training, Jai alai.

My Favorite Encounter: One-day catamaran to Ft. Jefferson on Dry Tortugas National Park, a brick fort that seems to be floating on the water.

Mexico's Western Resorts Rating: 27   Best Touring Season: Year-round

South of the border, down Mexico way, that's where I fell in love
when stars above came out to play.
–Frank Sinatra

Highlights: A well-planned playground particularly suited for incentive groups and meetings. Visit Los Cabos area, including Cabo San Lucas & San Jose Del Cabo at the end of the Baja California peninsula, a dry cactus land with championship golf and great fishing, large beach resorts on the corridor between the two towns; Puerto Vallarta has traces of Old Mexico, colonial church & village; Acapulco features cliff diving & long resort beach, good Mexican food & shopping.

My Favorite Encounter: Early morning fishing in Cabo–caught a striped marlin, swordfish, and two dorados in one hour; my arm was ready to fall off.

Mexican Riviera Maya   Rating: 29   Best Touring Season: Year-round

Among these temples ... whose grandeur of architectural details,
no human tongue is able to describe.
–Hernando Cortez

Highlights: Cancun is a vacation getaway with many impressive resorts, shopping & restaurants. Take a boat excursion to Isla Mujeres, a clear water Island, or the Riviera Maya, which stretches down the coast with all-inclusive resorts combining value and luxury, water activities, golf and day excursions to Xelha for snorkeling & hammocks, Mayan ruins at Chichen Itza, Tulum & Coba. Cozumel Island for quaint Mexican towns & very good scuba.

My Favorite Encounter: I climbed to the top of Kukulcan Mayan pyramid in Chichen Itza and took time to view ruins as far as the eye could see.

Caribbean

Northern Caribbean Cruise   Rating: 26   Best Touring Season: Year-round

Yellow bird up high in banana tree, yellow bird you sit all alone like me.
–Traditional Jamaican song

Highlights: Cruise the colorful Bahamas, private cruise islands for a great beach day; Nassau & Paradise Island with large resorts; white sand beaches, casinos and fascinating aquarium at the resort Atlantis. Other ports-of-call include: St. John, Virgin Islands, for non-stop shopping; Puerto Rico for Old San Juan, Spanish forts of El Morro & San Cristóbal, and El Yunque Rain Forest. Jamaica for a Dunn's River Falls climb & Martha Brae slow rafting; Cayman Island for diving & turtle farm.

My Favorite Encounter: Got captured by the evening with a calypso steel band mixed with Planters Punch rum–"Ya Mon, very nice indeed".

Southern Caribbean Cruise   Rating: 26   Best Touring Season: Year-round

This is my island in the sun, where my people have toiled since time begun.
–Harry Belafonte

Highlights: A cruise experience from Puerto Rico to St. Kitts; visit Brimstone Hill Fortress and watch the green Vervet Monkeys; Dominica for deep forest and rivers with over-sized frogs; St. Lucia for two scenic mountain peaks - Petit Piton & Gros Piton; Martinique's infamous Mount Pelée volcano & Creole culture; Barbados for flying fish, Sam Lord's Castle and miles of sugar cane fields; St. Vincent and the Botanical Gardens; Dutch Aruba for shopping and Bonaire for diving flamingos and the salt works.

My Favorite Encounter: During a stop in Martinique, climbed up and in Mount Pelée, whose eruption killed 30,000 people in 1902.

Cuba   Rating: 26   Best Touring Season: Year-round

I was a man lucky enough to have discovered a political theory
... like finding a map in the forest.
–Fidel Castro

Highlights: Start in Havana, drive down the Malecón promenade and tour the huge Spanish forts that protect the harbor, walk through old town where Ernest Hemingway wrote and drank mint mojitos, listen to Cuban music that reminds you of Ricky Ricardo, or take a vintage 1950s American car taxi. Ride the Hershey Train and rest on the beaches of Varadero with European resorts and gala stage shows. Visit the colonial town of Trinidad, then drive south to Santiago de Cuba and see the old Bacardi Rum factory, large Spanish forts and a view of Teddy Roosevelt's San Juan Hill & U.S. Guantanamo Naval Base.

My Favorite Encounter: As a journalist, toured Santiago de Cuba and drove up San Juan Hill, taken by Teddy Roosevelt's Rough Riders, but the guide only talked about the Cuban soldiers.

Central America

Guatemala   Rating: 28   Best Touring Season: Year-round

Suddenly we glimpsed at an awe inspiring sight,
four of the great pyramids of Tikal.
        –Sir Eric Thompson

Highlights: A land of volcanos, natural beauty & Mayan ruins. Start in Guatemala City, full of multi-colored buses, Spanish aqueducts, National Palace and plenty of Marimba bands. Chichicastenango Indian Market with burning incense and locals in colorful outfits, Lake Atitlan, pristine water with backdrop of three volcanos and Indian villages; Antigua - old Spanish colonial capital of Central America with cobbled streets, numerous churches and Casa Santo Domingo Hotel - a former monastery; Tikal's great Mayan ruins with five pyramids, ballcourt & 3,000 buildings plus deep Petén Itza jungle & lake.

My Favorite Encounter: Finally made it to the great Tikal ruins deep in the Petén forest, with howler monkeys that make scary hooting sounds.

Costa Rica   Rating: 26   Best Touring Season: Year-round

Pura Vida. (full of life) –Costa Rica's common greeting

Highlights: Start in the capital of San Jose for year-round spring-like weather, shop for hammocks or miniature oxcarts, then visit Poás or Irazú Volcano. On the Pacific Coast, Peninsula Papagayo for a choice of resorts with nice beaches, golf, zip line Canopy Tour, whale & dolphin watching; Palo Verde National Park river cruise to see pink spoonbills, white egrets, green macaw, crocodile and green & black iguanas.

My Favorite Encounter: Snorkeling in the Bay of Papagayo flanked by a humped back whale and her calf.

South America

Brazilian Amazon   Rating: 23   Best Touring Season: Year-round

If you're going to live by the river, make friends with the crocodiles.
–Local proverb

Highlights: Fly into Manaus on the Amazon – the most powerful river on Earth, ten times greater than the Mississippi. Tour the Manaus Opera House built by rubber barons, then stay in a room high in the tree canopy above dense jungle to experience tropical birds and monkeys. Start your river cruise expedition – good accommodations & Zodiac landing boats going where your big boat cannot. In the rain forest see local tribes, tropical plants and wildlife of every shape and size.

My Favorite Encounter: I walked by a rushing river with a local Indian who split a brown stone, exposing pure green jade. I still have it as a memento from Amazonia.

Machu Picchu & Cusco, Peru   Rating: 28   Best Touring Season: Year-round

It seemed like an unbelievable dream ... what could this place be?
–Hiram Bingham

Highlights: Cusco is the ancient capital of the Inca Empire and situated at 11,200 feet in the mountains of Peru. Start in the old town and visit the Plaza de Armas with a Spanish cathedral and many walls built by the master Inca builders, visit the ruins of Sacsayhuamán or shop for soft alpaca sweaters. Take the morning train into the Urubamba Valley, arriving at the station below the lost city of the Incas – Machu Picchu, discovered by American Hiram Bingham; wander through the stone structures with trapezoid-shaped windows, climb to the Sun Gate or the steep Huayna Picchu for a view of the ruins and valley, drink a pisco sour at the Sanctuary Lodge.

My Favorite Encounter: Early morning, I took a group of 30, including my three boys, and climbed the slippery and dangerous Huayna Picchu Peak.

Rio de Janeiro & Iguazu Falls, Brazil   Rating: 31   Best Touring Season: Year-round

Tall and tan and young and lovely, the girl from Ipanema goes walking.
–Stan Getz

Highlights: Rio is a dramatic port with rising mountain peaks, great long beaches and vibrant local people called Cariocas, who dance the samba and sing - particularly during Carnival; shop for Brazilian jewelry at H. Stern or eat at a churrascaria, with meat cooked over a roasting pit; visit Sugar Loaf Mt. via a gondola, Christ the Redeemer statue on Corcovado Mt. or wander around the Jardin Botanic Gardens. On Copacabana & Ipanema watch guys play soccer and gals strut down the beaches; fly to Iguazu Falls in the jungle to see one of the world's greatest waterfalls. You can also drive across the bridge and visit Argentina & Paraguay.

My Favorite Encounter: At the brink of the Iguazu Falls with a local guide, we paddled a dugout canoe to an area called Devil's Throat - very scary; you can look straight down into the mouth of the waterfall.

Argentina   Rating: 23   Best Touring Season: Year-round

Don't cry for me Argentina, the truth is I never left you.
–song from "Evita"

Highlights: A country that stretches down the Atlantic Ocean full of scenic lakes, mountains and great waterfalls. Arrive in Buenos Aries and tour the Pink Palace, stately Teatro Colón Opera House, the fashionable Jockey Club Race Track; dine on Argentine beef and wine on Boca Calle Florida boulevard. And, of course, try your best tango steps. The Falls of Iguazu are but a flight away; the Pampas is known for gaucho cowboys and estancias, or large ranches. South in the country is the Patagonia region, where glaciers create a stunning landscape, and Bariloche; a ski resort in the Lake District, it looks like an Alpine village where lakes meet mountains.

My Favorite Encounter: After a tango show, shared conversation and dined on bife de lomo steak complemented by local red wine on the fashionable Boca Calle Florida pedestrian street.

Antarctica

Antarctic Cruise   Rating: 22   Best Touring Season: Winter only

Lands doomed by nature to everlasting frigidness.
–Capt. James Cook

Highlights: Fly to Tierra Del Fuego at the end of South America and board your ship in Ushuaia, Argentina, and sail the Beagle Channel into the Drake Passage (can be calm/can be rough); past loose iceberg fields and enter the water of Antarctica - a forlorn land un-inhabited except for research stations (some you can visit). The large penguin nesting areas are sometimes off the coast on islands like Elephant & Deception; take pictures of many varieties of seals and board zodiac rubber boats to find spouting whales. Rogue glaciers and the occasional storm can add adventure to this unique voyage.

My Favorite Encounter: On two different trips, took a swim in the Antarctic Sea at Deception Island, very cool!

Atlantic Ocean

Bermuda   Rating: 25   Best Touring Season: Spring, Summer, Fall

Bermuda is essentially a small town in a glamorous setting.
–David Shelley Nicholl

Highlights: An island in the Atlantic Ocean that boasts British and American heritage; a small population but large in natural beauty. Dress in Bermuda shorts, rent a moped for an island tour. At the east end find Fort St. Catherine and charming St. George's Harbor; in the middle play golf near beautiful Harrington Sound; visit Crystal Caves or shop in the capital city, Hamilton. The beaches are rivaled only by the sparkling blue water. Drive the west end and find Horseshoe Bay, grand resorts, lighthouses and the Royal Naval Dockyards.

My Favorite Encounter: As a Tourism Cares volunteer, we cleared brush from a national park woodland, then jumped into the ocean to cool off.

Iceland   Rating: 26   Best Touring Season: Summer

Iceland is the best land on which the sun shines. –Icelandic proverb

Highlights: A non-stop flight from the East Coast to this Atlantic Ocean island is only five hours. The ride from the airport to the capital of Reykjavik reveals lava fields without trees, but beautiful in its bleakness. This Scandinavian country has a tectonic plate running up the middle of the island, and volcanic activity is common. The Blue Lagoon is a thrilling geothermal area used for swimming, so if you get cold just dip under the steaming water. Geyser hot springs blow water into the sky, but the highlight is mighty Gullfoss Waterfall plunging and cascading down barren land, an awesome force of water in a fascinating part of the world.

My Favorite Encounter: Climbed beside windblown Gullfoss Waterfall, held on & took photos; the sound takes your breath away, and the wind can put the fear of God in you.

Europe

Scotland   Rating: 30   Best Touring Season: Spring,
                                                 Summer, Fall

*My heart's in the highlands, my heart is not here;
my heart's in the highlands a chasin' a deer.*

- anonymous poem

Highlights: Bonnie Scotland - begin in Edinburgh and walk the Royal Mile on High Street, passing St. Giles Mother Church and up to Castle Rock & Edinburgh Castle; in August enjoy the Military Tattoo with brilliant regalia of bag pipers and drums, say "hi" to the queen at Holyrood Palace or stroll Prince Street by Balmoral Hotel and stop at Sir Walter Scott Monument. Shop for cashmere sweaters and if time allows, board the royal yacht Britannia. Head west to Loch Lomond & the Trossachs with green pastures sprinkled with white sheep, travel north for a ferry ride to the Isle of Skye and back to the shores of Loch Ness for possible monster feeding. Golf links start with the home of golf - St. Andrews. Go north of the Firth of Forth and play Carnoustie or south to exclusive Muirfield. In the middle lands you will find Gleneagles or west to Turnberry, then north to Royal Troon and Prestwick. Dine on fresh salmon or haggis with your morning eggs and scones, enjoy a dram of single malt Scotch whisky.

My Favorite Encounter: Dressed in kilts and sporran for a formal dinner at Sterling Castle complete with bagpipes and drums. Note for gentlemen: no undergarments please.

England   Rating: 31   Best Touring Season: Spring, Summer, Fall

This blessed plot, this earth, this realm, this England. - William Shakespeare

Highlights: Take the circle route of jolly old England. Begin in London with the house of Parliament on the Thames; Westminster Abbey and Big Ben; theatre district of Piccadilly Circus; Buckingham Palace & the changing of the guard; the prime minister's residence at #10 Downing Street; Tower Bridge and the Tower of London, home to Britain's Crown Jewels; the British Museum & St. Paul's Cathedral. Just outside of London - Windsor Castle & St. George's Chapel & Hampton Court with breathtaking ornamental gardens, then off to prehistoric Stonehenge, gothic Salisbury Cathedral and the Georgian city of Bath and the famous Roman baths. Up through the Cotswolds to Shakespeare's birthplace Stratford-Upon-Avon, medieval Chester & the Lake District, and Wordsworth's beloved Grasmere, cross to the east arriving in York and visiting the medieval York Minster Cathedral; next south to the university cities of Cambridge & Oxford and Sir Winston Churchill's birthplace at Blenheim.

My Favorite Encounter: Flying my employees across the pond to watch the changing of the guard and live theatre British style.

Ireland   Rating: 32   Best Touring Season: Spring, Summer, Fall

Oh Danny boy, the pipes, the pipes are calling, from glen to glen and down the mountain side. −Old Irish song

Highlights: Start in Dublin's fair city−known for its glass-laced doorways, Trinity College & Book of Kells, St. Patrick's Cathedral, Phoenix Park and O'Connell Street. Drive to Kilkenny where the River Nore winds below the castle perched on the hill, then on to the early Viking river port of Waterford. See famous Waterford Crystal's showroom, Old Jameson Distillery, then on to Cork area to kiss the Blarney Stone, giving you the gift of gab; on to charming Kenmare and around the Ring of Kerry for a landscape of rugged beauty with spongy peat bogs. Killarney offers horse-drawn jaunting carts to Muckross House, charming shopping streets & lovely lakes; stop at Dromoland Castle for a game of golf and an Irish coffee, then to the coast for a look at the Cliffs of Moher −a towering sight on the Atlantic Ocean; continue by Galway Bay to Ashford Castle on Lough Corrib, live like a king, cruise the lake, golf or ride horses−a fitting end to the Emerald Isle.

My Favorite Encounter: Shared stories with my Irish friends in a small pub, around a peat fire with Irish stew and a pint of dark Guinness.

Northern France   Rating: 33   Best Touring Season: Spring, Summer, Fall

I love Paris in the springtime; I love Paris in the fall. – Cole Porter

Highlights: "We'll always have Paris"–Begin where 12 streets meet at the Arc de Triomphe, and stroll down the Champs-Elysées. The symbol of Paris is the Eiffel Tower, so take the elevator for a panoramic view; tour Notre Dame Cathedral with medieval gargoyles that watch down from above. The City of Lights also offers Hôtel des Invalides, Napoleon's Tomb, the Louvre Palace Museum - Place de la Concorde with the Egyptian obelisk, Basilique du Sacré-Coeur in Montmartre, Opera Garnier and charming little Sainte-Chappell. Take evening cruise of the River Seine. Day trips include Claude Monet's Giverny Gardens, Chantilly equestrian riding school or a day at Versailles, the palace of Louis XIV - the Sun King with the Hall of Mirrors and formal gardens, or spend a day in Reims in the Champagne region, have a glass of Dom Pérignon, sparkling Moet & Chandon, then drive west, see where Joan of Arc was burned at the stake in Rouen. Visit the Bayeux Tapestry Museum, the picturesque Harbor of Honfleur and the Normandy beaches, including D-Day's Omaha Military Cemetery. The Benedictine Abbey at Mont St. Michel is almost surrounded by water and a thing of beauty. Travel in Brittany to see Angers' city walls & fortress and the chateau country of the Loire Valley featuring Chenoneaux on the River Cher & Château de Chambord hunting lodge. Next, the gothic Chartres Cathedral with stained glass rose windows and enormous Fontainebleau Palace.

My Favorite Encounter: Standing in the military cemetery overlooking Omaha Beach, where my father landed 1944.

Southern France   Rating: 32   Best Touring Season: Spring, Summer, Fall

Boy, those French. They have a different word for everything. –Steve Martin

Highlights: Consider a barge cruise or balloon ride near Bordeaux, take in a walking tour and wine tasting, but don't miss Biarritz Atlantic resort and St. Bernadette grotto at Lourdes. Spend a day or two at my favorite medieval walled town of Carcassonne, which sits on a hill with towers and bridges and battlements, then marvel at the triple-arched Roman aqueduct at Pont du Gard, the Palace of the Popes and bridge over the Rhône in Avignon or steal away to the La Bastide de Gordes overlooking a lovely valley and gorge. On the French Riviera, or the Côte d'Azur, walk Promenade de la Croisette in Cannes and stop at the Carlton Hotel, wander the cobblestone streets of Nice and shop for perfume in Grasse. Or dine in the medieval town of Saint-Paul de Vence; try the lawn bowling or Pétanque in the town square. Your next stop is Monte Carlo resort for the jet-set crowd, featuring a royal palace, Oceanographic Museum, Grand Casino, and Grande Corniche. Drive north into the French Alps to Grenoble and Chamonix ski resorts, where on a clear day you see Mount Blanc. Then a gastronomic meal in Lyon and finish with a TGV high-speed train back to Paris.

My Favorite Encounter: In the double-walled city of Carcassonne, enjoyed a cassolette meal of ham, duck and beans in a stone-walled bistro.

Northern Italy	Rating: 33	Best Touring Season: Spring, Summer, Fall, Winter skiing

I saw the angel in the marble and carved until I set him free. –Michelangelo

Highlights: The city of Milan boasts a magnificent gothic cathedral with spires pointing to heaven, glass-domed Galleria for shoppers, the famous La Scala Opera House and the Last Supper painting. An hour north is Lake Como and stunning Villa d'Este Palace Hotel on the lakeshore. Drive the winding road and take a short boat ride to Bellagio, a resort town on the tip of a peninsula; for lunch try local perch and risotto. Lugano in Switzerland is just over the border, or travel by Lago di Garda to Venice and the maze of islands with canals and bridges, palaces and churches. Center your tour at St. Mark's Square and the Doge Palace, Bridge of Sighs, Campanile bell tower, Byzantine St. Mark's Basilica and plenty of pigeons. The home of Marco Polo and Antonio Vivaldi are on the lagoon cruise through the Grand Canal and Rialto Bridge. Take in the view across the water to Santa Maria Della Salute Cathedral and visit a glass-blowing factory on Murano Island. Going down the coast, the little Republic of San Marino and two castles sit high on Mount Titano. Arrive in the Renaissance city of Florence - the splendid capital of Tuscany. The Arno River runs through the city, and, over the water, the Ponte Vecchio Bridge provides jewelry shopping. Michelangelo's statue of David awaits you, Uffizi Gallery, the Piazza del Duomo with the baptistery and Bronze Doors of Paradise. Santa Maria Del Fiore is covered with green, pink and white marble; the Campanile or Bell Tower is the tallest structure, but take time for the Palazzo Pitti and Basilica of Santa Croce, where famous Italians are buried. If you stand at a tilt, the Leaning Tower of Pisa looks level; it's a bell tower next to a cathedral and baptistery. Lucca is a well-preserved walled city and the home of the opera composer Giacomo Puccini. Cinque Terre (five lands) are cliff villages overlooking the sea and can be reached by boat or train. Santa Margherita is a resort town with trompe l'oeil, or paintings on buildings to fool the eye. Take a short boat ride and you're in magical Portofino, a small, u-shaped port with charming fish restaurants.

My Favorite Encounter: From the Venice airport, I took a thrilling boat transfer through the Grand Canal to St. Mark's Square, then across the bay to the Cipriani Hotel.

Southern Italy	Rating: 32	Best Touring Season: Year-round (winter is chilly)

"SPQR" - In the name of the Roman Senate and people.
—Motto of Rome found on buildings and streets

Highlights: All roads lead to Rome. The Eternal City is steeped in history, so start with the Roman Forum, then the Colosseum and walking around the great amphitheater to appreciate its size, Circus Maximus and Trajan's column. The Pantheon has a hole in the top, while the Ponte St. Angels Bridge leads by Hadrian's Mausoleum, the walled city of the Vatican, St. Peters Basilica and the Sistine Chapel. In the evening at Piazza Novena try veal scaloppini, maybe some Chianti and gelato for dessert. End your walk at the Spanish Steps and beautiful Trevi Fountain, with lights shining on the statues. A day trip north to Tivoli and the Fountains of Villa d'Este is a day well spent. Go south to Naples Bay and focus on Pompeii, a preserved Roman city covered by ash from Mount Vesuvius. After the tour, visit the National Archaeological Museum to view the great treasures of Pompeii, including mosaics and the nobles' wealth in the silver room. Herculaneum is another site well worth seeing before you boat to the Isle of Capri, a jet-set hang-out with a blue grotto and high, picturesque cliffs. Stop in Sorrento for oranges, then drive the striking Amalfi Coast, shop in the town of Amalfi or Positano for a refreshing lemonallo drink or relax at a trattoria for local fish and pasta. Taormina in Sicily has a view of the sea from 800 feet; the town is near Mount Etna. Additionally, the island is full of Greek archaeological sites. Take a ferry to Olbia and the Costa Smeralda in Sardinia. The aquamarine waters and Mediterranean resorts await you.

My Favorite Encounter: Standing in the grandeur of St. Peter's Basilica with spiraled columns, marble inlaid walls and priceless art.

Switzerland   Rating: 30   Best Touring Season: Late Spring,
                                                      Summer, Early Fall, Winter skiing

Mountains are the beginning and the end of all natural scenery. - John Ruskin

Highlights: A landlocked country of green valleys and the white Alps. The people speak French, Italian, Romansh and German and excel in banking and Swiss-army knives. From stately Zurich, ride south on smooth Swiss National Railroad to Lucerne at the base of the Alps. Along with boat rides on Lake Lucerne, visit the Chapel Bridge, Lions Monument and ride a gondola to Mount Pilatus and enjoy hot chocolate and a breathtaking view of the Alps. Wind down into Interlaken with a view of the Jungfrau summit. Then it's on to Geneva and Lac Léman, or Lake Geneva, with its 400-foot lake fountain. Two charming towns await you - Lausanne, home to the International Olympic Committee (IOC), and Montreux, famous for the Lord Byron poem "Prisoner of Chillon." Go into the Alps by train and transfer to a cog-wheel train climbing up to Zermatt, a ski resort at the base of the Matterhorn. Try some cheese fondue, and before leaving Switzerland ride the Glacier Express train to the posh ski resort of St. Moritz.

My Favorite Encounter: Full-day excursion from Geneva, partly by cog-wheel train, to the ski town of Zermatt and the Matterhorn.

Spain   Rating: 31   Best Touring Season: Spring,
                                                      Summer, Fall

Three Spaniards, four opinions. – Spanish proverb

Highlights: Madrid is a lively city full of beautiful fountains, including the Plaza de España, monument to Cervantes and the Cibeles Fountain. Wander through the Prado Museum to admire the paintings of Velazquez and Goya and much more. Palacio Real, the Royal Palace, is full of elaborate room displays. If you're in the city on Sunday, consider the bull fight; it's a special event lasting two and a half hours. Travel north to the medieval walled city of Avila, constructed of brown granite with 88 towers. Segovia has the famous Alcazar, plus 2,000-year-old Roman aqueduct stretching the length of the valley. Bilbao is a port city of the Basque region. Visit the Guggenheim Museum there. Pass through San Sebastian and its Bahia de la Concha beach and stop in Pamplona, where the running of the bulls occurs every July. Barcelona is a large city on the coast with a long beach promenade, with the Columbus Monument and Sagrada Família - Antoni Gaudi's cathedral masterpiece. Head south to the capital of Valencia, stopping in the old quarter for a refreshing glass of orange juice and on to Costa Del Sol, or the sunny coast. The Moorish city of Granada is perched on a hill. Tour the Alhambra and the Court of the Lions and water gardens. The Andalucia resort towns of Malaga and Marbella attract visitors in the warm months, so allow relaxation time and watch a flamenco dance. Drive to Seville, a wonderful city for architecture, and visit the cathedral with the tomb of Christopher Columbus. Near Madrid, spend time in Toledo, which is surrounded by the Tagus River and capital of Castile-La Mancha. The 13th century cathedral is one of Europe's best and almost overpowering in its size. One other visit is to El Greco's home, where you can view some of his paintings. If time allows, take a side trip to the Monastery of El Escorial, the Valley of the Fallen.

My Favorite Encounter: Watching the precise flamenco dancing or the spectacle of a Sunday bull fight in Plaza de Toros de Las Ventas.

Germany   Rating: 29   Best Touring Season: Spring,
                                                          Summer, Fall

Germany has been born anew. -Robert Ley

Highlights: Berlin, once split in half, is a vibrant city with a view to the future. The Brandenburg Gate is the symbol of the city, with a four-horse statue above the arch, near the Reichstag Building and lovely Teirgarten Park. Walk down Unter Den Linden Boulevard past Humboldt University to the large Berlin Cathedral Dome, where you can climb to the top and walk around the rotunda. It's a short distance to the Pergamum Museum to see the Greek altar to Zeus and the gate of Babylon. Before you leave the city, visit the Berlin Philharmonic, Kaiser Wilhelm Memorial Church or Ku'damm and the Agyptisches (Egyptian) Museum with the bust of Nefertiti and her graceful neck. Outside the city in Potsdam is Frederick the Great's royal palace, Sans Souci, a fine example of Rococo architecture with landscaped gardens, fountain and grand staircase, so don't miss this grand Schloss. Lutherland with historic Wittenburg, Eisleben and Eisinach, and with Wartburg Castle on a mountain peak. Another masterpiece is the Zwinger baroque palace in Dresden on the Elbe River. South to Nuremberg with the massive medieval fortress and the Zeppelin Field, used by the Nazis as a parade ground. The Romantic Road stretches 180 miles, and among the many medieval towns and castles, stay in Rothenburg with cobblestone streets, archways and long walls. Munich, the Bavarian capital, is the home of Oktoberfest. The Glockenspiel clock, Marienplatz, Hofbräuhaus beer hall, and Nymphenburg Schloss (Palace). Go south to visit Mad Ludwig II fairytale Neuschwanstein Castle and the small but elegant Linderhof Palace, or Herrenchiemsee on the lake. The Black Forest is well named for its dense trees and is a resort spa area famous for wooden cuckoo clocks. Heidelberg is a university town on the Necker River.

Visit the castle and university or have a stein of beer with a friend or a prince. A Rhine River cruise is one of the original grand tours of Europe. The river boats dock in Mainz for the Gutenberg Museum. Near Mannheim, cruise by vineyards and castles such as the Lorelei and the Mouse Tower. See the Deutsche Eck (German corner) in Koblenz, and Cologne's gothic twin tower cathedral, one of the most impressive in the world.

My Favorite Encounter: Led a Lutheran group to Wittenberg and listened to a sermon in the City Church.

Danube Cruise & Tour	Rating: 31	Best Touring Season: Spring, Summer, Fall

Edelweiss, Edelweiss, every morning you greet me.
–From "The Sound of Music"

Highlights: The Danube River starts in Germany and flows through the lovely Wachau Valley of Austria, then makes a bend into Hungary and continues to eastern Europe, flowing out into the Black Sea. One of the most popular cruise itineraries starts in the capital of Hungary. Budapest has a striking parliament building on the Danube River where the Chain Bridge gracefully crosses from Buda to Pest. Ride the funicular up to the Buda Palace and visit St. Matthias Church and Fisherman's Bastian for great photo ops. On the Pest side don't miss St. Stephen's Basilica; it has been renovated with gold-leaf interior. There is a synagogue with a memorial garden to the Jews who died during the Nazi occupation. To get the full flavor of Budapest, order a goulash soup with gypsy violins, it's always in style. Cruise past the Danube bend to the imperial city of Vienna, Austria, home to Mozart, Beethoven, Strauss, Freud and the Habsburg royal family. A grand tour of a grand city includes the Hofburg Winter Palace, Vienna State Opera House, the Ring-strasse Boulevard, Prater Park and giant Ferris wheel, St. Stephan's Cathedral with zigzag roof and Spanish Riding School with Lipizzaner white horses. There are two outstanding palaces, Belvedere and Schonbrunn; the latter has beautiful formal gardens and an ascending hill with a decorative gloriette. Across from the cathedral, enjoy a very Austrian chocolate Sacher torte with whipped cream and coffee. Dürnstein in the heart of Wachau Valley has to be the cutest village in Europe with its blue-domed church with maypole in the town square. The Benedictine abbey in Melk dominates the hillside with its large white and mustard-colored walls. Regensburg, Germany, has Roman ruins, but this city's highlight is St. Peter's twin tower cathedral, and the Thurn and Taxis Castle offers an in-depth tour. Nuremberg is where the Rhine-Main-Danube Canal meets and has the large Zeppelin Field used by Nazis as a parade ground. The old town has massive thick towers and walls, with medieval forts. Drive into the Czech Republic and enter the city of a hundred spires, Golden Prague. Nothing beats the charm of Tyn's church in the main square along with the astronomical clock. Stroll Wenceslas Square, you know, "good King Wenceslas," cross the Charles Bridge with multiple statues and visit St. Vitus Cathedral and Prague Castle. A side trip includes the Bohemian towns of Kutná Hora, a well-known silver town, and Heritage site Český Krumlov.

My Favorite Encounter: Last-minute ticket to the opulent Vienna State Opera House, Sacher torte and coffee after the performance.

Greece   Rating: 29   Best Touring Season: Spring,
                                               Summer, Fall

The great wellspring of Western thought. –Historical saying

Highlights: Start your Greek odyssey in Athens, and from the hill of Acropolis tour

the Parthenon, Erechtheum, Agora market, Theater of Dionysus and the night life of the Plaka neighborhood. Before you leave, spend time in the National Archaeological Museum or watch the Edzen Soldiers, who guard near Constitution Square. The Roman Temple of Zeus should also be on your tour list; the temple columns are enormous. Drive south to the temple of Poseidon at Cape Sounion and try to arrive before sunset, because it is a spectacular event over the Aegean Sea. Travel to the cradle of Greek civilization, the Temple of Apollo at Delphi, the historical home to the ancient oracle. Wander the hills and ancient city and visit the Charioteer Statue in the Delphi Archaeological Museum. North to the city of Kalambaka, you will find fantastic landscape of Meteora with more than 20 monasteries on top of rock pinnacles. Although not as well-known, put Meteora on the top of your Greek tour list. In Peloponnese there is another spectacular sight, the Corinth Canal, with its deep cut canal allowing mid-size ship passage and can be viewed from one of several bridges. Visit ancient Corinth with its impressive collection of statues in the local museum. The epic poet Homer tells us, Mycenae was the Kingdom of Agamemnon, who led his army across the sea to Troy. Heinrich Schliemann, a German archeologist rediscovered the city, including the Lions Gate entrance, making for an interesting half-day tour. The great theater of Epidaurus is well-preserved; stand in the middle of the stage and your whisper can be heard on the top row. Olympia was the site of the early Greek athletic games and here you will find the Temple of Hera and Zeus. Many great works of art, including the statue of Hermes, are displayed in the Archaeological Museum of Olympia.

My Favorite Encounter: Invited to stay overnight at a Greek monastery; joined in the prayers and a humble dinner, with bearded monks.

Aegean Cruise   Rating: 26   Best Touring Season: Late Spring,
                                                          Summer, Early Fall

I still sigh for the Aegean. Shall you not always love its bluest of waves?
–Lord Byron

Highlights: If sailing the islands of the blue Aegean doesn't captivate a traveler, then the addition of a wealth of historic sites creates a grand tour almost anyone will appreciate. Swing past Athens and sail to Corfu in the Ionian Sea, an island of cyprus and olive trees surrounded by ideal blue water. Two fortresses protect Corfu's old town, and it has a grand esplanade for shopping and dining. Overlooking the city is the Achillion Palace created by Sissi, Empress of Austria. This is a fanciful palace not to be missed. Picturesque Paleo Beach offers a European beachside resort and hilltop monastery. Jet-set Mykonos has white stone streets, pelicans wandering the beach, scenic windmills and white, cube-shaped houses. Take a short boat ride to Delos, the ancient Greek religious island and the birthplace of Apollo. Ephesus, Turkey, is an extensive Greek and Roman ancient city that is still being restored. Walk down the old street by the Odeon, Trajan's fountain and stone toilets. The centerpiece of the city is the multi-arched library, and beside it is the agora market and great theater. Outside the site is the cottage of the Virgin Mary and the remains of the temple of Artemis, one of the ancient Seven Wonders of the World. Patmos is known for the cave and monastery of John the Evangelist. Timos is a Greek Orthodox holy island. On the island of Rhodes, visit the picturesque Acropolis at Lindos and the impressive crusaders' Palace of the Grand Masters, built by the knights of St. John. The huge colossus of Rhodes is long gone, but this resort island has a walled city and resort beaches. Sailing into Santorini is a mystical experience, for here a volcano exploded thousands of years ago and left an eerie fishhook island. The black volcanic rock and white Greek buildings on the very top of the cliff make a dramatic color contrast. This island is sometimes called Thera and may be the lost city of Atlantis. Santorini is a tourist's slice of heaven, and to get to the top, take a mule ride or healthy walk, or an easy cable car ride (but that of course is cheating). Crete is the original island of Greek civilization. King Minos Palace at Knossos is an interesting tour, as is the museum with the Bull Fresco above it. Two outstanding beaches draw large European crowds in the summer months.

My Favorite Encounter: A choppy boat ride from Mykonos to Delos with my son and wife to wander the open-air temple ruins.

Russia   Rating: 26   Best Touring Season: Summer

Somewhere my love, there will be songs to sing,
although the snow covers the hope of spring.
–from "Dr. Zhivago"

Highlights: Peter the Great called his city St. Petersburg, the "Window on the West." Tourists to-day also say it is the Venice of the North, primarily because the Neva River separates into many canals and a bay that opens onto the Gulf of Finland. Things to see: the Hermitage, or Winter Palace, is a fantas-tic green and white museum, including the Palace Square and Nevsky Prospect; St. Isaac's Cathedral has green malachite pillars; Peter and Paul fortress is the tomb for the tsars; Spilled Blood Church has been beautifully restored and is next to an attractive water canal, as is the Admiralty, and the old Soviet battleship Arora. You will find the graves of Tchaikovsky and Dostoevsky and monu-ments to the poet Pushkin. Outside of the city is the fabulous Peterhof Palace (formerly Petrodvorets) of Peter the Great, with grand gardens of statued fountains. Catherine the Great Palace, Oranienbaum, is also well worth the visit. The capital of Russia is Moscow and the center of the city is the Kremlin and Red Square. Inside the walls are the bell tower of Ivan the Great, the Palace of Congresses and the Armory Chambers with the Faberge egg collection. Just outside the wall is St. Basil's onion-domed church, Spassky Gate, Lenin's Tomb, Gum's Department Store and, nearby, the Bolshoi Theater. Joseph Stalin began a building project and created high-spired buildings locally known as Stalin gothic, which are spotted throughout the city. A new grand statue of Peter the Great stands beside the Moscow River. The Volga and Sari Rivers offer boat trips from St. Petersburg to Moscow, including Lake Onega; this is a gentle way to explore Russia by river boat. The Golden Ring is a tour of the traditional Russian churches and mon-asteries, and includes stops in Sergiyev Posad, Vladimir and Suzdal. The churches can be visited within a few days and this is another way to explore the history of Russia.

My Favorite Encounter: In the Soviet era, bartered my blue jeans with a Soviet soldier for his brass belt buckle in front of the gates of the Kremlin.

Scandinavian Cruise   Rating: 29   Best Touring Season: Late Spring,
                                                 Summer, Early Fall

... wonderful, wonderful Copenhagen. –song and local saying

 **Highlights**: The Little Mermaid statue sits graceful-
ly on a rock in Copenhagen's port, a fairytale symbol
for well-mannered Scandinavia. Start in Denmark's
elegant city with spires and towers reaching toward
the sky. Copenhagen offers lots of treats, including
Ny Haven, with fishing and sailing boats, the Strøget
pedestrian shopping street and the town hall with its
tall, imposing tower. Don't miss Tivoli Gardens, an early entertainment park, the Børsen
stock exchange building with dragon-tail spire, Amalienburg Palace with soldiers in traditional uniforms, the four fierce-looking bulls of Gefion Fountain, and remainders everywhere of beloved children's writer Hans Christian Andersen. Have a Carlsberg beer
on the brewery tour, or travel to Frederiksborg Castle and Kronborg Castle for a nice
one-day trip. Cruise the scenic coast of Sweden into Stockholm, a city of canals and
lakes. Old town Gamla Stan Island is your best bet for a look at the Royal Palace and
cathedral. Stockholm City Hall hosts the yearly Nobel Prize awards; and the one-of-a-
kind Vasa maritime museum offers a look back in time, with a huge warship preserved
underwater for hundreds of years. You can boat out to Drottningholm, the home of the
Royal Family, and enjoy the yellow and white palace with its formal gardens. Helsinki,
Finland, is a handsome port with neoclassic senate square with a stately Lutheran
Church. There is a monument to composer Jean Siblelius, Finlandia Music Hall and the
Church in the Rock, plus an inexpensive trolley ride where you can see many other city
highlights. Sail into Oslo fjord and you're in the capital of Norway – a seafaring country that has Viking blood in its veins. The Viking Ship Museum has well-prepared 9th
century Viking burial ships, and the Kon-Tiki Museum has Thor Heyerdahl's hand-made
reed boat. Frogner Park is a must, with many statues including the Angry Boy and a tall
monolith in the center of the park. After a harbor cruise, visit a Norwegian stave church
or look down the very long ski jump shoot. At the end of your Scandinavian cruise, find
your way over to Bergen and take a one-day "Norway in a Nutshell" tour with train, boat
and motorcoach to on gorgeous Sognefjord, a true wonder of nature.

My Favorite Encounter: Flight from Oslo to the high arctic island of Svalbard to take a
day hike, being aware of aggressive polar bears.

Orient Express Rating: 31 Best Touring Season: Spring, Summer, Fall

I start getting restless whenever I hear the whistle of a train.
- from the song "Far Away Places"

Highlights: Agatha Christie's mystery book "Murder on the Orient Express" helped inspire thousands of people to experience the luxury of a grand European train ride. The most famous route is the Simplon-Orient Express from Venice to London. This is a trip that combines the legendary train with deluxe services and the finest in dining. You might start your journey with a night or two at the Cipriani Hotel, which faces St. Mark's Square in Venice. A large pool and gardens provide a relaxing atmosphere. On departure day, boat to the train station, board your blue and white sleeper train and depart into the Italian Dolomites and then over the Alps through the famous Brenner Pass and into Innsbruck, Austria. It's time to dress to the nines in stylish gown or tuxedo, and gather in the bar car to have your favorite drink while the piano player plays your favorite songs. Enjoy a lobster and steak gourmet dinner, then let the roll of the train rock you to sleep. After a short stop in Paris, the train arrives at Calais, France, and you cross to England by the Chunnel, then board a historic British Pullman train that arrives in the afternoon at Victoria Station, London. This is a legendary journey never to be forgotten.

My Favorite Encounter: My wife and I lived in the lap of luxury, dining on lobster and mingling with the rich and famous.

Western Mediterranean Cruise Rating: 31 Best Touring Season: Spring, Summer, Fall

The grand object of traveling is to see the shores of the Mediterranean.
- Samuel Johnson

Highlights: No other tour can match the discoveries on a Mediterranean cruise. Begin from Civitavecchia, the nearest port to Rome. Sail south and look for the volcanic fireworks on the Italian island of Stromboli, then pass through the Straits of Messina into open sea, to the Fort City of Valletta, Malta -- with high ramparts built of tan Malta stone. This small but intriguing country gets part of its heritage from the British and the medieval Knights of Malta. Next port stop, Tunis, Tunisia, on the north coast of Africa. Visit the ruins of Carthage, a city destroyed by the Roman legions during the Punic War. Detailed Roman mosaics are displayed in the city museum. Cruise to Palma de Mallorca, Balearic Islands, Spain, for a true jet-set beach location. Tour the round fort and cathedral in Palma, then into the country with many windmills, fig tree orchards and well-known pearl factory. Near the sea, the Caves of Drach are filled with formations, with an underground lake and a soothing violin concert. Gibraltar is a British outpost that guards the straits between Europe and Africa. Near the Rock visit St. Michael's Cave and a colony of protected Barbary Apes. The ship then sales to Africa, docking at Casablanca, Morocco, which has a long ocean coast and an enormous Hassan II Mosque built at the edge of the water, which can hold 70,000 worshipers. Dinner with a tajine pot filled with chicken and couscous, and for dessert – almond pastries. Stop in Portimão on the Algarve Coast of Portugal, relax on the alluring warm beaches, sip local wine and eat fish cooked in olive oil, or play a round of golf on one of the many championship courses. There is distinctive Moorish-style design in the chimneys of many of the houses. Finish your cruise in Lisbon on the River Tagus. Don't miss the coach museum and wander into the Alfama old town for a late-night meal.

My Favorite Encounter: The Caves of Drach in Majorca and the underground lake with a string quartet playing Chopin.

Africa

Egypt   Rating: 28   Best Touring Season: Year-round
                                                 (summers can be very hot)

All things dread time, but time dreads the pyramids. –Anonymous

Highlights: Time has proven the most celebrated landmark in the world is the Pyramids of Egypt. If arriving by ship, Port Said or Alexandria might be your first look at Egypt. Port Said is the gathering area for the Suez Canal, a busy port night and day. Cairo, the largest city in Africa, is on the edge of the great Sahara Desert and where the Pyramids of Giza have stood for 2,500 years. You can walk or ride a camel or Arabian stallion to the base and climb into one of the tombs – nearby the Sphinx looks out over the desert. It has the Pharaoh's head and the body of a lion. Here you will find a wonderful museum displaying a burial felucca boat for the use of the Pharaoh in the afterlife. The pyramids transcend all manmade landmarks. Tutankhamen's treasures await you at the museum of Egyptian Antiquities. Shop for an oval cartouche, usually made of gold, worn as a necklace. You may also buy a turquoise scarab bug pin or wander into a perfume shop in the Khan el-Khalili bazaar district; it's noisy but exciting. The Citadel and Mosque of Ottoman Muhammad Ali and the city of the dead are well worth your time. Take a look at Egypt's oldest stepped pyramids in Sakkara and Memphis, and then fly to Luxor (the ancient city of Thebes) for an open-air museum tour. Visit the Temple of Karnak and the row of Rams-Headed Sphinxes. Then cross the Nile to the Valley of the King and pass by the Colossi of Memnon and Queen Hatshepsut Temple to tour one of the underground pharaoh tombs. Now sail down the Nile like Cleopatra for a cruise to Aswan and the High Dam; the unfinished obelisk in the quarry area is most interesting, as is the Temples of Philae Island. Have tea at the old Cataract Hotel perched on a hill, take a felucca boat to the Aga Khan III tomb on an island in the Nile, and fly into the desert for a visit on the Shores of Lake Nasser to the relocated Ramses II Great Temple of Abu Simbel. For a final experience, fly to the Red Sea to a resort in Sharm el-Sheikh for snorkeling or scuba in the clear blue waters.

My Favorite Encounter: Rode to the pyramids on an Arabian horse, climbed to the top then went inside.

Morocco   Rating: 29   Best Touring Season: Year-round

We're on the road to Morocco. – Bing Crosby and Bob Hope

Highlights: When the Moors left Spain for what is to-day Morocco, they brought a culture full of ideas and unique art and architecture. Today, influences from the Arab, Berber and French cultures make up the land of the Moors. Casablanca is a major port, and its lovely beaches stretch for miles down the Atlantic coast. Bogart and Bergman may be gone, but there are plenty of tourists to replace them. Relax on the beach, drink local wines and visit the large Hassan II mosque or local souq. If you drive to the capital city of Rabat, watch for the Arabian horse soldiers guarding the former king's mausoleum. In Fes, the old-est imperial city and religious center, stay at Palace Jamai, the former royal palace, and watch from your balcony as the sun sets over this bowl-shaped town. A journey to Marrakech, the red city, is the highlight of a Moroccan odyssey. In the souq, watch snake charmers and shop keepers selling rugs and ceramics, desert wood trays. In the narrow streets are food stalls, with plenty of crowds. Spend the afternoon at La Mamounia Hotel surrounded by gardens of roses, and enjoy mint tea and almond cook-ies, sit on Moroccan stools and plan an excursion into the beautiful but rugged high Atlas Mountains, visit romantic Berber tents and desert hospitality. For a change of pace and a bit of a surprise, there are many golf courses well-designed and ready to play.

My Favorite Encounter: From a special dining room, looking down on the bowl-shaped holy city of Fes, I was a guest after sunset for a delicious Ramadan meal - with special dishes served only during the holy month.

Kenya   Rating: 27   Best Touring Season: Year-round
                                                    (spring & fall can be rainy)

There is something about safari life that makes you forget all of your sorrows.
–Karen Blixen, author

Highlights: Jambo "welcome" - Kenya is the home of the safari! The great white hunter has faded away and a new generation of safari photographers are filling vans and land rovers to capture wildlife in a natural setting. Most safaris start in the interesting East African city of Nairobi. Start by visiting African writer Karen Blixen's house – she wrote the book "Out of Africa." Feed the tall giraffes at Giraffe Manor by climbing up to a high balcony. Fly north and live in luxury at Mount Kenya Safari Club near the slopes of majestic Mount Kenya. Pool, golf and horseback riding are at your fingertips. Continue north to Samburu Game Reserve. From a comfortable veranda, look to the muddy riverbanks for large crocodiles that crawl out of the river right on time for a raw dinner. Flying to the Masai Mara over scenic Great Rift Valley is a treat in itself. The Mara is the extension of the Serengeti Plains and is the home to the great African migration. Many tented camps accommodate your Kenya experience, and safari vehicles drive across the Mara searching for the abundant game, including, in-season, the awesome experience of 1 million wildebeest, zebras, gazelles, elephants, giraffes and impalas. Cheetahs, lions, hyenas and jackals stalk for prey, and the Mara River is full of hippos and crocodiles. Hot-air ballooning, particularly at dawn, is a must. Nothing can compare with a peaceful ride just above the animals. The Masai people protect their land and their wildlife. Men are brightly dressed in red and carry long spears. Make a visit to a village with their mud huts and protective brush fences. Food is fresh, people are polite, safari is great -- everything is hakuna matata, or "no worries." In Amboseli National Park, look for umbrella or acacia trees, swamps and scrub brush, with the backdrop of Kilimanjaro offering a photographer's paradise. The open plains allow super big-game viewing plus large groups of baboons, fast-running ostriches, storks and the bizarre-looking Topi antelope.

My Favorite Encounter: My kind, gentle, loving wife on safari ... "Hope we see a kill today."

Tanzania   Rating: 27   Best Touring Season: Year-round
                                                 (spring & fall can be rainy)

Dr. Livingstone, I presume. –Henry Stanley

Highlights: The snows of Kilimanjaro still cap the great mountain that rises to 19,340 feet, highest in Africa. For the ambitious hiker, a five- or six-day climb can be arranged with porters and guides hiking the Marangu Trail. Not for everyone, the trek has some obstacles, starting with acclimation to altitude, and sun exposure. After three days, put on your Gore-Tex suit and you may reach Gillman's Point at the crater's edge. With about half of the normal oxygen, hike around the rim line and snow glaciers to Uhuru Point, with Tanzania and Kenya below the clouds. In the middle of the country, check in at one of the lodges situated on the rim of Ngorongoro Crater, sometimes called the Garden of Eden. Look down on a wonder of nature, a huge, extinct volcano with 20,000 animals in a protected caldera. Drive down switchback roads into a world of rhinos and elephants, lakes with flamingos and monkeys of every variety. Here you can see many animals and particularly birds that are seldom seen in other game reserves. Now fly to the famed Serengeti Plains for the migration and discover a land brimming with wildlife. If you stay at a lodge by the river, you get an evening serenaded by snorting hippos, but do not wander out of your Boma tent for an evening stroll -- it's hostile territory.

My Favorite Encounter: Five-day climb up Mount Kilimanjaro to stand in the snow at the highest point in Africa.

South Africa, Botswana & Victoria Falls Rating: 27   Best Touring Season:
                                                           Year-round

This is by far the greatest collection of animals left in the world. – Elspeth Huxley

Highlights: A land of exquisite natural beauty, dramatic mountain ranges, magnificent coastline and wildlife savannah plains. With Table Mountain serving as a dramatic backdrop, Cape Town is a port city and gateway to a South African adventure. Start with Victoria and Alfred Waterfront, then take a cable car ride to the top of Table Mountain for a panoramic view, or a picnic maybe with a bottle of local Riesling wine. Sunsets disappear over the oceans, mountains and peninsula. Allow for a full day to Stellenbosch or Franschhoek wine country; includes wine tasting and lunch at a Cape Dutch Vineyard and try local bobotie, a spiced minced meat. It's another day's drive to Cape Point, where the Atlantic and Indian Oceans meet at the legendary Cape of Good Hope. Stop for a fresh lobster feast and snap close-up pictures of small Ferry Penguins on a beach reserve. The Garden Route from Cape Town is a 130-mile road that winds east along coastal terrain of lakes, mountains and picturesque bridges, wild flowers and golden beaches. For train buffs, board the Blue Train and take the 28-hour deluxe ride that stops along the way at Kimberly Diamond Mine. The train, featuring overnight sleeper cars, arrives in Pretoria or continues on to Victoria Falls, Zimbabwe. Johannesburg is known as the city of gold and has large hills of mine tailings scattered around the city. Fly or train to Kruger National Park for some of the best game viewing anywhere. Stay at one of the splendid private game reserve lodges. Here is a golden opportunity to experience exhilarating game runs looking for the big five: elephant, rhino, cape buffalo, lion and leopard. Fly to the Okavango Delta in Botswana, a game-rich area with floodwaters that allow viewing, particularly in a local mokoro dugout canoe. Check into an isolated game-viewing camp surrounded by water and, many times, hippos. If you get to Chobe National Park in Botswana, try a boat ride where, sometimes, large elephants swim next to you as they cross the river. Victoria Falls is one of the three greatest falls in the world. Take a guided tour and get very wet from the mist on both sides, Zimbabwe and Zambia. Watch bungee jumping off the Victoria Falls Bridge or river raft the Zambezi River. The Victoria Falls known locally as Masi-oa-Tunya, (the Smoke that Thunders) can also be enjoyed from a distance at the very British Victoria Falls Hotel.

My Favorite Encounter: Sitting around an evening campfire, we were instructed to move slowly and stay calm as hippos grazed some 10 feet from our fire.

Middle East

Turkey   Rating: 30   Best Touring Season: Spring,
                                                        Summer, Fall

Istanbul, it is more like some enduring city out of a thousand and one nights.
      –Demetrius Coufopoulos

 **Highlights**: Asia Minor was the early name for Turkey, but there's nothing minor about a country that has more Greek ruins than Greece and more Roman ruins than Italy. Influenced by Tartars, Persians, Greeks, Romans, Ottomans and Europeans -- Turkey holds great treasures of the past and present. Istanbul (not Constantinople) on the Bosporus is straddled by the New Galata Bridge. On the European side, an old walled city with historic Pera Palas Hotel of Agatha Christie fame, with wooden elevators and rooms that look down on the Golden Horn Inlet. Hagia Sophia, or St. Sophia, is the symbol of the city along with the Blue Mosque; there is a garden walk between the two magnificent structures. Topkapi

Palace is where Ottoman sultans live with their harems. The display of jewelry, including the Topkapi dagger with enormous emeralds, and the ample grounds offer an open museum to the opulent Ottoman past. In the Grand Bazaar, carpets and ornaments are sold everywhere and local restaurants serve kabob lamb and beef with a stiff Raki drink. The capital of Turkey is Ankara, which was a stop on the Old Silk Road and is in approximately the middle of the country. Here you can visit a museum with Hittite artifacts and the remains of King Midas, the ruler with the golden touch. Wander the many acres set aside for the mausoleum for Turkey's first president, Kemal Atatürk. Travel to Cappadocia for moonscape pinnacles and early Christian cave churches. The caps and cones of the pinnacles can be best seen on a thrilling hot-air balloon ride. The former Roman baths at Hierapolis also display an amazing natural wonder, Pamukkale "cotton castle," which contains hot springs and terraces of carbonate minerals left by flowing water. The whirling Dervishes of Konya are a sect of Islam who spin around and around in long white robes. Go to the Aegean Coast and walk between Greek and Roman pillars down the streets of Ephesus; it is one of the best-preserved cities in the Mediterranean, and nearby are lovely sea resorts.

My Favorite Encounter: Riding the old wooden elevator at the Pera Palas Hotel of Agatha Christie fame.

Israel / Jordan

Rating: 27   Best Touring Season: Year-round
                    (winter can be cold)

...A land flowing with milk and honey... –Bible verse (Exodus 3:8)

Highlights: A holy land for three religions, Israel offers pilgrimages for Jews, Christians and Muslims. Ensconced in the walled city of Jerusalem are areas sacred to half the world's population. For Jews the holiest sight is the Western Wall, which is the remains of the Temple Mount. For Christians, the Via Dolorosa is the path that Jesus walked carrying his cross, on the way to his crucifixion and burial. For Muslims, the Dome of the Rock is the sight where Mohammed ascended to heaven. This is why it's called the Holy Land. Here are important highlights, including: the Dead Sea Scrolls, the Garden of Gethsemane, the Mount of Olives and Bethlehem. Masada is a rock fortress rising above the Dead Sea. The Roman legions won a three-year battle, but the Jews chose death over capture. The pledge of new Israeli soldiers is that "Masada will never fall again." Bet Shean & Caesarea are two well-protected Roman cities. Acre in the north is a crusade town with gigantic walls, a UNESCO World Heritage Site. Visit the holy sites of Nazareth and the Sea of Galilee, where Peter cast his nets, Capernaum in the north, and the Jordan River flowing south. The Hashemite Kingdom of Jordan has long desert lands with a wealth of historical sites. Amman, or the old name Philadelphia, is a clean, almost European-looking city with open-air cafés and a modern feel. Jerash is a well-preserved Roman city with a triumphal arch and the Temple of Artemis. The ancient city of Petra was an active trading city and located south of Amman. It is known as the rose-red city and one of the great wonders of the world. Petra was left to deteriorate but today is being restored. Enter by the narrow canyon Siq on horseback like Indiana Jones and come upon the Treasury, a large temple cut out of the red rock walls. Many other buildings can be visited and, for the hiker, an invigorating walk to view Petra from the high rocky points. This is a Bedouin land with small villages, and herds of sheep roam the sparse countryside.

My Favorite Encounter: After the sun set, sat around an outside table on the shores of the Sea of Galilee and shared stories and wine with the priests who had the stewardship of Capernaum, site of the remains of the synagogue where Jesus taught.

Arabian Peninsula	Rating: 25	Best Touring Season: Spring, Fall, Winter (summers are hot)

All roads lead to Dubai when it comes to money. –Patrick Jost

Highlights: Saudi Arabia is the cradle of Islam and the guardian of the holy cities of Mecca and Medina. Generally they are visited from Jeddah - if, of course, you are a Muslim. The Jeddah fountain is in the bay and is one of the world's tallest. The capital, Riyadh, has impressive modern homes, office buildings and an elaborate airport. The Sultanate of Oman has a history of shipping and commerce due to its location on the Gulf of Oman. Muscat is the modern capital, but with old Portuguese watch towers on the hills that are lit at night, giving the city an Arabian Nights feeling. Dhow boats still ply the seas, and visitors can spend time on the old corniche and souq. Dubai in the United Arab Emirates is the grandest city for unique architecture. Start with Burj Al Arab the world's tallest hotel, shaped like a traditional Dhow sailing boat. The ultimate in luxury - it has an atrium lobby that rises 600 feet. There are manmade islands, and an extensive gold market and a multitude of dramatic architectural structures from hotels to office buildings, including the world's tallest building, Burj Khalifa. When the oil runs out, this Emirate will still be the talk of the world.

My Favorite Encounter: In Muscat, walking through the souq to view the old Portuguese watch towers and sultan's palace.

Asia

The Five Stans–Uzbekistan, Turkmenistan, Kazakhstan, Kyrgyzstan, Tajikistan
Rating: 22   Best Touring Season: Spring,
Summer, Fall

For the lust of knowledge … we take the golden road to Samarkand. - J.E. Flecker

Highlights: Here are the five land-locked countries that are little known and get less attention, but have surprising and interesting natural and man-made wonders. The first is the desert Republic of Turkmenistan, whose capital, Ashgabad, is noted for an Asian bazaar that might remind you of the Old Silk Road with booths stocked from floor to ceiling with carpets. Before departing for the long ride over the desert, dine on fresh black sturgeon caviar from the nearby Caspian Sea. Take the road over the Kara Kum desert passing mostly transport trucks, stop by the forgotten ruins of Mary & Merv, and wander through the abandoned towers, then onward to Bukhara, Uzbekistan. An important road caravan city on the Silk Road is Old Bukhara - it still has a caravanserai, or lodging for people and their animals, many Madrasah (Islamic universities), the oversized Ark Citadel and the Tower of Death. The great city of Samarkand holds the mausoleum of Tamerlane the Conqueror, who ruled over most of the five Stans, and Ulugh Beg Observatory, which is now a museum of astronomical equipment. The grandest of the grand is the Registan public square with incredible madrasah domes of blue and turquois ceramic tiles. Kazakhstan is the world's largest land-locked country, a bleak nation that stretches for endless steppes. Kyrgyzstan is a mountainous country and a throwback to Mongols' pastoral nomadic life. When you enter the city of Osh, you find bearded men with fur hats and women festooned with bright jewelry. A very special place right out of central casting, but it's not Hollywood, it's real. Tajikistan is 90 percent mountainous with blue lakes, and all roads lead to the Dushanbe, a mystical and at times unstable capital city. After you've seen the rest of the grand tours, don't forget to gaze your eyes on mystical Samarkand.

My Favorite Encounter: Talking with an elder in the old commercial market of Osh - a town where men wear fur headdresses and the women are bedecked with bobbles, bangles and beads.

Iran   Rating: 20   Best Touring Season: Spring,
                                                 Summer, Fall

Persia, a country embarrassed with mountains, open to the sea
and in the middle of the world.
–Francis Bacon

Highlights: The great Persian Empire that invaded the Greek city states and battled Alexander the Great is today modern Iran. Old Persia, the exotic land that is home to one of the oldest civilizations, still cradles fabulous architecture. Tehran is a busy, modern capital highlighted by the graceful Freedom Monument near the airport. Enter the National Museum and go back in time where the famous Peacock Throne captured from India is surrounded by rooms of jewels. North in the country, the Caspian Forest & Sea attract hikers and adventure travelers, but fly south over the desert to Shiraz, "city of poets." and tour mosques with inlaid mosaics displaying magnificent tile arches. Find a tea house and have a cup of Chai tea or on a hot day chopped ice faludeh, a dessert-like drink. The extensive ruins of Persepolis built by Darius the Great in 512 B.C. is worthy of a grand tour all by itself. Bas-relief carvings on pillars, statues and the walls of the palaces depict battle, heroes and gods. Unfortunately, the ruling Ayatollah spends little money on non-Islamic monuments, but when you visit the Muslim city of Isfahan, the former capital, it's a great experience. Imam Square is striking. One of the biggest squares anywhere - the city's mosques and palaces are built in a rectangle around the square, where hundreds of people gather night and day. Colorful tiled buildings are a picture-takers dream, and the 400-year-old bridges over the Zayandeh River are arched to allow the fast-moving water to pass. Walk down to a fascinating tea café just a foot above the water, but no alcohol is allowed anywhere in the country and women, even tourists, must wear a scarf over their heads. This is a land where the people are under the control of religious leaders, but the rich cultural landmarks are worth the journey.

My Favorite Encounter: Walked alone in Isfahan's Imam Square and met countless Iranians who wanted to use their English and seemed to love Americans.

India   Rating: 28   Best Touring Season: Oct - Feb
                                             (monsoon season June-Oct)

This is India, land of dreams and romance,
of fabulous wealth and fabulous poverty.
                    –Mark Twain

Highlights: When Shah Jahan's beloved wife died in childbirth, the great Moghal Emperor built a tomb in her honor. Today the Taj Mahal in Agra is considered the most perfect architectural monument in the world. The white marble building has three domes and four minarets, a reflecting pool and, not often photographed, two red buildings flanking either side, plus a meandering river just below the tomb. India is an experience to be enjoyed from October through February. Delhi, or Old Delhi, includes the impressive Red Fort, the Pearl Mosque, India Gates and Presidential Palace. If you fly to Varanasi or Benares, you're entering a holy Hindu city where the Ganges River flows. Witness Hindus at prayer in the water of the river's west bank, boat along the waterway to see hundreds of bathers, temples and hear the sound of bells ringing out the daily religious events. In the State of Rajasthan you will find the Pink City of Jaipur, home to the elaborate five-story Palace of the Winds and the Hawa Mahal with its lacey ornamental domes. The City Palace Museum has an old observatory that rivals the one in Samarkand, and the Amber Palace and City Palace are pure India design and can be entered on the back of a decorated elephant. There is a wonderful abandoned city Fatehpur Sikri, beautiful Victoria Monument in Calcutta, a palace on an island in Udaipur and rock-cut Hindu, Jain and Buddhist manmade caves of Ellora and Ajanta – a short flight from Mumbai. Some of these marvals can be enjoyed on luxurious private railway cars – called the Palace on Wheels. For travel in southern India, the Meenakshi Temple complex is just one of many Indian sites to be appreciated.

My Favorite Encounter: Rode to the Amber Palace in Jaipur, swaying back and forth on a lumbering Indian elephant.

Southeast Asia   Rating: 30   Best Touring Season: Nov-April
                                               (monsoon's June-Oct)

*On the road to Mandalay where the flying fishes play and the dawn comes up
like thunder over China cross the bay.*
–Rudyard Kipling

Highlights: Long before the Colonial French and British influence on Southeast Asia, there were great empires that rose and fell in what is today's Indochina. Burma, or Myanmar, is a magical land and had a glorious Golden Age during the Anawratha Empire. The magnificent ruins of Pagan (Bagan) date to the 11th century, and today they can be found on the banks of the Irrawaddy River, where 2,200 clay brick temples and pagodas dot the plains. Mandalay has the most important Buddhist monasteries in the country, and sightseeing includes the Royal Palace with 12 miles of moats, Mandalay Hill (a great place to watch the sunset), a long teak bridge over the river with working water buffaloes, and the world's largest stone book. Golden-domed Shwedagon Pagoda is in the heart of the largest city, Rangoon (aka Yangon). Chaukhtatgyi Pagoda holds a colossal reclining white Buddha statue 265 ft. long. Sule Pagoda sits on a main road in the middle of traffic, and the National Museum holds the magnificent golden Royal Lion Throne. Thailand, or Siam, has several ancient capitals but none finer than Bangkok on the Chao Phraya River. Walk from your hotel to the long tail boat that cruises by the solitary Temple of Dawn. Enjoy a tour of Bangkok's famous Emerald Buddha, Golden Buddha and Reclining Buddha temples. Visit the spectacular Royal Palace or take a day trip to the Bridge on the River Kwai, or busy Floating Market & Rose Garden Country Resort. Fly north to the hills of Chiang Mai & Wat Phrathat Doi Suthep hilltop temple. Ride an elephant into the jungle trails or take in a Kantoke dinner with traditional Thai dancing. Complete your visit and fly south to Phuket Island for beach or water sports. It's a short flight from Bangkok to Siem Reap, Cambodia - to discover its magnificent temples of Angkor Wat, the jewel of the Khmer Empire. This vast temple complex including Angkor Thom, Banteay Srei and tree-covered Ta Prohm were dug out of the jungle by the French at the turn of the 20th century. If you fly south to the capital Phnom Penh on the Mekong River, you'll visit the Silver Pagoda Royal Palace, and if you'd like, the killing fields of the Khmer Rouge. Laos is many things, a culture of Theravada Buddhists and a country of meditating monks, and in the mountains, wild herds of elephants still roam. Vietnam is developing into a modern country - so see it soon before the memories of Saigon, the boat cruises on the Mekong Delta, and the memories of American soldiers disappear.

My Favorite Encounter: Wandered through Cambodia's Ta Prohm temples, which are engulfed by immense banyan trees that wrap around the temple ruins.

China   Rating: 28   Best Touring Season: Spring,
                                               Summer, Fall

There lies a sleeping giant, let him sleep for when he wakes
he will move the world.
–Napoleon Bonaparte

Highlights: Welcome to the Middle Kingdom, to the land of Emperor Qin Shi Huang - builder of the Great Wall. The all-powerful emperor Kubla Khan, builder of Xanadu, the philosopher Confucius and chairman Mao Zedong - welcome to China and 5,000 years of history. Arrive in Beijing, formerly Peking, capital of the largest population on Earth. Stand in colossal Tiananmen Square and enter the Forbidden City with hundreds of buildings and palaces. In and around the city visit the round Temple of Heaven and the Summer Palace of Empress Dowager with its Marble Boat in a lake, Jade Bridge and Long Corridor. The Ming tombs can be visited, and great marble carvings line the Avenue of the Animals. Walk up and down from one watch tower to another on the Great Wall, which winds over 3,700 miles. In Shanghai, visit the old European Bund business district and ride from the airport on the world's first commercial magnetic levitated train. Xian is the cradle of Chinese civilization and the start of the Silk Road. There is a walled city and the Wild Goose Pagoda, but first of all there are the famous army vault pits with 8,000 terra cotta soldiers. They guard Emperor Qin along with terra cotta horses and bronze chariots. Take a river cruise on the Yangtze, going by the new dam and Three Gorges, a place of real beauty. The River Li in Guilin is at the top of the list with the natural pinnacle rock formations. Kunming has a stone forest (shilin) with rock formations protruding from the ground like stalagmites; the Qinling Mountains to Chengdu's north are protecting pandas in the wild. Two other historic cities are Hangzhou, which has the West Lake, and Suzhou, which has the Grand Canal. End your China odyssey in Hong Kong, one of the profoundly beautiful harbors in the world. Grab a water taxi to Victoria and Repulse Bay, then a 10-course Chinese meal on the Jumbo Floating Restaurant.

My Favorite Encounter: Dining on Peking duck with my family in a five-story restaurant dedicated exclusively to pressed duck dining.

Himalaya Kingdoms   Rating: 24   Best Touring Season: Late Spring,
                                                       Summer, Early Fall

The sight of snow wipes out the sins of the world. – Hindu proverb

Highlights: Climb to the roof of the world and discover Shangri-La! Tibet, Nepal and Bhutan offer a path to natural beauty and enlightenment. There are many ways to see the mountain kingdoms; let's start with Tibet, land of the Yellow Hat Monks. Although the Dali Lama lives in exile, he has spiritual rule over the Tibetans, and you can visit Lhasa's world-famous Potala Palace, a massive, 1,000-room structure. Tibet's holy shrines where pilgrims worship are scattered about the city, but sometimes it's hard to catch your breath at 11,540 feet, so take it slowly. Maybe try dining on yak soup and keep your eye out for Mount Chomolangma or Mount Everest when your plane departs this mountain kingdom. Katmandu, Nepal, sits in a green valley with mystical stupa Buddhist eyes looking down upon all pilgrimages and tourists. Journey to Durbar Square and feel the good vibes of the temples, shrines and palaces. There is a living goddess whose feet should never touch the ground, and out of town find Patan, a large temple area with long-roofed palaces. An optional morning flight around Mount Everest, the world's highest mountain, is an epic trip, so no need to climb 29,000 feet and take on oxygen or hire Sherpas. Royal Chitwan National Park is a protected forest and grasslands area for the preservation of animals. Check into Tiger Taps Jungle Lodge and you get keys to your thatched hut room, which comes with an elephant and mahout for riding through tall grass to look for Indian rhinoceros, deer and sometimes Royal Bengal tigers. For years the kingdom of Bhutan was isolated from the outside world, but today one can visit the dzongs fortresses or temples, watch colorful festivals or marvel at the Bhutan architecture, particularly in Thimph, the capital. Paro is the airport town and home to the Taktshang Monastery, also known as the Tiger's Nest. It is situated cliff-side near the Chomolhari Mountains, rising 24,000 feet. The Himalayan people of Bhutan are gentle, caring people who refuse tips and want only a smile and friendship. This is Shangri-La!

My Favorite Encounter: I walked through Tibet's Potala Palace, a huge but mystical place and talked with Yellow Hat monks who profoundly believe in peace and harmony.

Indonesia   Rating: 30   Best Touring Season: Year-round
(festival dry season June-Oct)

This is the morning of the world. –Prime Minister Nehru

Highlights: The fabled East Indies, or Indonesia, consists of 17,508 islands that lie south of Indochina in an archipelago that includes Sarawak and Sabah, Malaysia, Brunei and Indonesia. They offer the traveler a variety of culture and religion from Hindu and Islam to Buddhism and Christianity. The island of Sumatra has rich agricultural land and an abundance of wildlife, including elephants, rhinoceroses, orangutans and tigers. Medan with its Dutch heritage is the largest city and gateway to large plantations of rubber, cocoa and palm oil. Tourists will enjoy a tour to Samosir Island and meeting the indigenous Batak people, who are an unusual protestant sect. They are famous for building long swayback houses where many people in the village live, like a commune. Jakarta is the capital of the country, but the cultural center is Yogyakarta in central Java, where you'll find Borobudur, with world's largest Buddhist temple monument. It was hidden in the jungle for many years and rediscovered by Singapore founder Stanford Raffles in the early 19th century, and restored over years of work – even enduring an earthquake setback. It consists of nine platforms, decorated with thousands of panels and more than 500 Buddha statues. Nearby, the Prambanon Hindu Temple ruins tell the story of Ramayana in bas-relief carvings. All of this in a predominantly muslim country. You can feel the pulse of Bali by viewing her thousands of Hindu temples and her verdant green rice paddies terraced down the hillsides. Spend leisurely days on the popular beaches at Nusa, Dua, Kuta, Sanur or Jimbaran; or shop for hand-crafted Balinese arts & crafts. Spend evenings watching the sunset or the Ketjak monkey dance of 100 or more performers. Bali is one of the most special relaxing spots to be found anywhere. West Papua, formerly West Irian Jaya, has primitive tribal dancing, and the island is shared with Papua New Guinea. Komodo Island is where the carnivorous Komodo dragons stalk the landscape hunting for deer and small animals. These huge lizards can weight 300 pounds and measure 11 feet. "The wild man of Borneo" is actually the orange orangutans that live in the Indonesian forests and can be seen in wildlife parks. For indepth explorers, many more island cultures await you in the land once known as the Spice Islands.

My Favorite Encounter: After dark watched 100 dancers swaying the Ketjak monkey dance, telling the story of Ramayana.

Japan   Rating: 29   Best Touring Season: Spring,
                                              Summer, Fall

The land of the rising sun. –Historical phrase

Highlights: Here is an island nation once closed to the outside world and therefore a culture created within its own borders. The isolated Japan creates a unique offering from other parts of the world. Kabuki theater, Sumo wrestling, lodging in a ryokan, which are traditional Japanese inns, and the deep love of beauty in nature. If Tokyo is your first point of entrance, you may feel the crowding and fast-paced lifestyle a bit too much, but give Japan a longer look. The Ginza area has stores with young girls wearing white gloves to help you find items for purchase, and at night neon lights pulse with the excitement of restaurants and bars. Before leaving the city, spend time at the Gardens of the Meiji Shrine, Imperial Palace and Tokyo Tower. Traveling by train is a pleasure; the system runs on time and is always clean. Take it to the Nikkō National Park and visit the intricately carved Toshogu Shrine, Sacred Stable and the three carved monkeys "hear, see and speak no evil." Wander through the cyprus trees or climb to the top of the hill to see Tokugawa Ieyasu's grave. Kegon Falls pours water from Lake Chuzenji and the surrounding forest, it's truly lovely. Out of Tokyo board the Shinkansen bullet train that passes by Mount Fiji on its way to the Kanto Plain & Lake Ashi. Hakone Open Air Museum features re-created famous statues from other parts of the world. In Kamakura stands the great 43-foot Buddha bronze statue, Daibutsu. He was built in 1251 and remains the symbol of Japan. Continue south to the ancient capital of Kyoto. Tour Nijō Castle and the Golden Pavilion set in a Japanese garden. Historic Nara has Tōdai-ji Temple, the largest wooden building in the world and a huge bronze image of the sitting Buddha. Nara Park has ponds, lakes, trees, temples and famous tame deer roaming the grounds. Okayama has Kōraku-en Garden, Hiroshima the Atomic Bomb Dome and there is a Snow Festival north in Sapporo. Osaka Castle is dramatically beautiful and one of Japan's most famous, it sits on a hill overlooking the city. Discover the polite and very clean people who may seem in a hurry but will take time to help you and politely bow.

My Favorite Encounter: I slept at a ryokan inn, where all eat together, and slept on tatami mats.

Pacific Ocean

Hawaii   Rating: 30   Best Touring Season: Year-round

Dreams come true in Blue Hawaii. – Elvis Presley

Highlights: Hawaii may be the best sun & fun destination on Earth. What more could one ask for - warm tropical weather year-round, off-shore breezes cooling the islands, white and black sand beaches, small islands, clean blue water, polite Polynesian people and endless numbers of eloquent resorts. Local foods include mahi-mahi fish, macadamia nut ice cream, fresh pineapples, plus outdoor luaus with fire torch dancers and lovely girls in grass skirts. Our 50th state is a delightful paradise, and Honolulu on the island of Oahu is a great place to start a vacation. Take an outrigger canoe ride on Waikiki Beach near Diamond Head. Put on your Hawaiian shirt and tour Pearl Harbor with the Arizona Memorial and the USS Missouri battleship, Iolani Palace, Punchbowl Crater Cemetery, Sea Life Park and the North Shore, and take in an enthusiastic show at the Polynesian Cultural Center. Fly to Kauai, the Garden Isle, for a spectacular helicopter tour over Waimea Canyon - known as the Grand Canyon of the Pacific, the dramatically beautiful Nā Pali Coast and Mount Wai'ale'ale - the wettest spot on Earth. The island of Lanai still has pineapple fields and beautiful tropical resorts. The island of Molokai has a great one-day mule ride down the Kalaupapa Pass, and the island of Maui is noted for well-organized whale watching in the winter months. Explore Īao Valley, while Mount Haleakala is known for its sunrises and hiking, and you can take a van up the mountain and bike down -- it's lots of fun and offers great vistas. Lahaina is known for its shopping and restaurants, the beaches of Kaanapali and Kapalua for golf and spectacular beach resorts. The Big Island, Hawaii, has the Kona Coast for resorts and black lava golf courses, Volcanoes National Park or a helicopter ride over Kilauea molten lava caldera. Hilo and the rainforest valleys have deep waterfalls and two great mountain peaks, Mauna Kea and Mauna Loa. Say aloha to the Islands of Hawaii.

My Favorite Encounter: Fun for the whole family, took an outrigger ride on Waikiki, paddled fast to catch a ride on a long-breaking wave.

Tahiti   Rating: 31   Best Touring Season: Year-round

I do believe God has a condominium on Bora Bora. –Gig Gwin

Highlights: Heaven has divine clouds, but Tahiti has Bora Bora! It is said that beauty is subjective until you boat in the lagoons of Tahiti. Located in the South Pacific, the Society Islands of French Polynesia sparkle in the warm tropical sun. Created by nature, crafted by the Tahitian people and protected by the French government, this is the "Queen of the Pacific." The international airport in Papeete welcomes flights from around the world. Many are honeymooners looking for a slice of paradise. On the island of Tahiti, get a feel for these South Sea Islands with a circle tour, driving past natural blow holes, then stop at Paul Gauguin Museum for a tour or lunch. Boat or fly to nearby Moorea with its spellbinding natural, beauty. The Pineapple Island has two striking bays – Cook and Opunohu, which are cut deep into the island's lush interior. A jeep safari takes you up to the rainforest of Belvedere lookout or for a lagoon adventure. Swim with the sting rays and black-tipped sharks on a boat trip that ends on an isolated motu sand island for a picnic lunch. Play the new golf course by the airport or watch an evening Tiki village show. Huahine, the Garden of Eden Island, has lush forests; Raiatea, the Sacred Island, has a river cruise; Tahaa has vanilla farms; and distant Fakarava has good diving in the atoll and a black pearl underwater farm - all are replete with top-rated resorts. Bora Bora has a verdant volcanic peak, Mount Otemanu, crystal clear lagoons, over-the-water bungalows and remote sand motus. The resorts are some of the finest in the world. Have dinner at Bloody Mary's Restaurant with fresh fish and tropical fruit, or just wander the beaches of these turquoise blue lagoons. If paradise exists, you will discover it in Tahiti.

My Favorite Encounter: In the bay near Opunohu, swam with numerous black-tipped sharks that eat fish, not tourists.

Australia   Rating: 30   Best Touring Season: Year-round

Waltzing Matilda, waltzing Matilda, you'll come a-waltzing Matilda with me.
- Australian bush ballad

Highlights: The land down under is quite different from the land up top. In Australia there are miles and miles of red outback, dry, desert-like areas with little water or people. Sitting in the middle of the continent is the great red monolith Ayers Rock. It is a spiritual place for local Aborigines; they call it Uluru. Early in the morning it appears dark, but as the sun takes hold it becomes red. Climbing to the top requires steady hands and a touch of courage. One hour up, great view, take photos and go down slowly - it is 350 feet high and nine miles around. It's best to be done before noon as the temperature can reach 110 degrees. The other dramatic rock formation is Kata Tjuta (a.k.a. The Olgas) - it has 36 dome-like formations. When the sun sets, that's the time to see the Milky Way; it's so bright it appears like a giant skylight. Fly to the east coast to Cairns, take a drive to Daintree Rainforest or get on the antique train to Kuranda. Then board the large catamaran for a 1-hour cruise to the Great Barrier Reef, the largest reef in the world. Scuba, snorkel or take a glass-bottom boat and see an underwater world of reefs brimming with colorful fish and coral. Staying at an island resort is another way to experience the Great Barrier Reef. Need beach time? Fly to the Gold Coast for fun in the sun, or out to Norfolk or Lord Howe Islands. Sydney has a world-class opera house, Bondi Beach for swimming, the Rock for history and dining. The Sydney Bridge can now be booked as a tour; you can walk up and over the span, and down the other side. Melbourne has great parks and zoo, and a strange way to play football, or maybe it's soccer; well it's called Australian football and a lot of fun to watch. Canberra, the capital, is well worth a stop, but Tasmania is full of national parks with unique flora & fauna, kangaroos and Tasmanian devils.

My Favorite Encounter: Started as dawn broke, climbed hand-over-hand up Ayers Rock for an endless view of the Outback and distant Olgas formation.

New Zealand   Rating: 29   Best Touring Season: Year-round

It's not the mountain we conquer, but ourselves. –Sir Edmond Hilary

Highlights: New Zealand is sheer beauty, the fairest land of all. Auckland is the gateway city, located on the North Island. After a museum stop to get acquainted with the Māori culture, drive north where islands dot the coast. Deep sea fishing and sailing are excellent. If you go south by the fast-moving Waikato River, you arrive at Waitomo Glowworm Cave. Boat in silence, and the roof of the cave, with its glowworms, lights up like stars; clap your hands and the worms go dark. Rotorua is a thermal area and the center of Māori culture. Take time to enjoy the Māori village and gushing geysers, which have a unique odor. Wellington is a capital that boasts a fine botanical garden and cable car ride, a great wharf and the port for Cook Strait leading to the South Island. The very English-like Christchurch has a gothic cathedral. Take time to stay at a sheep ranch or drive along the meandering Avon River. Mount Cook tops 10,000 feet with a national park full of glaciers and alpine lakes. Queenstown is a famous tourist town and known for the triple challenge, where you buy one tour that includes jet boat spins, fast current rafting and a helicopter ride through the canyon of the Shotover River. Bungee jumps can make it the awesome foursome. Take a cruise on Lake Wakatipu on the coal-burning TSS Earnslaw, go trout fishing, ride a cable car to the top of the mountain or become a bush walker and hike the many trails from Te Anau. You may fly from Queenstown over the breathtaking lakes and mountain peaks to Milford Sound. This is fjord country, and the majestic mountain is called Mitre Peak. During your boat cruise, waterfalls and playful dolphins are part of the nature show. If you go to New Zealand, the best time of year is our winter ... their summer. "It's an unforgettable trip, mate."

My Favorite Encounter: The triple challenge in Queenstown: Shotover River rafting, jet-boat spinning and canyon helicopter ride.

Galapagos Islands   Rating: 28   Best Touring Season: Year-round

A separate area of creation. –Charles Darwin

Highlights: The Galapagos Islands are an open-air zoo without fences or walls. The animals have little fear of people, the birds are tame and occasionally curious toward tourists and cameras. Charles Darwin, the English naturalist, researched the wildlife of these islands that sit alone some 600 miles off the Ecuadorian Coast. He published "The Origin of Species" and shook the establishment dogma of the day. The island remains isolated and protected, thanks to Ecuador's National Park rangers. But this animal wildlife area is primarily explored from cruise ships. Most visitors enjoy a daily hike on one of the moon-like landscaped islands, then back on board to clean up, have a sundowner and enjoy dinner aboard ship. Twelve main islands are open for viewing, and the most popular of these are Isabela, Fernandina, Bartolomé, San Cristóbal and Santa Cruz. So stay on the trail and enter the world of 400-pound, 150-year-old tortoises, land and marine iguanas, sea lions, small penguins, blue & red footed boobies, flamingos, flightless cormorants and the orange-colored Sally Light Foot crabs – leaving only your foot prints behind. Get as close as you want without touching – swim with the sea lions, climb volcanic hills and learn the art of wet landings. Because of its proximity to Peru, this trip can be combined with Cusco and Machu Picchu, or you may choose the Ecuadorian capital city of Quito as another stop on your grand tour.

My Favorite Encounter: With a group of 30, looked and listened as a 400-pound turtle lumbered toward us in the tall grass.

The Grand Tours of the World can serve as a life-long source for future journeys. I feel comfortable the great and wonderful trips that await you are included in this list. Before giving my final stamp of approval, it was reviewed by eleven of the best travel people in the industry. So this is a solid composite from travel experts. As a bonus I've added my favorite grand tours from around the world. I have been able to tour each one of these at least three times, so I hope this will help with your next vacation.

My Top 20 Grand Tours

After 40 years and 178 Grand Tours personally taken, the tours in this chapter were the best. And for the best of the best, here is my top 20:

1. Italy
2. Northern France
3. African Safari
4. Canyon Country USA
5. Greece
6. China
7. Egypt
8. England
9. New Zealand/Australia
10. Machu Picchu, Galapagos
11. Alaskan Cruise
12. Hawaii
13. Tahiti
14. Ireland
15. Germany
16. Danube Cruise
17. Canadian Rockies
18. Spain
19. Southeast Asia
20. Israel/Jordan

To travel hopefully
is a better thing than to arrive.

–Robert Louis Stevenson

Chapter 5:
Planes, Trains, Ships & Cars

W e're living our dream," said a couple as they depart-
ed the train station in Durango, Colorado; they had
just completed a full-day excursion on the Durango &
Silverton Narrow Gauge Train – and were delighted with their
historic transportation. "We're from Bristol, England, and this
is a highlight of our Western U.S. holiday." They paid homage
to the beautiful Colorado Mountains, smiled and strolled away.
Many times, outstanding transportation can be a rejuvenating
power and a memorable grand tour.

In your planning process, always put the modes of transportation on your short list. Begin with trains, ships, cars, and planes
as options to set a foundation for trip planning. Driving vs.
flying, cruising vs. motorcoach tour or train trip. Each has its
own rewards. Does cruising get high marks, and would you
like to glide to majestic places or jump ship at the first port-of-
call? Train trips…do they conjure up romance of the rails, or of
clunky old dinosaurs? Automobiles…the freedom of the road
or boring interstate highways? This chapter explores planes,
trains, ships and automobiles, and presents you with an intriguing array of transportation choices.

The Evolution of Railroads

You leave the Pennsylvania Station 'bout a quarter to four,
read a magazine and then you're in Baltimore.
Dinner in the diner, nothing could be finer, than to have your ham an'
eggs in Carolina.

–from "Chattanooga Choo Choo"

A benchmark in tourism came with the development of rail-roads. Tourism in early times was limited to general transportation of the day. It was not a pretty picture for even the most intrepid voyager; no one was pleased over the lack of comfort on small ships bouncing around the open sea. Roads were plagued with potholes and dust, and travel after dark—well, beware. The dawn of the railroads brought an enlightened, albeit smoky future. English engineers invented all-iron rails and train engines capable of using high-pressure steam. Shortly thereafter, creative American entrepreneurs started to develop advanced locomotive and rail systems, primarily on the East Coast. At first safety seemed to be a problem, as many of the trains had trouble staying on the tracks. The great railroad barons disregarded newspaper articles reporting jack-knifed passenger cars and passengers asphyxiated by black, sooty smoke. The object of the day was faster trains and bigger profits. Undaunted by derailments and the occasional Butch Cassidy and Sundance Kid robberies, the American railroad progressed at a rapid rate. The "little train that could" kept going; "I think I can, I think I can, I think I can" might have been the slogan of the day.

In the 1860s, the U.S. government recognized the great potential of railroads and authorized that a rail line be built across America from East Coast to West Coast. But who would build such a back-breaking rail system across windswept prairies and over the imposing Rocky Mountains? Well, let's see ... how about European immigrants starting from the East and Chinese laborers from the West. Two advantages — cheap labor and a whole bunch of new citizens. They met at Promontory, Utah, in 1869 and marked the event with a famous golden spike, which celebrated the completion of the world's first transcontinental rail line.

As rider-ship increased, quality passenger service became the hallmark of American railroads. As passengers boarded the trains, they would be met by stately black porters in white gloves welcoming families and business travelers to a ride on the rails in luxury. The trains offered fine dining and the comfort of retiring to Pullman sleeping cars. Sleek new engines, like the Streamliners, pulled trains that set the standard for excellence. Legendary trains competed for rider-ship, including the Burlington Zephyr, the Union Pacific City of Salina, the Santa Fe Super Chief, the Illinois Central City of New Orleans, the Milwaukee Road Hiawatha and the New York Central Twentieth Century Limited. The American traveler was now able to ride in comfort, and the popularity of passenger rail travel continued as a practical means of transport from coast to coast..."All Aboard!"

Today, vacation rail travel survives as a patchwork of vintage trains providing nostalgic memories of bygone days. Passengers still flock to board the Canadian Rocky Mountaineer between Vancouver, Banff; and Jasper; the Alaskan Whitepass and Yukon Train from Skagway; and the Anchorage-Denali-Fairbanks Alaskan Railroad – and Amtrak, although a semi-government owned monopoly, is continuing to improve their vacation travel experience. Many niche markets draw train buffs, including Colorado's Durango-Silverton narrow-gauge train. This one-day round-trip excursion is my favorite for family adventure. Board the train in the frontier town of Durango, where a uniformed conductor gives commentary as the train moves through a river valley, then climbs to frightening heights before chugging down into the old mining town of Silverton. Two cog-wheel trains – one at Pikes Peak, Colorado and the other at Mt. Washington, New Hampshire, are always popular with travelers. Also on the A-list of train tours is the luxurious Blue Train South Africa from Cape Town to Pretoria and the elegant Royal Scotsman, which travels through the Scottish Highlands. Two other favorites are the rail trip in Mexico's Copper Canyon and the Swiss Alps' picturesque Glacier Express. The most romantic and maybe the most expensive train is the Simplon Orient Express from Venice to London. I took this trip with my wife and found it to be a historic and romantic two-day trip. We viewed the Alps and dined on culinary delights before a motor coach transfer through the Chunnel and arrival at Victoria Station in London.

High-speed trains that provide superb service can be found in various areas of the world, including Europe and Asia, but change is in the air. Today, Shanghai has inaugurated a state-of-the-art magnetic levitation train, called Maglev, from its international airport to the downtown station. Maglev works on a positive/negative floating magnetic force, and the ride is seamless and comfortable. This marvelous innovation has the potential of alleviating congested airline travel, because a train can add passenger cars. Another feature of Maglev: It is not tethered to heavy wheels and traditional tracks; it can therefore develop blurring speed. The downside: Because of high speeds, the trains need to be elevated and the cost of construction and land acquisition runs high. Do the advantages outweigh the costs? Only tomorrow will tell the tale, so listen for the whistle to blow on the future of train travel.

She'll be comin' 'round the mountain when she comes.

–American folk song

Cruising and Crossings

I must go down to the seas again, to the lonely sea and the sky,
and all I ask is a tall ship and a star to steer her by.

"Sea Fever" - John Masefield

Cruising is my favorite way of seeing the world; pull the anchor, I'm ready! To start, let's give credit to the British, who have distinguished themselves in transportation throughout the centuries. They were first in railway development, first with the commercial Comet jet, co-builder of the super-sonic Concorde, creator of the functional London taxi cab and double-decker bus, and pre-eminent in the evolution of ocean liners. Great Britain led the world in the development of sea-going ships. Cunard and White Star lines were the frontrunners in ocean-going liners that stressed luxury with various classes of service. The Queen Mary and Queen Elizabeth passenger liners were built as elegant floating hotels. This English seafaring tradition has been a hallmark of ocean-going vacations. Hail Britannia, Britannia rules the waves.

It's fair to say that substantial passenger improvements have been made since the Niña, the Pinta and the Santa Maria sailed across the Atlantic. At the turn of the 20th century, the Cunard and White Star lines dominated trans-Atlantic crossings. Later, the Germans, French, Italians, Swedes, Greeks, Canadians, Dutch and Americans entered the race for passengers – and the ships became larger, faster and more luxurious. Just as things seemed to be going quite splendidly, old chap, ocean liners suffered a major setback. When the Titanic – on its maiden voyage – struck an immovable iceberg, the "unsinkable" ship with 1,500 passengers was lost to the icy North Atlantic. An outraged protest forced new international maritime laws, adding more lifeboats and other safety standards to protect passengers and crew.

The French SS Normandie and the American USS United States were to become the pride of their nations. These grand ships crossed the pond, carrying their passengers to & from Europe and the United States. Here a distinction should be made between cruising and crossing. On a crossing, guests may be in the lap of luxury with comfortable deck chairs, gourmet meals and plush cabins, but at the risk of detail, this is not cruising. A crossing is from point A to point B, for the purpose of transportation, and not specifically sightseeing. Cruising vacations, on the other hand, serve the purpose of touring and many cruises start from and return to the same port.

During the late 1960s, ships began to be built from the keel up to service the growing cruise market. Brochures for this all-inclusive style of travel started to appear in great numbers on travel agents' racks. One of the leading upstarts was Carnival Cruise Lines. They sold 'fun' and flooded the market with reasonably priced seven-day cruises that were affordable for families. This appealed to a mass market and allowed millions of new travelers to take part in the cruise experience. When I escorted cruises the first-time passengers, at times, would ask the most interesting questions, such as, "Does the crew sleep on the ship?" or "Does the water go completely around the island?"

Today, tourists have a wide range of ships plying the Caribbean, Alaska, Panama Canal, Mediterranean, Baltic, Asia and the Pacific, plus a new, growing market in river cruising. Seasonal river cruising is now available in Europe on the Rhine, Danube, Seine and Rhone rivers, to name just a few. In Egypt, cruise the Nile; in Brazil, the Amazon; in Asia, China has developed river cruising through the Three Gorges on the Yangtze. Russian river cruises have also become popular, and this gentle style of touring is taking the travel community by storm.

If variety is the spice of life, modern cruises offer a rich and spicy menu. Jumbo-sized ships might sound ugly as sin, but there is strength in numbers. The mega ships have an economic advantage: Sheer scale drives down the cost per person. Today, most vacationers from any walk of life can afford a cruise experience. Big ships also offer an impressive choice of public spaces, including atrium lobbies with spiral staircases, multiple restaurants and bars, casinos, spas, theaters and the ever-popular lido deck with pools and lounge chairs to soothe the soul. Smaller ships tend to cater to the upscale and adventure markets, and they have the ability to maneuver into smaller ports, providing a more flexible itinerary.

River cruising has grown in popularity primarily because it provides touring of cities that are inland from the sea. River boats and romance are synonymous, with gentle-water riverbanks close enough to touch. I recall cruising a particularly lovely stretch of the Austrian Wachau Valley, and my wife made note of the large number of cyclers riding parallel to the river. We waved hello to folks strolling the shoreline; we could almost have had a conversation. By design, river boats are low, long and narrow to fit through the frequent locks. River cruising has become popular, in part, because many little towns grew into great cities along the river banks and have charmed tourists for centuries. So if this is your escape from everyday life, consider a river journey and add to your store of knowledge about river sights around the world.

Today, you are in the Golden Age of Cruising and it's in full swing. You can glide from one port-of-call to another, so climb the gangway and enter the comfort of modern cruising. Your ship is about to depart and your cabin is waiting

America's Love Affair with the Automobile

And I can't wait to be on the road again.
On the road again,
Like a band of gypsies we go down the highway.

"On the Road Again" - Willie Nelson

America's love affair with automobiles is a major chapter in tourism. This story of sports cars and minivans, Mustangs and Eldorados might best be found on bookstore shelves under the heading of romantic novels. The Italians love their pasta and the Irish their Guinness, and the great American passion is automobiles. The American car defines our culture. It's independent transportation, it's pride of ownership, it's bragging rights and sometimes almost a part of the family. As our nation expanded in the 20th century, the automobile became a symbol of the American way of life and, for millions of families, the freedom of a driving holiday.

People of other countries at times refer to the United States as a nation on wheels; we've come a long way from the Stanley Steamer and the Model T. The horseless carriage of yesterday is today a technical marvel of design and comfort, a mobile resort with GPS and sound systems, and safety blended with horsepower.

The American romance with the road has its origins in World War II and Allied Supreme Commander Dwight D. Eisenhower.

The German highway network made a lifelong impression on the general with its high-speed efficiency. Ike went from soldier to politician and decided to emulate the Autobahn road system. President Eisenhower persuaded Congress to establish the Interstate Highway System. The government spent billions building a reticulated pattern of superhighways as a necessary component of a national defense transportation system. This lofty engineering project gave Americans the freedom of the roads, with Ford, Chrysler and General Motors providing the backup.

Today, touring through American with your beloved buggy has never been easier, yet one caveat to this "honeymoon of highways" is that road speed and safety have almost eliminated scenic landscapes. CBS correspondent Charles Kuralt said it best, "Thanks to the interstate highway system, it is now possible to travel from coast to coast without seeing anything." Here's a thought...next time the family and faithful car set off on a driving odyssey, consider the alternatives—some picturesque roads, those blue and red highways on your map, will help you discover some of the quaint, little-known stopping places. As for those efficient interstate highways, they'll get you swiftly to your destination, hopefully without hassles. So Mr. President, for your vision of America on wheels and the nationwide road system, and for expanding our mobility and freedom...thank you. In short—I like Ike.

The next generation of cars will address fuel economy over style and speed. Gas prices have been the millstone around the neck of the traveling public as costs move up and down like a yo-yo. The frustration with petroleum has sparked a renaissance in new technology. What powers your next automobile may not be gasoline but rather fuel cells or batteries. The hybrid has emerged as a practical solution after a culling process of alternative fuel candidates. Plug-in hybrids may emerge as the next driving giant where the power source comes ultimately from coal, nuclear, solar or wind farms. Would Henry Ford have envisioned a wind-powered automobile? The stakes are very high; the profit potentials are at the beck and call of the next generation of intuitive engineers.

Traveling at Jet Speed

Come fly with me, let's float down to Peru
In llama-land there's a one man band and he'll toot his flute for you
Come fly with me, let's take off in the blue.

"Come Fly with Me" - Frank Sinatra

The growth of flight began in 1903 when two American bicycle makers, Orville and Wilbur Wright, made the first airplane flight in history over the sand dunes of Kitty Hawk, North Carolina. This modest flight of 120 feet was the origin of the aviation industry. Subsequently, almost every new plane flew faster and farther than it had the year before. In the early days, barnstorming tours dazzled crowds, and aviator Charles Lindbergh put the stamp of approval on flying in 1927 when he made the first solo flight across the Atlantic Ocean in the Spirit of St. Louis, a single-engine airplane. Lucky Lindy became a hero in the Roaring Twenties, in a time of heroes that set the stage for future passenger service.

Propeller aircraft soon emerged into prominence. New aircraft were introduced into the market, including the legendary DC3. This sturdy, large-winged plane was so flexible it is still flying today at third world airports. Some people may connect with this plane – you may remember walking uphill to your seat. Pan Am and TWA battled for air dominance and were pioneers in international destinations. The Pan Am Clipper "flying boat" forged a new era for tourism, particularly to the Orient. If you should ever journey to Midway Island, there are remnants of a water-landing dock, where in the '30s the China Clipper landed and refueled on its way to Asia.

One of the next notable aircrafts was a creation of Howard Hughes; he fostered the graceful Super Constellation, a sleek, four-engine craft with three distinct fins on the tail. The range of the "Connies" made Atlantic Ocean travel affordable, but travelers noted that the plane wasn't much wider than a pencil.

The year 1958 saw the beginning of the Jet Age, the transition from propeller to jet aircraft. The jet provided a quantum leap in speed, not to mention comfort and passenger appeal. The world had shrunk! The Boeing 707 roared successfully through the 1960s, and in January of 1970, Pan Am and TWA launched the wide-body era, inaugurating 747 service.

Rapid improvements continued, and six years later, British Airways and Air France began supersonic Concorde service between the U.S. and Europe. Without the jet, there would be no six-hour trip to Europe, no expansion of tourism and no Gig Gwin visiting all countries on earth.

Oh 707, what a noble silver bird, we salute you and give tribute to the aircraft that took people around the world through the speed of your wings. Boeing's super commercial aircraft was a harbinger of things to come; it has placed an indelible mark upon the altar of travel. For inexplicable reasons known only to me, I have spent the last 40 years hanging in the air, chalking up 3 million miles and traveling to all corners of the earth. I was born at the right time. This would have been impossible without the advent of jet travel. I've been fortunate to live during a time that moves at jet speed.

Shine up the crystal ball and look into the future of flight. Today, most commercial aircraft look similar, as all current Boeing and Airbus designs have engines mounted on the wings. Venerable 727s and DC9s have rear-mounts, but all have a look-alike appearance. The new generation 787 with its carbon fiber skin and the jumbo airbus 380, from a distance, look like carbon copies of their predecessors; the future belongs to jets with blended styling, with engines incorporated into the wing, looking less like a jet and more like a space shuttle. This next technical advance will provides less drag and lessens city noise abatement problems. Already, private enterprise has successfully flown sub-orbital flights, and when technology catches up with Star Trek dreamers, look for orbital flights that will shrink flight times into an almost unnatural phenomenon.

Welcome to the hotel California,
such a lovely place, such a lovely face,
plenty of room at the hotel California,
any time of year, you can find it here.
–The Eagles, "Hotel California"

Chapter 6:
Lodging Made Memorable

To fully experience lodging, momentarily let go of what you know – feel only the moment. If you're spending a long week in Denmark or jet-setting to the Greek Islands of Mykonos or Santorini, the same resort rules apply. I recall check-in at the front desk of the Intercontinental Hotel in Bora Bora, where a young soft-spoken Polynesian woman handed me keys to my room. She then pointed in the direction of the Bora Bora lagoon. Dog tired from a 10-hour flight to Tahiti, I trudged out of the lobby and slowly lumbered down the wooden walkway leading to the water. Then my sluggish brain began to focus and delightedly I realized that my room was not just a room, but an over-the-water bungalow. My slumped body changed abruptly. Standing a little taller I strolled out toward the bungalow; I began to pick up my pace and add a slight shoulder swagger to my walk.

Opening the door to my room was like opening the gates of paradise. A large, elegant sitting room led to an oversized bedroom with local Tahitian tapa décor. My outside balcony resembled a nature sanctuary. Below the deck lay a shallow lagoon with multi-colored fish and a lazy leatherback sea turtle swimming gently between the balcony posts. In front, the water color blended from turquoise to teal to cobalt until the reef met the land, which rose dramatically to the verdant volcanic peak, Otemanu.

I became a quick-change artist, and my swim suit was barely on before I plunged off the balcony and spent carefree moments swimming between curious schools of fish. Upon returning to my deck, I shut my eyes and let the sun turn my lily white skin into a healthy looking blush. The grand finale to my first day in paradise was a Polynesian sunset that lasted a good 30 minutes. During this gloaming, images of a simpler time in life wandered through my mind. I even conjured up a dream of becoming a Tahitian beach bum and never returning to the real world. Such are the hob-goblins of one's mind, tempting all your senses. The resort presented me with a sublime way to spend my vacation days - a grand tour of relaxation and a promise of doing absolutely nothing.

The choice to stay at a hotel, motel, inn or resort is as personal as your own toothbrush. Each traveler approaches lodging in a different way. I wish I could flatter myself by predicting the wants and needs of all clients as they walk into my office, but it's an impossible task – I have no crystal ball to see into their minds. Personal finances, of course, often is a factor in hotel selection, so no matter if you are a rich man, poor man, beggar man, thief ... you want the biggest bang for your vacation buck. Yet cost is only one ingredient in the selection of lodging.

 **Economy Lodging**—Under the harsh light of scrutiny, lodging is simply temporary quarters to provide a roof over one's head. It can be as sparse as a tent for hiking or a European economy room with the bathroom down the hall. The thrifty traveler may view his room as merely a place to sleep and a launching pad for day trips. Standard comments include "we're not going to spend much time in our room" or "I want to use my money on things other than fancy resorts." Motel 6 and other thrifty hotel chains provide a great value for your hard-earned dollars. I have noticed some people tend to be embarrassed to book or even talk about low-priced lodging. Hey, maybe you're working on a shoestring; it's your money, so stand tall. You're not going to be put on double secret probation, and it's not going on your permanent record.

The world is full of one- and two-star properties ready to provide a clean bed. Motels in particular are convenient, with close parking, basic amenities and fast check-out. If I'm on a business trip, motels are my first choice; I have developed a stingy attitude toward business costs and an appreciation for convenience.

 **Bed-and-Breakfast Lodging** — For holiday travelers, consider bed-and-breakfast lodging. Usually moderate in price, B&Bs provide a local charm without an eye-popping price tag. In a nutshell, most B&Bs are private homes that wear two hats — living quarters for the owner and rooms for rent, plus breakfast. From large cities to one-horse towns, their popularity has grown rapidly, partly because savvy B&B owners have banded together and formed associations that set common standards.

Bed-and-breakfast lodging came of age not with large advertising campaigns but rather by word of mouth. The signature attraction of B&Bs is the local, friendly experience that travelers rave about. Gathering around the breakfast table with other guests opens the door for conversation and sharing of vacation ideas. Suggestions from the owner and a smattering of map directions can lead to a splendid day. Case in point, wife Terrie and I joined close friends for 10 days of touring in the Canadian Maritimes, and we selected B&Bs from the local association list. Each morning we gathered little travel nuggets and feasted on local breakfast specialties. On one particular morning, all fired up over our day-tripping, we ventured out through the rolling hills of Prince Edward Island. We visited the Anne of Green Gables home, temporarily got lost, ate steamed mussels at a great restaurant, got lost, and found our way back home to our cozy B&B before nightfall.

Mid-level hotels are the standard for most travelers. Well-managed chains offer a wide variety of amenities at a moderate cost. Hotels and resorts have evolved through trial and error into quality properties, many with cracker-jack service and dining to please the most discerning guests. This very popular level of three- and four-star properties combines the best of both worlds — fusing the otherwise tight-fisted traveler with the more affluent traveler and giving both reasons to spend a little more to enjoy things you don't do every day. Holiday Inn, Hyatt, Marriott, Hilton and Sheraton are standard bearers and represent a sampling of quality places to lay your head. Hotels around the globe have jumped on the bandwagon, elevating their properties to seduce the international traveler. Old World or Third World inns are no longer tired old buildings frozen in time. Many have had a full makeover, and the results have been impressive.

Luxury Properties — Ooh la la! Let's now talk about the crème de la crème of lodging, the posh world of luxury hotels and resorts. The boomer generation and generations X and Y, represent new luxury clients. Many of these affluent people have come up the ranks as creative entrepreneurs who are not so much impressed with status, but are yearning for adventure and knowledge.

Historic grand hotels boast a long heritage of elegance and service for the rich and famous, most notably at city properties. In recent years Four Seasons and Ritz Carlton successfully started a building trend, expanding 5-star properties to resort areas. The luxury market seems to be increasing like the sorcerers apprentice with a never-ending building spree; enough travelers have shown they will pay the price for luxury and quality.

Hotels and resort properties cater to the public in countless ways. To list all the traveler wants and needs would take a Herculean effort. Wants and needs are two different human expressions. No person explained wants and needs like my father, Dr. Jimmy Gwin – he taught an enthusiastic graduate marketing course and dedicated two full lectures to our human desires. Given the topic of lodging, he might start with a traveler's basic need for beds, bathrooms and possibly parking. I might add cleanliness, for we Yanks insist on healthy, tidy surroundings. Those are some of the basic needs. My father explained that wants expand our desire to dream of nice things; but remember, you get what you pay for. Today, I marvel at the diversity of answers when I ask what's important for guests at a lodging property. Sometimes I get an answer like soft sheets with a thread count of 450 or better, and they might add, "I want to pick my own pillows." This person may request soft surroundings, a heavenly bed, a cozy bathrobe and an abundance of fluffy towels. Others desire blissful relaxation and utter serenity for their domicile; therefore an adults-only resort might be in order. Hot tubs relieve my lower back pain, so I put this high on my personal want list, along with a morning newspaper. What's on your want list: bigger lobby, choice of eateries, fancy spa or business center? The list goes on and on.

I started compiling my list of favorite lodgings more than 40 years go, realizing that some of these properties listed below may have fallen on hard times, or even closed their doors to the public—yet some are the hallmarks of their community or country. In selecting your next Grand Tour, you might refer to this collection of properties. If you choose wisely, one of these hotels or resorts might be the highlight of your next Grand Tour.

The "A" List for Memorable Lodging

North America

Fairmont Chateau Whistler–BC, Canada
Stately ski resort where spa and ski run meet.

Fairmont Empress–Victoria BC, Canada
Grand lady on the harbour, arrive by float plane.

Fairmont Banff Springs–Banff Canada
Castle-looking gem built on the side of a mountain overlooking Bow Valley.

Fairmont Chateau Lake Louise–Alberta, Canada
On the shore of a turquoise lake surrounded by mountain peaks.

Fairmont Chateau Frontenac–Quebec, Canada
High on a hill, the landmark of this charming French Canadian town.

Lake Quinault Lodge–Quinault, WA
On the lake in the Olympic National Forest, relax on the large lawn.

Crater Lake Lodge–Oregon
View of the sapphire volcanic lake with hiking trails lookouts & snow drifts.

The Westin St. Francis–San Francisco, CA
Historic building on Union Square, with cable cars & hilly walks.

The Ahwahnee Hotel–Yosemite Nat'l Park, CA
Surrounded by vertical canyon walls, a deluxe touch in the national park.

The Beverly Hilton Hotel–Beverly Hills, CA
Hollywood's best known address - stars and style, glitz and glamour.

Waterton Lakes Resort–Alberta, Canada
Perfect lake location with wandering wildlife.

Lake McDonald Lodge–Glacier Nat'l Park, MT
The national park's pride and joy, with historic red bus tours.

Amangani Resort–Jackson, WY
Deluxe suites with perfect view of the Grand Teton Range.

Jenny Lake Lodge–Grand Teton Nat'l Park
Rustic elegance - log cabins in the woods, hiking trails to the lake.

Jackson Lake Lodge–Grand Teton Nat'l Park
Great floor to ceiling view of the Grand Teton & Jackson Lake.

Coeur d'Alene Resort–Northern Idaho
  Modern resort on the lake with well-kept course, featuring a floating golf hole.

El Tovar Hotel–Grand Canyon Nat'l Park, AZ
  A modest lodge looking over a Grand Canyon.

Majestic View Lodge–Springdale, UT
  Long beautiful view of natural wonders just outside the park.

Zion Lodge–Zion Nat'l Park, UT
  A comfortable park lodge in the heart of Zion Nat'l Park.

The Boulders Resort–Scottsdale, AZ
  Creative architecture, graced by twelve-million-year-old granite formations.

Arizona Biltmore Resort–Phoenix, AZ
  "The Jewel of the Desert", with Camelback Mountain backdrop.

Wigwam Motel–Holbrook, AZ
  An oddity on Old Route 66, Tepee shaped rooms with 1950's cars.

The Ritz Carlton, Batchelor Gulch–Avon, CO
  Top-drawer luxury nestled in an exclusive enclave on Beaver Creek Mtn.

New Sheridan Hotel–Telluride, CO
  Historic hotel in an old mining town, with drop-dead beauty & free ski lift.

The Broadmoor Resort–Colorado Springs, CO
  Elegant styling, mountain golf, 3000 acres at the Cheyenne Mountain base.

Hotel Santa Fe–Santa Fe, NM
  Centrally located, adobe design in this capitol city of galleries.

The Driskill Hotel–Austin, TX
  Elaborate woodwork & balconies, classic styling & color of Texas Hill Country.

Hyatt Regency–San Antonio, TX
  Modern hotel overlooking the meandering Riverwalk and near the Alamo.

InterContinental Hotel–Chicago, IL
  On Michigan Ave, grand lobby with historic Olympic indoor pool.

The Wheeler Mansion–Chicago, IL
  A boutique hotel, 12 rooms, 1 block from McCormick Place.

Omni Royal Orleans Hotel–New Orleans, LA
  In the heart of the French Quarter decorated with wrought iron balconies.

The Grand Hotel–Mackinac Island, MI
>   Long graceful balcony on an Island without cars, "America's summer place."

Monmouth Plantation–Natchez, MS
>   This plantation house was built when cotton was king, circa 1818.

Pinehurst Resort/Holly Inn –NC
>   Old Southern charm and luxury, 8 golf courses through the long-needle pines.

The Sanctuary Hotel–Kiawah Island, SC
>   Ocean front resort on a beautiful Island, complete with golf and kayaking.

The Mansion on Forsyth Park–Savannah, GA
>   Magnificently restored Victorian mansion, excellent food, excellent city.

Casa Monica Hotel–St. Augustine, FL
>   Historic Moorish revival architecture, set in the oldest US city.

Disney's Contemporary Resort–Orlando, FL
>   Family hotel with a monorail running through the property.

Disney's Grand Floridian Resort–Orlando, FL
>   Stately red-gabled building, the best of Florida architecture with boats transfers.

Don Cesar Beach Resort –St. Pete Beach, FL
>   Large pink resort on St. Pete beach, a family favorite.

The Greenbrier–White Sulphur Springs, WV
>   A Georgian style masterpiece nestled in the mountains with golf & mint juleps.

Williamsburg Inn–Williamsburg, VA
>   On the Nat'l Historic Registry; stately, with gracious accommodations.

The Willard InterContinental–Washington, DC
>   Crown jewel hotel of Pennsylvania Ave., overlooking the National Mall.

Waldorf Astoria–New York, NY
>   A legendary city hotel–serving a wonderful salad of apples & walnuts.

The Plaza Hotel–New York, NY
>   Commanding the corner, overlooks Central Park; a prestigious address for years.

Bellagio Hotel–Las Vegas, NV
>   Rich accommodations, luxury on the Las Vegas strip with dancing fountains.

Caesars Palace–Las Vegas, NV
>   Roman styling including naughty nooks and cranny's.

Luxor– Las Vegas, NV
> Egyptian architecture complete with a multi-story pyramid.

Fairmont Acapulco Princess–Mexico
> At one time the best atrium resort to be found, 15-story Aztec pyramid.

Las Hadas Resort–Manzanillo, Mexico
> Arabian-style mystical resort with tents on the beach, don't miss the sunset cruise.

Secrets Maroma Beach–Riviera Maya, Mexico
> All-inclusive resort with a romantic feeling–a honeymoon heaven.

Ritz Carlton–Cancun
> Leading hotel with turquoise beach–a bit rough for swimmers, great pool.

The Caribbean

Atlantis–Nassau, Bahamas
> Fanciful resort on Paradise Island, one of a kind, best-in-class aquarium.

El Conquistador Resort - Puerto Rico
> Perched high on a hill overlooking blue waters, with splendid golf.

Hotel El Convento–San Juan, Puerto Rico
> Restored convent in the heart of Old San Juan, short walk to the Spanish forts.

Hostal Nicolas de Ovando–Santo Domingo, DR
> Located in the colonial quarter, a World Heritage sight and a true gem.

La Samanna Resort–St. Martin
> Luxury Caribbean resort–very French, with ocean panoramic view.

Caneel Bay–St. John's, Virgin Islands
> Originally a Rock Resort getaway for quiet times, and perfect beach.

Sam Lords Castle–Barbados
> Stately mansion built by a buccaneer, winding coves and beaches.

Central America

Hotel Casa Santa Domingo–Antigua, Guatemala
> Part of the Spanish-Colonial period, a converted convent with candlelight dinners.

Four Seasons–Papagayo Peninsula, Costa Rica
> Pristine natural setting, unspoiled beaches, championship golf, tropical forest.

South America

Waku Lodge–Canaima Falls, Venezuela
>   Waterfall & jungle lodge, gateway to Angel Falls - tallest in the world.

Hotel Monasterio–Cusco, Peru
>   Over 400 year old building, two blocks from the Plaza de Armas central square.

Sanctuary Lodge–Machu Picchu, Peru
>   Overlooking the ruins & endless miles of jungle mountains, a view like no other.

Copacabana Palace–Rio, Brazil
>   On the most famous beach with a view of Sugar Loaf Mountain.

Hotel Das Cataratas–Iguazu Falls, Brazil
>   Tropical jungle and a view of the mighty orange colored falls.

Antarctica – (No Hotels / by Cruise Ship only)

Atlantic Ocean

Fairmont Southampton–Bermuda
>   Tall and elegant with a British flare and a gentle beach, perfect for relaxation.

Reid's Palace–Funchal, Maderia
>   Sitting on a steep cliff, the hotel commands a view of this Island of flowers.

Europe

Sheen Falls Lodge–Kenmare, Ireland
>   Stone bridge with cascading water to the lake - gateway to the Ring of Kerry.

Park Hotel–Kenmare, Ireland
>   A noble hotel with gardens flowing down to green fields, and a wonderful spa.

Dormoland Castle–Limerick, Ireland
>   Live like a noble, play golf like a pro.

Ashford Castle–Cong, Ireland
>   2 lakes and a stream by a medieval castle–my very favorite place.

The Ritz-Carlton Powerscourt–Enniskerry, Ireland
>   Palladian-style architecture, beautiful golf at Druids Glen Country Club.

Culloden Estates–N. Ireland
>   A lovely setting in a beautiful manor house complimented by a flowing stream.

Merchant Hotel– Belfast, N. Ireland

    Restored building in the heart of Belfast, grand lobby and great location.

Slieve Donard Hotel–N. Ireland

    40 shades of green around historic Royal County Down Golf Club.

Turnberry Resort–Scotland

    Overlooking famous golf courses and the Irish sea and Alisa Craig Island.

Gleneagles Hotel–Scotland

    In the middle of Scotland, golf, equestrian stables & more golf, simply stunning.

Balmoral Hotel–Edinburgh, Scotland

    Take a stroll down Prince Street or a view of Edinburgh Castle.

Old Course Hotel–St. Andrews Scotland

    Look down on the Old Course and Swilken burn, you're in golf heaven.

Carnoustie Golf Hotel–Carnoustie, Scotland

    Tiny town near famous link course–pure golf experience.

Borthwick Castle–Scotland

    Real medieval Scottish fortification near Edinburgh, old twin towers & grand dining hall.

Grosvenor House Hotel–London, England

    Across from Hyde Park ... "the place to stay governor."

Dorchester Hotel–London, England

    Very well appointed for every occasion, a place for the rich & famous.

The Claridge–London, England

    Located in Mayfair & home to royalty, called the extension of Buckingham Palace.

Bath Resort–Bath, England

    A Georgian resort for a charming Georgian town.

Le Manoir–near Oxford, England

    Beautiful English hotel and gardens, famous for its culinary delights.

Grand Hotel–Stockholm Sweden

    At harbors edge across the water from Gamla Stan Island and Royal Palace.

Hotel Dangleterre–Copenhagen, Denmark

    Landmark next to Ny Haven & Stroget Street, "wonderful, wonderful Copenhagen.

Hôtel de Crillon–Paris, France

    Overlooking Place de la Concorde ... a joy to behold, bourgeoisie luxury.

Hotel Ritz–Paris, France
>   Located on Place Vendôme - is this the best hotel in the world?

InterContinental Hotel–Paris, France
>   The Grand Ballroom dining room is a work of art with stained glass orb.

La Bastide de Gordes–Gordge, France
>   Overlooking the valley with historical buildings and great sunsets.

Hôtel de la Cité–Carcassonne, France
>   Double-walled medieval city, UNESCO site, the pride of France, not to be missed.

The Carlton Hotel–Cannes, France
>   Premier property at the centre of La Croisette Promenade.

Domaine de Divonne–Divonne, France
>   Art deco at its best with nearby casino and minutes from Geneva.

Hotel Du Palais–Biarritz, France
>   Historical palace on the water in French Basque Country.

Hotel de Paris–Monte Carlo
>   Across from the famous Grand Casino, a gathering place for the rich & famous.

Hotel Puente Romano–Marbella, Spain
>   Spanish beach resort with Roman ruins and meandering gardens.

Penia Golf Resort–Algarve, Portugal
>   Moorish style property, beautiful golf course & warm Mediterranean sun.

Villa d Este–Lake Como, Italy
>   Historic palace on a shimmering lake, 5-star hotel - one of the best.

Hotel Cipriani–Venice, Italy
>   Stay at the 'Chip", enjoy the large pool and boat to San Marco Square.

Hotel Weston Excelsior–Florence, Italy
>   Away from the crowds & across the street from the River Arno.

Hotel Hassler–Rome, Italy
>   Just above the Spanish steps, a diplomats first choice.

The Weston Excelsior–Rome Italy
>   "Magnificent white palace on Via Veneto", one of the world's great classic hotels.

Hotel Romazzino–Sardinia, Italy
>   Alluring hotel with lavish gardens- adorns seaside cliffs kissed by an emerald sea.

Hotel Cala Di Volpe–Sardinia, Italy
   Built by Aga Khan to be a jet-set get-a-way.

Platzl Hotel - Munich, Germany
   Charming Bavarian hotel in the center of Munich.

Buergenstock Park - Lucerne, Switzerland
   Overlooking Lake Lucerne, my honeymoon hotel, distant view of the white Alps.

Victoria Jungfrau - Interlaken, Switzerland
   Elegant hotel in a small town surrounded by the Swiss Alps.

Le Montreux Palace - Lake Geneva, Switzerland
   Luxury on Lake Geneva, a most romantic setting.

Hotel Imperial - Vienna, Austria
   City hotel in an imperial city, the Vienna Waltz originated here.

Hotel Sacher - Vienna, Austria
   Tasteful city surroundings, don't miss the Sachertorte.

Sacher Salzburg Hotel - Salzburg, Austria
   On the banks of River Salzach with view of Fortress Hohensalzburg.

Schloss–Dürnstein, Austria
   In the Wachau Valley, a perfect hideaway with Austrian hospitality.

Hotel Grand Bretagne–Athens, Greece
   Located on Constitution Square, a gathering spot for the well-to-do.

Andronis Luxury Suites–Santorini, Greece
   Situated high on the Island, the black rocks give way to the sea.

Grand Hotel Europe–St. Petersburg, Russia
   Well restored, an old world hotel & center-piece of the city.

Rossiya Hotel–Moscow, Russia
   Not the prettiest, this giant property is next to Red Square & most attractions.

Africa

Cairo Marriott–Cairo, Egypt
   Former Palace on the Nile, feel like a Sultan.

Old Cataract Hotel (Sofitel)–Aswan, Egypt
   From the balcony, watch Felucca boats sail the Nile.

Mena House Oberoi–Cairo, Egypt
> Green oasis set in 40 acres of gardens with the pyramids towering above.

Palais Jamai–Fez, Morocco
> Overlooking the holy city, don't miss the sunset & call to worship.

Hotel La Mamounia–Marrakech, Morocco
> A pink-walled city & a resort filled with roses and history.

Riad Jona–Marrakech, Morocco
> Large open-air common room with unique Moroccan design.

Hyatt Regency–Casablanca, Morocco
> Near the old Medina, feels like the movie Casablanca.

Mt. Kenya Safari Club–Mt. Kenya, Kenya
> Manicured lawns, Mt. Kenya backdrop, elegance in the jungle.

Norfork Hotel - Nairobi, Kenya
> Jambo–welcome to a historic city property, the starter hotel for safaris.

Kichwa Tembo Tented Camp–Masai Mara, Kenya
> Rondavals or round huts near the open plains, full of animals.

Serina Mtn. Lodge–Mt. Kenya Nat'l Park, Kenya
> Keep it quiet as wild game come to you at the watering hole.

Ngorongoro Lodge–Tanzania
> Incredible view of the crater, African interior with large tubs, not to be forgotten.

Grumeti River Lodge–Serengeti, Tanzania
> Camp next to a river filled with hippo, don't go walking around at night.

Marangu Hotel–Kilimanjaro, Tanzania
> Modest hotel with vibrant atmosphere for climbers going up & down Kili.

Victoria Falls Hotel–Victoria Falls, Zimbabwe
> For over 100 years a very British hotel, have high tea with wandering monkeys.

Thornybush–Near Kruger Nat'l Park, S. Africa
> Dine alfredo as antelope & zebra wander by–my family's favorite safari lodge.

Mount Nelson Hotel–Cape Town, S. Africa
> Table Mountain dominates the skyline, enjoy the local lobster and wine.

Khivai River Lodge–Okavango River Delta Botswana
> Elephant, hippopotamus & lions roam around the camp, you're in their backyard.

Palace of the Lost City–Sun City, Bophuthatswana
> Resort with a flair for Hollywood, game parks, casino and a lot of fun.

Middle East

Pera Palas Hotel–Istanbul, Turkey

>   Frozen in time with wooden elevator, it's near Bosporus and Golden Horn.

Gamirasu Cave Hotel–Cappadocia, Turkey
>   Sleep inside a stone spire & become a Troglodyte, it's one of a kind.

Al Bustan Palace IHC–Muscat, Oman
>   Built around the water, hotel mosaics inside and out, with mountain backdrop.

Burj Al Arab–Jumeirah, Dubai
>   The fanciest hotel anywhere, the view from the top is unreal.

Indian Ocean

Four Seasons–Private Island, Maldives
>   Private coral island, very exclusive with speedboat transfer accompanied by flying fish.

La Galawa Beach Hotel–Comoros
>   White sand beach, self-contained resort, a popular place for South Africans.

Le Méridien Fisherman's Cove–Mahé, Seychelles
>   Set amidst tropical garden, exotic vegetation, view of the Indian Ocean.

Cinnamon Lodge–Habarana, Sri Lanka
>   Modest property set in a garden, great location for excursions to wildlife and temples.

Asia

Taj Mahal Palace & Tower–Mumbai, India
>   A showcase of India art and artifacts, it offers large rooms & garden dining.

Rambagh Palace–Jaipur, India
>   Former palace of a Maharaja with indoor swimming pool & gardens.

Lake Dal Houseboats–Dal Lake Srinagar, Kashmir
>   Created for the British, elaborate boats with hand-carved bedrooms, quite mystical.

Hotel Yak & Yeti– Kathmandu, Nepal
>   5-star oasis, black/orange interior, don't miss the Dynasty Crystal room.

Sedona Hotel–Mandalay, Burma
>   A rich hotel in a poor land, with a view of royal palace grounds.

Sakura Sanctuary Resort–Pagan, Burma
    A great view of the temples and the Irrawaddy River.

Four Seasons–Chiang Mai, Thailand
    Thai thatched huts placed around rice paddies and hilltop dining, very peaceful.

Peninsula Hotel–Bangkok, Thailand
    Superb service, stunning view of the Chao Phraya river with local long-tail boats.

Oriental Hotel–Bangkok, Thailand
    Riverside deluxe property with legendary deluxe service and historic charm.

Raffles Grand Hotel–Angkor Wat, Cambodia
    A hotel with a heritage, stopping off point before the temples.

Raffles Hotel–Singapore, Singapore
    The lodging place for many famous travelers, try a sling at the bar.

Island Shangri-La–Hong Kong, China
    Luxury retreat in the heart of the city, views of the city & Victoria Harbour.

Peninsula Hotel–Hong Kong, China
    Erected in the 1920's, a landmark surrounded by large skyscrapers.

Shangri-La Hotel–Xian, China
    Luxury hotel in a very poor part of town, indoor pool to cool you off.

Radisson Hotel–Shanghai, China
    Ride the Mag Lev train near the hotel that overlooks the restored Bund and the Huangpu River.

Fujiya Hotel–Near Lake Ashi, Japan
    Held in a time warp of the 1920's, great gardens & mountain hike.

Imperial Hotel–Tokyo, Japan
    Frank Lloyd Wright architecture in the neon Ginza.

Nikko Prince Hotel–Nikko, Japan
    On the edge of the Lake Chuzenji, near Nikko National Park.

Ryokans–All across Japan
    Family style Japanese inns with "tatami" mat beds and family bathing.

Pacific Ocean

Ritz Carlton–Bali, Indonesia
> Gentle beaches, gentle people & sunsets.

Palau Royal Resort–Koror, Palau
> A panorama of Rock Islands in Micronesia.

Hyatt Regency–Garapan, Saipan
> Gardens for Japanese visitors with balconies, great adult-sized swing.

Maui Prince Hotel–Makena, Maui, Hawaii
> Secluded crescent beach, at the foot of Haleakala, meditation garden with multi-colored carp.

Ritz Carlton–Kapalua, Maui, Hawaii
> Large horizontal property with gracious rooms and golf with a view of the ocean.

Grand Hyatt Kauai–Poipu, Kauai, Hawaii
> Lush grounds, wonderful spa, near National Tropical Botanical Gardens.

St. Regis Princeville at Hanalei–Kauai, Hawaii
> A setting for South Pacific movie and a great resort.

Four Seasons Lodge at Koele– Lanai, Hawaii
> Birds roam the beautiful grounds a touch of heaven and a hilly golf course.

Sheraton Waikiki–Oahu, Hawaii
> Big & busy, but the location is great, a view of Diamond Head from the Hanohano Room.

The Royal Hawaiian Resort–Waikiki, Oahu, Hawaii
> The pink palace of the Pacific, a treasure of Hawaii.

Navy Barracks Eastern Island–Midway Island
> Northwest of the Hawaiian Islands, with the world's largest Albatross population.

InterContinental Resort–Bora Bora, Tahiti
> Overwater beach & garden bungalows, great view of the Mt. Otemanu.

St. Regis Resort–Bora Bora, Tahiti
> Over the water bungalos, it's honeymoon heaven.

Novotel–Queenstown, New Zealand
> On the shores of Lake Wakatipu, surrounded by hills and mountains.

Bed & Breakfast–Lord Howell Island, Australia
> Pristine natural beauty, crystal clear waters –perfect hideaway.

Oh beautiful for spacious skies,
for amber waves of grain,
for purple mountains majesty,
above the fruited plains.

–Katharine Lee Bates

Chapter 7:
America's National Parks

America, a nation of boundless dreams, multi-national heritage and immense natural wonders, deserves a guardian for its national treasures. We as a people, as a nation, entrust this sacred responsibility to our National Park Service, to protect our past and be the stewards of 300 hundred years of achievements.

As our fledgling colonies shed the shackles of European governments, a new nation of opportunity blossomed. Given free reign, the American dream evolved at exponential speed. Yankee ingenuity spawned writers, artists, business tycoons and experimental religions creating bedrock of democracy, and shaped a government "of the people, by the people and for the people." Our nation created an impressive list of firsts that amazed historic Europe and priestly Asia. To protect and display our treasures, early American conservationist John Muir and Stephen Mather, who became the first director of the National Park system, recognized our magnificent scenery and applied their tremendous energy to protect our national gems. Today a polished team of motivated national park employees welcomes millions of tourists to our national sites.

America, with its burgeoning economy, set aside funds to protect and promote our national heritage: a land of deep forests, sandy deserts, rivers flowing thousands of miles, purple mountains majesty, great lakes and waterfalls, tranquil prairie lands, eerie everglades, a warm gulf, two oceans with endless seashores and a truly grand canyon. Preservation of this immense land mass blessed with a dizzying variety of topography was a formidable task for our government.

For the National Parks Service, natural wonders and national parks have tended to evolve together. These gifts of nature are complemented by our historical landmarks (Mesa Verde National Park was the first historic site in the world to be so protected). We have protected such varied areas as the Little Big Horn, Theodor Roosevelt's Sagamore Hill and Ft. McHenry, where Frances Scott Key wrote "The Star-Spangled Banner." These are but a few shining examples, a passel of sights that gained significance in a relatively short span of history.

I have asked Bob Hoelscher to share the experience of America's national parks with you. He has been in the travel industry for many years and has built a successful tour company. Bob is a past chairman of the National Tour Association (NTA), and we have nurtured a friendship spanning 40 years. While I was visiting all of the world's countries, Bob was traveling to most of the American national parks. At present, his explorations have led him to more than 325 national park units in the United States. A scintillating conversationalist with a strong conviction in his opinions, Bob is a joy with his varied interests.

I'm sure Bob Hoelscher's passion and intellectual curiosity will eventually take him to all of our national parks. When that journey is complete, Bob with his collection of national parks, and I with my countries, will share a cold one while embellishing our tales of exploration. It is an honor that Mr. Hoelscher has contributed his insights about our heritage. As owner of Flemming Tours, Bob provides commentary presented through the window of an observer who receives daily feedback from travelers. Therefore, from the insight of a traveler with a fervent respect for our national parks, please enjoy the following special section.

America's National Parks

by Bob Hoelscher, CTC, CITE, CTP, MCC

When reminiscing about travel experiences, I remembered a "run of the mill" workday that became something really special simply because of my love for America's great and varied national parks. After making a pair of lecture presentations to a group of travel coordinators in Harrisburg, Pennsylvania, I decided to journey to nearby Gettysburg, not to again wander through its storied battlegrounds, but instead to explore the home of one of America's most popular 20th-century leaders, which is nestled nearby among the lush, rolling hills in the southern part of the state. In 1950, at what is now Eisenhower National Historic Site, General and Mrs. Dwight D. Eisenhower purchased a handsome farm and house, the latter which, unfortunately, turned out to be unsound structurally and had to be rebuilt almost completely. There they retired in 1961 after his 50 years of service to the American people had concluded with two terms in the White House. My tour was a truly memorable one, and not only because the farm is a charming and historic place.

Some might justifiably contend that one of the greatest entertainment bargains in the U.S. today is the annual "America the Beautiful" National Parks and Federal Recreational Lands Pass, which any of us can purchase for $80. This handy little plastic card allows the holder and as many family members as he or she can cram into the family vehicle unlimited entrances for a full 12 months into all of our nation's parklands that charge an admission fee, plus sites administered by the Forest Service, Bureau of Land Management, Bureau of Reclamation and Fish and Wildlife Service, as well as discounts for guided tours at sites like the Eisenhower Farm. By comparison, the charge for one person to visit one of the theme attractions that make up the Walt Disney World complex in Central Florida for one day is, as of this writing, a cool $79, not counting parking fees and over-priced incidentals that few visitors can resist. Regarding the rel-ative value of the actual experience one encounters in a vaca-tion centered on one or more of our great national treasures, as opposed to the commercial attractions of the Orlando area, beauty is obviously in the eye of the beholder. Since you already know the orientation of this essay, you also know where my sympathies lie, but please read further and honor me with the opportunity to convince you, too.

Before going further, it is important to note that our National Park Service manages many more sites than those that are offi-cially called national narks. Everyone has heard of great scenic areas like Yellowstone, Grand Canyon, Yosemite, Crater Lake and Great Smoky Mountains National Parks, but most people do not realize that of the 392 NPS units, only 58 of them are actu-ally designated as national parks. The rest of the NPS collection includes areas with some 30 different descriptions, including National Monuments, National Memorials, National Historical

Parks, National Historic Sites, National Battlefields, National Military Parks, National Recreation Areas, National Seashores, National Lakeshores, National Rivers, National Scenic Trails, National Reserves, National Preserves, even Parkways! While there are a host of qualifications that determine which specific designation a particular NPS unit is given, here it's sufficient to note only that whatever type of scenic or historic attraction you can imagine, you are likely to find fine examples of it under NPS administration.

Do you crave thrilling views of massive, sheer-walled canyons? Do you like to climb mountains or hike through remote forests? Are you a photographer? Do you appreciate canoeing down a peaceful river? Is American history your specialty? Can you best contemplate the mysteries of the universe alone, surrounded by the stark landscape of towering sand dunes? Interested in geology? Want your kids to learn something worthwhile on their summer vacation? Might you like to actually see the millions of stars in the heavens from a place where there is no pollution and no bright lights? Consider yourself a battlefield buff? Intrigued by the prospect of learning more about famous Americans of the past, or of actually walking in their footsteps? Want to get up close and personal with an extraordinary example of nature's river of ice, the glacier? Need to really "get away from it all"? Or have you just had enough of fast-food restaurants, T-shirt shops, plastic water slides (rather than natural ones), outlet malls, flashing signs, whole towns of tourist traps,

or slot machines and Indian casinos (as opposed to Indian culture)? If you even think you might answer any of these questions in the affirmative, you really must investigate the opportunities available to you in our national parks!

In fact, the range of options available among those 392 NPS sites is staggering, as the agency's domain has continued to expand rapidly during its existence of almost 100 years. In 1849, the Department of the Interior was given responsibility for managing the nation's internal affairs, so by 1872, with the rise of conservation as a noble goal, that department set aside 2 million acres as Yellowstone National Park "for the benefit and enjoyment of the people." Teddy Roosevelt, a New Yorker who traveled widely in the American West at a time when such trips were hardly easy or comfortable, was well known for his love of the great outdoors. Today, along with his friend, the great conservationist John Muir, he is given much of the credit for fostering widespread interest in the nation's scenic riches and their protection for future generations. The 1906 establishment of Mesa Verde National Park in Colorado also broadened the "park concept" to encompass America's diverse history and cultural heritage. Soon the Secretary of the Interior would challenge millionaire Stephen Tyng Mather to serve his country by coming to Washington, and Mather accepted by becoming both the driving force for the creation of the NPS and its first director when the service became a reality in 1916. In 1933, President Franklin D. Roosevelt transferred some 50 historical sites, the

Washington Monument included, to the NPS, both doubling the agency's size and making it truly national in scope. Part of Roosevelt's vision was that the duty of preserving and interpreting the nation's hallowed Revolutionary and Civil War battlefields should rightly belong to the NPS rather than the War Department (now the Department of Defense), where it previously resided.

Despite the rapid growth in the number of areas administered, however, the mandate of the NPS remains the same in the 21st century as it was back in 1916 . . . "to conserve the scenery and the natural and historic objects and the wildlife therein . . . to provide for the enjoyment of the same" and "to leave them unimpaired for . . . future generations." Today such varied sites as Brown v. Board of Education National Historic Site in Kansas, the USS Arizona Memorial in Hawaii, Women's Rights National Historical Park in New York, Obed Wild and Scenic River in Tennessee, and Wolf Trap National Park for the Performing Arts in Virginia stand side-by-side on the NPS roster with such well-known landmarks as Zion (Utah) and Sequoia (California) National Parks, Gettysburg National Military Park (Pennsylvania), plus Mount Rushmore National Memorial (South Dakota), Statue of Liberty National Monument (New York) and the Gateway Arch (Jefferson National Expansion Memorial) in St. Louis. Recent additions range from the result of a well-publicized, popular cause (the National World War II Memorial in Washington) to one of the country's newest but little-known "official" national parks, Congaree National Park (formerly Congaree Swamp National Monument) in South Carolina.

I've already mentioned how well the NPS is run. The reason for this happy state of affairs is simple: Thousands of committed, hard-working, friendly employees on all levels . . . national and regional directors, individual park superintendents, rangers and volunteers staffing the visitors centers, even maintenance workers . . . know how important it is to all of us that they protect, enhance and interpret our amazing wealth of park sites to the best of their abilities.

One only need look to the trendy, upscale resort community of Sedona, Arizona, for a "showcase" example of why our greatest scenic resources must be granted government protection to shield them from potential exploitation. This splendid area of red rock buttes, mesas and unique formations is now (and probably permanently) despoiled, not by the "bad guys" of "heavy" industry, but by largely unchecked, profit-before-preservation tourism interests that have similarly impacted places like Niagara Falls and the Gatlinburg/Pigeon Forge area of Tennessee. Unfortunately, the esthetics of a Kentucky Fried Chicken, a gift "Shoppe," or a Days Inn or Super 8 Motel, however neat and tidy, tend to add very little to one's experience when visiting a setting of uncommon natural beauty like Sedona. Similarly, it is no secret that haze resulting from emissions at coal-fired power plants is significantly obscuring visibility at a number of our greatest parks. Needless to say,

organizations like the National Park Foundation (which is actually chartered by Congress), the National Parks Conservation
Association, the Sierra Club, the National Trust for Historic
Preservation and even more specialized groups like the Save-
the-Redwoods League not only have their jobs cut out for them,
but also provide a necessary function within our system of
checks and balances of advocating either public education and/
or developmental restraint.

How can you find out more about our parklands and the NPS?
Since most folks seem to be computer literate these days (and
most more than I), a good place to start is either the NPS website, www.nps.gov, or the National Park Foundation's website,
www.nationalparks.org. Furthermore, in addition to boutique
travel book specialists, usually the big-city outlets of major book
stores, like Barnes & Noble and Borders, have extensive travel
sections with a variety of park guidebooks. I have found that
the best sources for parks-related materials of all kinds, however, are the shops to be found within the parks themselves,
usually at the visitors centers, although you are understandably
going to find a wider selection to choose from at, say, Glacier
(Montana) and Mount Rainier (Washington) National Parks
than you are at a Fort Davis National Historic Site (Texas) or a
Hopewell Culture National Historical Park (Ohio). But my personal preference is really not reading someone else's interpreta-
tion or background information on a particular park unit, but
experiencing the site and what it has to offer for myself. I guess

that explains why I'm now writing this essay just to whet your appetite, and not a complete book.

If you are a camper or a hiker, for example, you will obviously need technical information that others don't. Those who use cars to drive in and utilize standard hotel or motor inn accommodations, however, won't find better, more frequently updated basic information to describe our parklands and surrounding communities (with suggested lodging and restaurants), as well as summarize what can be seen and done there, than in the AAA Tour Books. If you happen to already be an AAA member, you won't find any books cheaper, either! On the other hand, although the AAA also offers fine maps and its unique "Triptiks" to get you to your preferred destinations, and not personally being a GPS fan, I much prefer the overall convenience and accuracy of the annual Rand McNally Road Atlas, which is available not only at virtually all bookstores but even at Wal-Mart

and Target stores nationwide for about $6. Incidentally, in addition to well-maintained campgrounds and picnic areas at many parks, a number of sites offer lodging and meals provided by contracted park concessionaires. Most are relatively modest and moderately priced except for a few upscale, historic properties like the Ahwahnee Hotel at Yosemite and the El Tovar Hotel on the South Rim of the Grand Canyon. If you want to stay in a particular park rather than nearby, either in a campground or a cozy bed, make sure to request your reservation early, as there are well over 300 million of us, but not nearly as many of them!

When can you go? Because our national parks are widespread both physically as well as in what they have to offer, you can include them in a trip (even a day trip) almost anytime. Obviously, some parks are closed during the winter simply for reasons of weather, for example, the North Rim of the Grand Canyon, Big Hole National Battlefield in Montana and Isle Royale National Park in Michigan, which is on a remote island in Lake Superior. Other places are hard to get to even in the summer, including a number of parks in Alaska where roads have yet to be (and likely never will be) built. Some sites just seem to be inconveniently located — places like Agate Fossil Beds National Monument in Nebraska, Organ Pipe Cactus National Monument in Arizona and Alibates Flint Quarries National Monument in Texas — and don't seem to be on the way to anywhere important. But many other units, like Petrified Forest National Park (also in Arizona), Colorado National Monument near Grand Junction, and Badlands National Park in South Dakota are situated right off major interstate highways. Of course, scores of NPS sites are located within the confines of our major cities themselves, places like Boston National Historical Park, the Lincoln and Jefferson Memorials in Washington, and Golden Gate National Recreation Area in San Francisco, almost all of which are easily accessible and open year-round. You can also easily visit a variety of our national parks and historical sites between "beach" days during visits to Hawaii or Florida, and even explore wonderful NPS areas when your cruise ship calls in Puerto Rico or the U.S. Virgin Islands!

With so many areas currently under the administration of the NPS, it is obviously impossible in a discussion of this length to do justice to or even list all of them. On the other hand, I would at least like to draw attention to some of the sites that you will surely find to be of interest. First, there are many justly-famous NPS units with which you likely already have some passing familiarity or basic knowledge, including a number that have been previously mentioned. Others, and the states they are in, might include . . .

"Official" National Parks: Acadia (Maine), Shenandoah (Virginia), Everglades (Florida), Big Bend (Texas), Carlsbad Caverns (New Mexico), Rocky Mountain (Colorado), Arches and Bryce Canyon (Utah), Grand Teton (Wyoming), Denali and Glacier Bay (Alaska), Haleakala and Hawaii Volcanoes (Hawaii), and Virgin Islands (U.S. Virgin Islands)

Other Scenic Places: Cape Cod (Massachusetts) and Cape Hatteras (North Carolina) National Seashores, White Sands National Monument (New Mexico) plus Glen Canyon (Arizona/Utah) National Recreation Area

Revolutionary and Civil War Sites: Minute Man (Massachusetts), Independence and Valley Forge (Pennsylvania), Colonial (Virginia) and Harper's Ferry (West Virginia) National Historical

Parks; Vicksburg National Military Park (Mississippi) and Antietam National Battlefield (Maryland)

Other Historic Places: Home of Franklin D. Roosevelt National Historic Site (New York), Fort McHenry National Monument and Historic Shrine (Maryland), Ford's Theatre National Historic Site (District of Columbia) and Wright Brothers National Memorial (North Carolina)

Secondly, there are many extraordinary NPS sites, the names of which are probably not on the tip of your tongue, if indeed you have ever heard of them at all. Of these, I'd like to mention the following as being particularly worthy of a visit . . .

Lowell National Historical Park in Massachusetts, where you can learn about the Industrial Revolution in America

Sagamore Hill National Historic Site on Long Island (New York), the handsome Oyster Bay home of Theodore Roosevelt

Hopewell Furnace National Historic Site, situated among very picturesque countryside, plus Johnstown Flood National Memorial, which tells the story of one of the nation's greatest disasters, both in Pennsylvania

Ninety Six National Historic Site in South Carolina, a remote but especially interesting Revolutionary War battlefield

William Howard Taft National Historic Site in Ohio, home of the only man who served his nation both as President and as Chief Justice of the Supreme Court

Pictured Rocks National Lakeshore, a magnificent wilderness area along the shores of Lake Superior in the Upper Peninsula of Michigan

"Official" National Parks that offer world-class scenic attractions but few visitors, perfect places to lose yourself amid the grandeur of nature . . . Great Sand Dunes and Black Canyon of the Gunnison in Colorado, Canyonlands and Capitol Reef in Utah, Great Basin in Nevada, Channel Islands and Kings Canyon in California, plus North Cascades (and adjoining Ross Lake National Recreation Area) in Washington

Several remote western National Monuments with splendid scenery that easily justify your departure from the "beaten path" ...Scotts Bluff (a towering landmark on the Oregon Trail) in Nebraska, Natural Bridges and Rainbow Bridge (the world's largest natural stone arch, a sacred site to the Navajos) in Utah, Devil's Tower (made famous by the motion picture Close Encounters of the Third Kind), the wonderfully varied John Day Fossil Beds in Oregon and Craters of the Moon in Idaho.

Scores of fascinating historic sites not only in the Eastern U.S., but across the West as well . . . the old cavalry outpost of Fort Union National Monument in New Mexico; Golden Spike National Historic Site, where the transcontinental railroad was symbolically completed in Utah; Hubbell Trading Post National Historic Site, still in operation today in the Navajo Nation (Arizona); plus Klondike Gold Rush National Historical Park in both Alaska and Washington

When making plans for a weekend "getaway" trip, you might also be surprised to find out just how close and how accessible some truly unique NPS sites are to your primary destination area. Here are just a few examples . . .

Visiting Boston? Both the faithfully-restored Saugus Iron Works National Historic Site and the home of two presidents, Adams National Historical Park, are both right outside the city proper.

Vacationing in the "Big Apple?" Why not pause to see where George Washington took the presidential oath of office (Federal Hall National Monument) or find out exactly who is buried in Grant's Tomb (General Grant National Memorial)?

Touring the Nation's Capital? Peaceful, isolated, densely-forested Theodore Roosevelt Island, reached from the Virginia side of the Potomac River, is right across from the hustle and bustle of downtown Washington, D.C.

Also nearby is the Lyndon B. Johnson Memorial Grove.

Heading to Missouri's Ozarks to take in some music shows? Convenient to Branson are George Washington Carver National Monument and two Civil War sites, Wilson's Creek National Battlefield and Pea Ridge (Arkansas) National Military Park.

After your visit to the Alamo in San Antonio, why not venture just a few miles from the downtown area and see one or more of the old Spanish missions that comprise San Antonio Missions National Historical Park?

Exploring the "City by the Bay?" San Francisco Maritime National Historical Park is filled with interesting old ships, boats and ferries, all located just steps away from Fisherman's Wharf and Ghirardelli Square. A short drive away across the Golden Gate Bridge are the towering coastal redwoods of Muir Woods National Monument.

Remember that our nation's parklands are most assuredly not just about and for white Americans whose ancestors came from Northern Europe. No matter what your ethnic background, you are likely to find NPS units that are of importance to your heritage.

African-Americans are sure to enjoy visiting such places of interest as Boston African American National Historic Site in Massachusetts, Frederick Douglass National Historic Site in the District of Columbia, Booker T. Washington National Monument and Maggie L. Walker National Historic Site in Virginia, Martin Luther King, Jr. National Historic Site in Georgia,and both the Tuskegee Institute and Tuskegee Airmen National Historic Sites in Alabama.

Americans of Hispanic descent can take pride in Castillo de San Marcos National Monument (Florida), San Juan National Historic Site (Puerto Rico), Chamizal National Memorial (Texas), Salinas Pueblo Missions National Monument (New Mexico), and Cabrillo National Monument (California).

Native Americans (and, of course, anyone interested in tribal history and culture) will especially appreciate Effigy Mounds

National Monument (Iowa), Nez Perce National Historical Park (Idaho), Little Bighorn Battlefield National Monument (Montana), Chaco Culture National Historical Park (New Mexico), plus Canyon de Chelly and Wupatki National Monument (Arizona).

Russian-Americans will be intrigued by Sitka National Historical Park in Alaska, French-Americans likewise by Jean Lafitte National Historical Park and Preserve in Louisiana. Japanese-Americans will be saddened by Manzanar National Historic Site, a World War II relocation camp in California. Of course, numerous Americans whose forefathers came from Ireland, Italy, Germany, Scandinavia and many other lands have at least some connection with Ellis Island in New York Harbor.

I'd also be remiss if I didn't mention a few of the national parks to be found within our North American neighbors . . .

Many of Canada's most famous parklands center around the spectacular Canadian Rockies, home to some of the most glorious mountain scenery on earth. Banff, Jasper, Yoho and Kootenay National Parks are the four contiguous units that straddle the Alberta/British Columbia border in the heart of this region, but Waterton Lakes in Alberta, plus Mt. Revelstoke and Glacier National Parks in British Columbia are also nearby.

The provinces of Atlantic Canada also offer a number of very popular park sites . . . Prince Edward Island National Park, Gros Morne and Terra Nova National Parks in Newfoundland, plus Cape Breton Highlands National Park and Fortress of Louisbourg National Historic Site in Nova Scotia.

Mexico also has quite a few national parks, the best known of which is likely the remote Copper Canyon (Parque Nacional Barranca del Cobre) in Chihuahua. Given the state of highway travel in our neighbor to the south, all but the most adventurous should likely consider a packaged vacation to explore Mexico's parklands.

Although not outside our borders, the Navajo Nation, which stretches across parts of Arizona, Utah and New Mexico, contains one of the most dramatic park areas to be found anywhere in the world. Monument Valley Navajo Tribal Park (not part of the NPS) contains gigantic, truly awe-inspiring red sandstone buttes and mesas that have been featured for decades in countless movies, television shows, commercials and other advertising. Also, near Page (Arizona), splendid Antelope Canyon is definitely worth a visit.

As I noted at the outset, as Americans we're all part owners of some 392 diverse park sites. Having been a tour operator and planner for almost 40 years, and as an individual whose schedule requires him to be almost constantly "on the road," I've had a unique opportunity to devote much more time to "park-hopping" than most. On the other hand, even I still have about 65 of them remaining to be visited before I can complete my "collection," should such a mission even be possible, given the apparently never-ending addition of new units to the NPS list. My point is simple…among our nation's parklands there are a wealth of extraordinary and incredibly varied places to go and things to see, all at a cost of little or nothing. These are places of great importance to you and your heritage…and time's a-wasting!

Among my favorite NPS memories are watching the sunrise from the crater rim at Haleakala National Park, as well as experiencing a glorious sunset while seated atop a towering dune among the quiet solitude of White Sands National Monument. I've hiked over "slickrock" to magnificent Delicate Arch in Arches National Park, and around sparkling alpine lakes to stands of ancient bristlecone pine in Great Basin National Park. Especially memorable were several trips in classic, roll-back-top "jammer" coaches across the "Going to the Sun" Road in Montana's Glacier National Park, as well as standing alone in the middle of the night before Daniel Chester French's massive seated figure of Abraham Lincoln in the Lincoln Memorial on the National Mall. In my home state of Utah, I've picked apples at Capitol Reef National Park and, happily, narrowly missed stepping on a rattlesnake at remote Hovenweep National Monument. Like me, you can discover pristine waterfalls in

the forests of Pictured Rocks National Lakeshore, plus walk the same country lanes where thousands fell in September, 1862, during the bloody battle at Antietam. And, with my good friend, Graydon "Gig" Gwin, I've explored the rain forests of Olympic National Park in Washington and visited imposing Fort Jefferson in Dry Tortugas National Park, an NPS unit in the Gulf of Mexico which is made up mostly of water, about 70 nautical miles west of Key West, Florida. Countless experiences like these can easily be yours, too, normally with just minimal effort and very little money.

Unlike big corporately-owned "theme" or "amusement" parks, casino operators, tourism promotion agencies or other commercial attractions, the NPS has virtually no money available for advertising or promotion to entice you to visit. You definitely won't be seeing huge billboards or computer-controlled electric signs along the highways and byways to point the way, and hopefully even your great-grandchildren and their heirs never will either. But even if your only reason to venture off of the interstate highway is prodding from a few zealots like me, what remaining justification is there for you not to get started soon? And if I can't entice you to try a completely different kind of vacation this or next year, well at least humor me and make a stop at one of your national parks along the way to wherever you were planning to go anyway. Not only won't you regret it, but I guarantee that you'll be back for more later!

- Bob Hoelscher

Here are the 58 officially-designated National Parks in the
United States and its dependent areas.

Park Name	Location	Established
Acadia National Park	Maine	1919
National Park of American Samoa	American Samoa	1988
Arches National Park	Utah	1971
Badlands National Park	South Dakota	1978
Big Bend National Park	Texas	1944
Biscayne National Park	Florida	1980
Black Canyon of the Gunnison National Park	Colorado	1999
Bryce Canyon National Park	Utah	1928
Canyonlands National Park	Utah	1964
Capitol Reef National Park	Utah	1971
Carlsbad Caverns National Park	New Mexico	1930
Channel Islands National Park	California	1980
Congaree National Park	South Carolina	2003
Crater Lake National Park	Oregon	1902
Cuyahoga Valley National Park	Ohio	2000
Death Valley National Park	California, Nevada	1994
Denali National Park and Preserve	Alaska	1917
Dry Tortugas National Park	Florida	1992
Everglades National Park	Florida	1947
Gates of the Arctic National Park and Preserve	Alaska	1980
Glacier National Park (part of Waterton-Glacier Int'l Peace Park)	Montana	1910
Glacier Bay National Park and Preserve	Alaska	1980
Grand Canyon National Park	Arizona	1919
Grand Teton National Park	Wyoming	1929
Great Basin National Park	Nevada	1986
Great Sand Dunes National Park and Preserve	Colorado	2004
Great Smoky Mountains National Park	N. Carolina/Tenn.	1934
Guadalupe Mountains National Park	Texas	1966
Haleakala National Park	Hawaii	1916

Park Name	Location	Established
Hawaii Volcanoes National Park	Hawaii	1916
Hot Springs National Park	Arkansas	1921
Isle Royale National Park	Michigan	1940
Joshua Tree National Park	California	1994
Katmai National Park and Preserve	Alaska	1980
Kenai Fjords National Park	Alaska	1980
Kings Canyon National Park	California	1940
Kobuk Valley National Park	Alaska	1980
Lake Clark National Park and Preserve	Alaska	1980
Lassen Volcanic National Park	California	1916
Mammoth Cave National Park	Kentucky	1941
Mesa Verde National Park	Colorado	1906
Mount Rainier National Park	Washington	1899
North Cascades National Park	Washington	1968
Olympic National Park	Washington	1938
Petrified Forest National Park	Arizona	1962
Redwood National and State Parks	California	1968
Rocky Mountain National Park	Colorado	1915
Saguaro National Park	Arizona	1994
Sequoia National Park	California	1890
Shenandoah National Park	Virginia	1935
Theodore Roosevelt National Park	North Dakota	1978
Virgin Islands National Park	U.S. Virgin Islands	1956
Voyageurs National Park	Minnesota	1975
Wind Cave National Park	South Dakota	1903
Wrangell-St. Elias National Park and Preserve	Alaska	1980
Yellowstone National Park	ID, MT, Wyoming	1872
Yosemite National Park	California	1890
Zion National Park	Utah	1919

*The discovery of a new dish
does more for human happiness
than discovery of a new star.*

–Anthelme Brillat-Savarin

Chapter 8:
Dining Around the World

One of the joys of traveling around the world is the opportunity to try new and exciting food. Thanks to my parents, who taught me to be adventurous at the dinner table, I can appreciate a plate of haggis in Scotland, sea eels in Tonga, conch fritters in the Bahamas or roasted rooster comb in Portugal.

Of course, I have to admit my courage was tested in Mongolia a few years back when the guide I had hired pulled the car off a countryside road and asked if I'd like to visit an encampment of nomads. While I hesitated to answer, a group of curious youngsters surrounded the car. I mustered a smile and was escorted into the round "ger tent" in which one extended family lived.

A ger tent covers a very small area, and we sat on low stools around a cooking fire. As my guide and the bearded elder talked, it became clear that my presence was causing a good deal of excitement. In a short time, the conversation became animated as the elder discussed the problems he was having with mountain lions attacking his cattle and yaks. During the discussion I observed a pot of bubbling white liquid covered by an unappetizing yellow film. As if the pungent smell wasn't enough, black flies darted back and forth, dive-bombing the soup.

Soon my worst fear was realized as the elder motioned toward the pot and back to me. I was being offered a bowl of yak soup. I can't recall ever being less attracted to food, but I couldn't refuse my host's hospitality. The first sip went down the hatch, and to my surprise, it wasn't all that bad—although, in a short time, my lips began to grow numb. As I took more sips, the numbing expanded to my chin and cheeks, for reasons I never understood.

I looked the elder in the eyes, held up my bowl and said, "You know, I might have another bowl of that white stuff."

The second bowl went down more smoothly, although I seemed to be developing a slight twitch in my right eye. Trying to be sympathetic to my host and fortified by the Mongolian mystery brew, I suggested we start a hunting safari to eliminate the lion menace. Yes, as more yak soup went down, my voice went up, and I insisted that we go get that damn lion right now. Wisely, my guide gently intervened and led me back to the car and my hotel.

Fortunately, most food in foreign lands is much more appealing.

I have eaten food from every corner of the world, from local bistros to elegant gourmet restaurants. As explorers of new places around the world, we travelers should consider local cuisine, one of the true enjoyments of a region or country. Dining abroad brings out the best in people. We learn new recipes, new tastes and often experience a whole different style of eating, but it can only be done if you start with a spirit of adventure.

Are you a little timid when it comes to eating? Are you someone who is not very comfortable when a menu is presented and you're faced with an abundance of strange words? Do you tend to shy away and ask for something simple? Have you fallen into the hamburger-or-pizza rut? If you have, it might be time to enter the delicious world of new food and, particularly, local dishes.

Remember, if you're in a strange place in the world and are offered local food, it's probably a dish that has been around for

hundreds, if not thousands, of years. It might have a flavor that's fairly compatible with your tastes, or it might be new and exciting. It may take you back to another time, and that local dish could become a part of your treasure trove of culinary knowledge. Do your homework. When you find yourself traveling to a new country, try to make dining an important event in your trip. Before you go, check the Internet or grab a book and do some reading on the local cuisine.

If you are staying in a fairly large hotel, the best way to experience local food is via a luncheon buffet. If it's a good restaurant, it will be replete with a variety of local food. Ask the waiter or maitre d' about the choice of dishes and the specialties of the house. Sometimes the restaurant will have little name cards to help with your decision. This also gives you a chance to try a little of everything.

If you're going out, you may want to choose a restaurant that is recommended by the locals. I try to look for a place where families eat. If you find an establishment with grandmothers, kids, aunts and uncles gathered around a table, you have probably found yourself a good place to eat with fair prices and a menu that will suit your palate (this also works in the United States).

It is also helpful to ask for recommendations from your hotel staff and concierge. First explain your price range, because a great gourmet meal totally out of your budget may leave you with a bad taste and do grievous harm to your wallet. On the other hand, if you can afford a great meal, consider the evening an investment in your travel dreams and memories. If needed, make a reservation. That prevents a lot of extra bar time, but if you find yourself in a holding area, try the local drink. I learned to enjoy ouzo in Greece, a pisco sour in Peru and plum wine in Japan.

Another rule of thumb is that any meal tastes a lot better if you're hungry. The French almost totally ignore breakfast, so when their lunch or late dinner approaches, they've eaten less and can appreciate the main courses a little more.

It doesn't hurt to blend in with the locals, particularly in your dress. If men are wearing slacks or jackets, then do the same. Remember, blue jeans with white tennis shoes say you are an American. If the dining is casual, fine, but consider that white "tennies" announce you as a foreigner.

In some warm climates, Brazil for example, they frown on coat and tie. You will find their dress is more casual, with men usually in open-collar elegant shirts. In colder climates, sweaters are always a good idea. But if coat and tie are the norm, that's what men should wear, and women should wear an appropriate style. The opposite of being too casual is to be overdressed. You can stick out like a sore thumb and can look a little clumsy or even pretentious.

When the food is presented, notice anything that is special. Sometimes the chef takes great pride in the colors of different foods and selections. A vivid display of colors can add to the evening enjoyment, although food with blue color never appeals to me.

A word of caution: In Third World countries, especially in countries whose governments aren't strict on hygiene, a meal at a roadside stand or grungy eatery may be a disaster. In 40 years of traveling internationally, I've rarely been affected by bad food. Of course, everyone's digestive system works a little differently. My bad experiences took place in Mexico and India. These two countries have, in the past, lacked proper sanitary laws. Both countries are improving, but there's good reason for the expressions Montezuma's Revenge and Delhi Belly. A good strategy for staying healthy is to wash your hands before eating; drink liquids only from bottles or cans that you open yourself (ask for no ice in your glass) and choose a respectable place to eat.

Exotic food — What is exotic food? Is it barbecued rattlesnake from Texas or precious truffles in southern France or flying fish in Barbados? The same goes for alligator steak in Florida, reindeer meat in Finland or ostrich in South Africa. This kind of food may be over the top for you.

Food that is little known to Americans is sometimes more of a challenge than a delicacy. For example, lots of people who have traveled to Hawaii refer to the white side dish, poi, as wallpaper paste. Hawaiians have been known to respond that people from the mainland must eat a lot of wallpaper paste. In any event, it's a bland, unusual food, made from the taro plant. Exotic? No. Tasty? Well, yes, particularly if you are Hawaiian.

Another uncommon food is Scottish haggis. It's one of those "looks bad, tastes good" foods. Haggis is made from the innards of a sheep, but you can easily become accustomed to its flavor, particularly with morning eggs.

The Chinese seem to favor obscure choices in the food groups. If you go to a Chinese market like the one I visited with my family in Xian, don't be surprised to see baskets of live turtles, frogs, snakes, cats, dogs and the ever-popular display of fish eyes. India also has an exotic menu. Since many Hindus are vegetarians, they have lots of wonderful non-meat dishes sometimes spiced with curry for a flavor that, once you become accustomed, will bring you back for seconds.

My biggest surprise in exotic food … ostrich. It tastes more like beef than bird, and it has a delicious flavor. Ostriches are being raised internationally and becoming regular fare in many fine restaurants. My least enjoyable food … Korean Kimchi, a hot pickled cabbage. Between the taste and smell, it can stop a charging water buffalo in its tracks.

One of my favorite eating experiences was in Nairobi, Kenya, a restaurant near the international airport called The Carnivore. It offers a large selection of skewered wild game roasted over hot coals and carved at your table. Slices of hot, steaming crocodile, antelope and zebra are offered along with the more mundane beef, chicken and pork. Camel also is on the menu, though it is so tough, it's like eating beef-flavored chewing gum, and you never quite get through it. This restaurant serves you one hot sizzling choice of meat after another, and it never stops until you show your table flag to say "OK, that's enough." No one seems to leave hungry at The Carnivore. You eat till your arms get tired and your tummy grows a little bigger. But keep in mind, in the immortal words of Miss Piggy, "Never eat more than you can lift."

Great Restaurant Locations with Meals to Remember

A loaf of bread, a jug of wine and thou beside me.
Rubaiyat of Omar Khayyam

The early Greek writers tell of the gods on Mt. Olympus and their grand feasts and lavish banquets of ambrosia. Imagine a divine dinner with a picturesque setting; clouded mountain tops overlook the azure blue Aegean Sea. Guests include Zeus and Hera sipping on an aperitif of nectar, served by Dionysus who is tending bar, while Apollo and Artemis are studying the heavenly menu. Aphrodite arrives in a stunning, revealing robe, while sadly Atlas appears to have the weight of the world on his shoulders, but that's another story for another day. As Poseidon orders the seafood entrée, Hermes runs around trying to play tricks on wise Athena. What a grand dining experience as the sun sets over ancient Greece and Mt. Olympus.

Nothing could be finer than a wonderful meal and a great venue; the combination is hard to beat. Over the years I've dined at some of the renowned restaurants of the world. In my early career as a travel director, I escorted business incentive groups to many exotic destinations. On most trips the program of events included great restaurant settings with meals to remember. These fine dining experiences left indelible memories. I've listed, by regions of the world, many favorites from then and now, and if you're a cosmopolitan person of the world, you may have dined at some of these eating establishments. As time goes by, some restaurants close, but here is a recap from the last 40 years of my travels.

The finest landscape in the world
is improved by a good inn in the foreground.

–Samuel Johnson

North America

Location: **Alaskan Salmon Bake Restaurant**, Fairbanks Alaska
Setting: Summer months - wilderness picnic style cookout, a little touristy but fun
Menu: Pink salmon, Halibut and Cod direct from icy waters; plus Frontier Theater

Location: **Nepenthe Restaurant**, Big Sur California
Setting: Overlooking the Pacific off scenic Highway 1
Menu: Wide variety from Ambrosia Burgers to prime rib
California wines including complimentary sunset

Location: **Allreds Restaurant**, Telluride, Colorado
Setting: At the peak of San Sophia Mountain, accessible by cable car
Menu: A variety of wonderful entrees, including local corn dish
Here is a wonderful restaurant with a view down the valley into Telluride

Location: **The Masters Golf Tournament**, Augusta, Georgia
Setting: Amen Corner, sitting in the stands between holes 11 & 12
Menu: Pimento cheese sandwich and a cold beer
Watching the world's finest golfers cross Hogan's Bridge

Location: **Commander's Palace** via street car, Garden District New Orleans, Louisiana
Setting: Tree-lined street corner with outdoor sign "Dedicated to dining in the grand manner"
Menu: Turtle soup, gumbo du jour, crab cakes, pecan pie and southern hospitality

Location: **Tides Restaurant**, Alma, New Brunswick, Canada
Setting: View of the Bay of Fundy and fishing fleet waiting for high tide
Menu: Local lobster fest, fish chowder, Digby scallops and the highest tides in the world

Caribbean

Location: **Richmond Hill Restaurant**, Montego
Bay, Jamaica

Setting: Overlooking the city, outside dining
with a warm Jamaican breeze.

Menu: Pepperpot soup, ackee spiced
rice, fresh Red Snapper fish, Blue
Mountain coffee, Tia Maria liqueur
and the rum is fine anytime of year.

Location: **Sam Lord's Castle Restaurant**, St. Philip, Barbados

Setting: 19th Century plantation great house, overlooking ocean, a sugar cane island
with British tradition and naughty pirates.

Menu: Flying fish eaten baked or fried, turtle steak with coconut bread.

Central and South America

Location: **LaPerla Restaurant**, Acapulco,
Mexico

Setting: Balcony seating for cliff divers
(last dive with torches)

Menu: Tortilla, thin corn pancakes with
meat and enchiladas cooked in
tomato sauce. Beverage - Cerveza
or Margarita

Location: **Sanctuary Lodge**, Machu Picchu, Peru

Setting: A view of the lost city of the Incas at 8,000 feet in the Andes jungle

Menu: Peruvian favorite - Pachamanca chicken, pork, sweet potatoes and yucca,
cooked in open pit over hot stones. Beverage - Pisco Sour

Location: **Rincao Gaucho Churrascaria**, Rio de Janeiro, Brazil

Setting: Large open pit meat restaurant with carnival atmosphere including Samba
dancers.

Menu: Skewered barbecued steak, pork and sausages with pepperonis. Sliced at
your table, the meals keep coming, the music keeps pulsating.

Location: **Many beef restaurants**, fashionable Calle Florida area, Buenos Aires, Argentina
Menu: Bifo de lomo, Pampas-bred steaks, excellent cut similar to filet mignon. Five course dinner starting with meat pie and large salad. Prices very reasonable; local red and white wines are very smooth.

Atlantic Ocean

Location: **Harbourfront Restaurant**, Hamilton Bermuda
Setting: Balcony overlooking the harbor, pink and white building and cruise ships.
Menu: Lobster with local onions and fresh seafood. Ladies may wear Bermuda scarves and gentlemen Bermuda shorts.

Location: **Reid's Palace Hotel**, Funchal, Madeira (Portuguese island)
Setting: Elegant British Style Hotel, overlooking the city and the sea. Embroidered tablecloths and wicker chairs
Menu: Espada - prehistoric looking fish caught in deep ocean; and "have a bottle of Madeira my deara".

Europe

Location: **Pump Room Restaurant**, Bath, England
Setting: Attached to Roman Baths, historic restaurant a must after touring.
Menu: Local lunch Shepherd's Pie, steak and kidney pudding or bangers and mash. Earl Grey tea or bottoms up with a pint of ale.

Location: **Nimb**, Copenhagen, Denmark
Setting: on the grounds of Tivoli Gardens, a historic amusement park
Menu: Smorgasbord open sandwich featuring herring, shrimp, cheese, eggs. Try a shot of cold akvavit and Carlsberg beer chaser.

Location: **Rhine River Cruise Boat**, Germany
Setting: Cruise the Rhine, viewing hillside vineyards and medieval castles
Menu: Venison in season, rabbit in sauce, bratwurst in profusion. Rhine and Moselle wine, light or dark beer in large painted steins.

Location: **Tre Scalini Restaurant**, Piazza Navona, Rome, Italy
Setting: Open-air tables facing Bernini's fountain of the four rivers; One of Rome's most beautiful squares full of tourist and Romans
Menu: Lasagna with ricotta and Tartufu chocolate ice cream.

Location: **Maxim's**, Paris, France
Setting: in the heart of Paris, elegant interior
Menu: Escargots in garlic butter, Pâté de foie gras, Chateaubriand. Treat yourself and add a bottle of Burgundy or Bordeaux.

Location: **InterContinental Hotel**, Athens, Greece
Setting: Top Floor Bar and Restaurant overlooking flood-lit Acropolis at night
Menu: Greek salad with feta cheese, lamb with a side of eggplant and baklava. Ouzo, the national aperitif is potent and can be taken with water.

Africa

Location: **Cataract Hotel,** Aswan Egypt
Setting: Terrace allows view of the Nile River and traditional felucca boats
Menu: Shish kebobs with pita bread, side of figs, dates and nuts. Hot day requires cold drinks; even Ramses II liked a cold Egyptian beer.

Location: **Palace Jamai**, Holy city of Fez, Morocco
Setting: Hilltop panoramic view of the oldest city in the land
Menu: Tajine pot filled with chicken and couscous followed by almond cookies.
         Enjoy mint tea or local wine and hear the call to worship from the minarets.

Location: **Outside terrace Victoria Falls Hotel**, Victoria Falls, Zimbabwe
Setting: Formal gardens and backdrop of billowing mist from the falls
Menu: White-glove English breakfast with kippers, omelets, toast and tea. Listen to the deep thunder of the falls.

Location: **Ngorongoro Crater Lodge**, Ngorongoro, Tanzania
Setting: Crater Rim restaurant perched over 10 mile wide green caldera. Evening symphony provided by jungle birds and monkeys.
Menu: Bananas and charcoal-broiled beef with mounds of fresh fruit.

Location: **Thornybush Lodge**, outside Kruger National Park, South Africa
Setting: Riverview of antelopes, zebra, lions, and more; after sunset. Avoid lions who are trying to dine on you!
Menu: Curried ground meat Bobotie, Kirk steaks, grilled warthog, Stellenbasch Wines.

Indian Ocean

Location: **Meridian Resort**, Seychelles Islands
Setting: Open air dining facing long crescent beach and granite cliffs
Menu: Smoked tropical fish, hearts of palm with mango salad. No special beverage but European bathers will keep your interest!

Asia

Location: **Rambagh Palace**, Jaipur India
Setting: former Maharajah's Palace with jewel encrusted pillars
Menu: Curry, of course. Mutton, chicken, fish and coconut, rice with grapes and cashews. Dessert gulag jamun (sounds bad, tastes good).

Location: **Chao Praya River Cruise**, Bangkok, Thailand
Setting: By moonlight pass the golden Temple of Dawn
Menu: Some spicy dishes, fried salted mackerel, crisp noodles and lots of rice. Sip a local brew or rice whiskey as riverboats chug by.

Location: **Jumbo Floating Restaurant**,
Aberdeen Bay, Hong Kong,
China

Setting: By night, water taxi transfer
to large multi-colored floating
dinner boat

Menu: 10 course Cantonese feast -
birds nest or shark fin soup,
sweet and sour pork. One of
the Orient's most famous dining experiences!

Location: **Peking Duck**, Beijing, China

Setting: Multi-story restaurant dedicated to duck, located in the maze of the City.
Busy Chinese night scene, try to blend in.

Menu: Famous pressed Peking duck with rice and mystery dishes (don't ask)

Location: **Fujiya Hotel**, Hakone, Japan

Setting: 1920 hotel frozen in time - Japanese Gardens and Waterfall

Menu: Sukiyaki-thin beef strips and vegetables with soy sauce. Near
Lake Ashi and snow-capped Mt. Fuji, great view on a clear day!

Pacific Ocean

Location: **Hanohano Room**, Sheraton Waikiki, Hawaii

Setting: Overlooking Waikiki Beach and Diamond Head Crater

Menu: Luau specialties - steamed pig, poi or Mahi Mahi fish.
Order a Blue Hawaiian and take in the Polynesian sunset.

Location: **Bloody Mary's Restaurant**, Bora Bora, Tahiti

Setting: Beautiful lagoon, Tahitian décor with sawdust floors

Menu: Displayed on ice—local fisherman catch, fresh fish of every color & size

Enjoying Local Beverages

There is a tavern in the town, in the town,
And there my dear love sits him down, sits him down,
And drinks his wine 'mid laughter free,
And never, never thinks of me.

–F. J. Adams, 1891 (drinking song)

Raise your glass and toast a colleague, a friend, a lover. Gently clink your glasses in celebration of a new destination. Perhaps your toast is a noon pick-me-up or a refreshing sundowner in the evening. Drinks with friends may gently signal the beginning of a relaxing interlude. Therefore, before you review the daily events, take stock of your vacation surroundings and request from the waiter a beverage that the locals are sipping. Boldly roll your tongue around the local brew; it is, for better or worse, what helps make up the tradition and fiber of almost any area. Eat, drink and be merry for tomorrow may launch new adventures. Throw down the gauntlet with conviction and order a strange-sounding drink, hoping for the best.

I've bellied up to the bar in numerous watering holes of the world. Yet I pride myself on temperance. "Moderation in everything" from the noble philosopher Aristotle still holds today — well, not every single time. So I'll reminisce about my past local beverage adventures and share with you some memories that echo in my mind.

Provence, France – I was a guest of the French Tourist Board in the medieval town of Carcassonne near the edge of the Pyrenees mountains. French gourmet dining was the protocol of the evening. All guests were in brilliant rega-

lia – gentlemen in dark suits, ladies in resplendent gowns. My place card flanked me between two prominent French travel executives. After seating, I could not help but notice the array of glasses set before me, not two or three, but five of various sizes and shapes. My first impression – ah, dining in the grand manner; second impression — ignorance must be bliss, for what purpose is there for so much glassware? Having a curious nature, I inquired of my host the purpose for each glass and he politely explained, "Largest glass – water; next, red wine, followed by white wine and an after-dinner cordial." All were carefully lined up in order of the meal service. To this day, I'm a bit foggy on the use of the fifth glass. Ah, c'est la vie, monsieur.

Havana, Cuba — Cuba is the last bastion for Fidel Castro and his people's revolution. It is one of a handful of outdated communist dinosaurs. I arrived from Nassau on Cubana Airlines flying a well-worn Russian aircraft. I linked up with Bahamian friends who had tight connections with Cuban officials. After a surprisingly easy customs procedure, we drove through the city visiting a private home and got acquainted with a local family. The father of the house was a retired colonel in the Cuban army and volunteered to show me Havana and its extensive historical sights. After a sweep down the Malecón seaside promenade, passing American 1950s-vintage automobiles, we parked near the old town and entered a bar. "Sit here," my friend insisted. "This is Ernest Hemingway's barstool. ... Now I'll order you a refreshing mojito; it was Hemingway's favorite drink." The tasty rum and sugar drink went down smoothly on a hot Havana afternoon. The drink is highlighted with fresh mint, and all ingredients are locally grown. Off to another bar, where we sat down at the exact table where Ernest wrote some of his famous books. So we ordered a second mojito. There was time to meander through narrow old Spanish cobblestone streets and a third hideaway where the colonel told more tales about this famous writer. With a grin on my face, I questioned his truthfulness regarding all these bar sightings – but the colonel reminded me that Mr. Hemingway did so enjoy his mojitos. So here's to the man who lived life to the fullest, he wrote and lived and drank with an infectious enthusiasm. This one's for you, Ernest!

 **Niagara-on-the-Lake, Canada** — A casual American might peg Canada as a hockey loving, Molson, Moosehead and Labatt's beer-drinking society. Yes, that holds true to a degree, but in your wildest dreams would the phrase "Canadian wine" cross your lips? Nay, nay, it's too cold for wine vineyards, you might say. Well, you're in for a pleasant surprise. Canada produces a sweet flavored ice wine that pleases most every palate. I discovered this tasty beverage at the Prince of Wales Hotel north of Niagara Falls in the quaint village of Niagara-on-the-Lake. Among its claims to fame, this Ontario town holds a yearly George Bernard Shaw Festival in the summer months and boasts the oldest golf course in North America. This area is truly a hidden gem and not to be missed if you're visiting Buffalo or Niagara Falls. In the surrounding countryside, vineyards and orchards cover the verdant fields. Winery stops are always in fashion, but the oak-paneled Churchill Lounge at the Prince of Wales is the perfect place for ice wine tasting. Picture yourself in a lovely pub surrounded by hand-cut oak from floor to ceiling, comfortable burgundy leather chairs and accented by a crackling fire. Now ask for the local drink and your server will suggest ice wine, a sweet dessert wine that complements pastries and petit fours alike.

There is one drawback; the cost can be a bit high because harvesting comes at a premium. It works out that only when the

grapes are cut frozen from the vine that the ideal chemical balance for ice wine is produced. Now I don't think you'd get my
friends and me out in the fields plucking grapes in sub-zero
temperatures. Can't you just picture reluctant workers, layered
in their Gor-Tex and fleece outfits, cutting frozen grapes hour
after hour? These guys must have less than a cheery tempera-
ment and are for sure not gleefully singing old Canadian folk
songs as they pluck frozen grapes.

List of Local Drinks Around the World

*Of all the gin joints in all the towns, in all the world,
she walks into mine."*

- Humphrey Bogart, Casablanca

The sip of a good local beverage can transform an ignoble bar
into the Garden of Eden. Combine a good drink with good company and you will mix up a refreshing tonic of camaraderie.
Many a good time can be had if you experiment with the local
nectar. To help stimulate your memory, I have a not-too-seri-
ous list of local drinks, enjoyed in special places I have visited throughout the world. Review my list and see if your mind
steers you back to the enjoyment of a local drink with good
company. Bottoms up!

Beverage	Setting	Place
North America		
Manhattan	The Oak Bar, Plaza Hotel	Near Central Park, NY
Fresh Cranberry Juice	Any Sidewalk Café	Edgartown, Martha's Vineyard, MA
Birch Beer Soda	Inner Harbor	Baltimore, MD
Mint Julep	Colonial Veranda	Greenbriar Resort, WV
Hurricane	Pat O'Brien's	New Orleans,LA
Coke and Ice	The Underground	Atlanta, GA
Budweiser Beer	Busch Stadium	St. Louis, Missouri
Maker's Mark bourbon whiskey**	Local Bars	Around Bardstown, KY
Huckleberry Daiquiris	McDonald Lake Lodge	Glacier Ntl. Park, MT
Caribbean		
Goombay Smash	Pool Bar - Atlantis Resort	Nassau, Bahamas
Planters Punch	Four Seasons Resort	Nevis Island
Bacardi Rum & Coke	El Convento, Old Town	San Juan, Puerto Rico
Mango Juice, freshly squeezed	Mt. Pelée volcano	St. Pierre, Martinique
Margarita (with lost shaker of salt)	Ocean terrace, Ritz Carlton	Cancun, Mexico
South America		
Black Raspberry Juice	Indian Market	Otavalo, Ecuador
Pisco Sour	Sanctuary Lodge	Machu Picchu
Coca Tea (for altitude)	Camino Real Hotel	La Paz, Bolivia
Akvavit with 1000 year old ice	Norwegian Cruise Ship	Antarctica
Coffee (with lots of sugar)	Sugar Loaf Mountain	Rio de Janeiro, Brazil
Atlantic Ocean		
Madeira Wine	Reid's Palace Hotel	Funchal, Madeira

Beverage	Setting	Place
Europe		
Coffee with whipped cream	Prater Park	Vienna Austria
Glenfiddich single malt Scotch whisky*	Rusacks Hotel pub	St. Andrews, Scotland
Irish Coffee	Ashford Castle	Cong Ireland
Pint of Guinness	Shelbourne Hotel Pub	Dublin, Ireland
Earl Grey Tea	Grosvenor House Hotel	London, England
Beer & Lime Juice	Local pub	Isle of Man
Bushmill Whiskey	Brewery Tasting Bar	Near Giants Causeway, N. Ireland
Wine, red or white	Any sidewalk café	Paris, France
Dom Pérignon champagne	Moët et Chandon winery	Champagne Region, France
Akvavit & Carlsberg beer chaser	Nimb Brasserie Tivoli Gardens	Copenhagen, Denmark
Steins of Beer	Hofbräuhaus	Munich, Germany
Hot Chocolate with marshmallows	Mt. Pilatus Observatory	Near Lucerne Switzerland
Original Budweiser Pilsner	Budvar Brewery	Budejovice, Czech Republic
Black Russian	Grand Hotel Europe	St. Petersburg, Russia
Valencia Orange Juice	Local Seaside Café	Costa de Sol, Spain
Sangria	Local Tapas Bar	Toledo, Spain
Peach Bellini	Harry's Bar (on the canal)	near St. Mark's Sq, Venice, Italy
Chianti Wine	Tre Scalini Ristorante	Piazza Navona–Rome, Italy
Lemoncello	Local taverna	Positano, Amalfi Coast, Italy
Licorice flavored Ouzo	Taverna, Plaka Area	Below the Acropolis– Athens, Greece
Africa		
King Tut Cocktail	Overlooking the Nile, Cataract Hotel	Aswan, Egypt
Moroccan Wine	Hotel La Mamounia	Marrakech, Morocco
Kilimanjaro Lager	Hotel Marangu (base camp)	Kilimanjaro, Tanzania

Beverage	Setting	Place
Africa (Cont.)		
Castle Beer	Camp Okavango (near hippo herd)	Okavango Delta, Botswana
Chai Tea	Blue People's Tent	Sahara Desert, Mauritania
Middle East		
Non-Alcoholic Champagne	Local Restaurant	Kuwait City, Kuwait
Chai Tea in porcelain cups	Bridge Tea House	Isfahan, Iran (Persia)
Raki Aperitif	Cave Restaurant	Cappadocia, Turkey
Asia		
Sake Rice Wine	Local Sake Bar	Nikko, Japan
Tsingtao Beer	Great Wall Restaurant	Great Wall near Beijing, China
33 Beer	Number 10 - GI bar	Saigon, Vietnam (not Ho Chi Minh City)
Singapore Sling	Long Bar of Raffles Hotel	Singapore
Coconut Toddy	Temple of the Tooth Parade	Kandy, Sri Lanka
Pacific Ocean		
Blue Hawaiian	Hanohano Rm, Sheraton	Waikiki, Oahu, Hawaii
Fosters Beer	Any Aussie Bar	Sydney, Australia

*whisky (Scotland & Canada)

**whiskey (everywhere else)

At last have made wonderful discovery
in Valley; a magnificent tomb
with seals intact;
re-covered same for your arrival;
congratulations.

–Cable sent by Howard Carter to Lord Carnarvon upon
discovering the tomb of Tutankhamen.
5 November 1922

Chapter 9:

Museums That Inspire

Ponder this thought: If we value beauty or history, or art, or engineering – then we, as a society, must protect our achievements. Without a firewall to wrap around our heritage, we lose our direction for the future. Museums are the road map to the past, a link to who we were and how we got to where we now stand. The pride of most nations is how they shoulder the responsibility of protecting their archives for future generations.

Need an example? Consider walking down Unter den Linden boulevard in Berlin, turning left at the Dom Church and discovering the treasures of the Pergamon Museum. In the larger than life exhibition room stands the Greek altar of Zeus, relocated stone by stone from Anatolia, or western Turkey. Walk another short distance in the museum and gaze at the entrance gate of Babylon. Museums open the doors to the trophies of lost civilizations. If you wonder about times past, then search no further than the museums of the world, which carefully protect their collections as a mother bear guards her cubs.

So let's go on a whirlwind museum tour; we'll pay the fee, get the entrance badge and enter into … wait a minute, this is our tour, we don't need no stinking badges. Enter the cradle of Chinese civilization in Xian, where 8,000 terra cotta soldiers still guard Emperor Qin. Smell the roses in the Tuileries Garden near the Louvre, where two ladies, Mona Lisa and Venus de Milo await you. Step into the American Museum of Natural History in New York City, guarded by a towering African bull elephant, or wander from room to room in Taipei's National Palace Museum with delicate jade carving and Ming porcelain. The gold mask of Pharaoh Tutankhamen awaits Egypt's travelers; or visit the "Attic of the British Empire" in London, the British Museum, and discover the Frieze of the Parthenon — also known as Lord Elgin's marbles. Study the mosaics of Pompeii at Naples National Museum and allow time for the Silver Room — a display of fabulous noble wealth.

Do you like wealth? Then let's enter the Tower of London to ogle the Crown Jewels, or visit the Topkapi Palace in Istanbul where precious stones are the size of golf balls. Now keep in mind, the treasures found in museums take a bit of time to be appreciated. Allow yourself the luxury of wondering the halls at a carefree pace.

Today's leading museums are interactive, with a broad range of exhibitions. Some museums rotate displays to keep that fresh appeal for visitors. Well-organized museums exhibit and create public awareness. Many art museums sponsor traveling exhibits, usually highlighting a specific artist or theme. Transportation museums sponsor events that whisk participants back in time with vintage train trips, auto shows, ship regattas and plane exhibitions. If you wander the galleries and halls, take time to watch small children sparkle with delight and teens soak up knowledge like a sponge, while parents take a trip down memory lane. It can all be found at your local museum.

World's Greatest Museum Treasures

Here is a mind-stretching exercise: imagine you're opening a brand new museum and have been given the power to choose any one item from any other museum in the world. No restrictions, no holds barred, just make your choice and it's yours. Since price is no object, I began making a short list of the best of the best, and here is my top five.

#5: Aztec Calendar Stone (Mexico City)

#4: Apollo 11 Capsule (Washington, DC)

#3: Mona Lisa Portrait (Paris, France)

#2: Statue of David (Florence, Italy)

#1: The Gold Mask of Tutankhamen (Cairo, Egypt)

Go ahead, challenge me. Make your own list. Let this be the inspiration for a museum visit on a future trip.

Early museums began as private collections, then starting in the 18th Century, the Age of Enlightenment, the first public museums opened in Europe. Museums are so popular, that they have become specialized to allow patrons to focus on different subjects. Here is a list of the museums by subject or type:

- Aerospace museums
- Airport Museums
- African American museums
- American national museums
- Art museums and galleries
- Biographical museums
- Creationist museums
- Jail and prison museums
- Natural history museums
- Philatelic museums
- Presidential libraries
- Railway museums
- Science museums
- Scouting museums
- Sculpture parks
- Ships as museums
- Transport museums
- University museums

Here are some of the most famous world museums. Should you be in one of the cities on the list, consider it time well spent in these fascinating museums.

North America

Metopolitan Museum of Art - New York City

Museum of Modern Art - New York City

American Museum of Natural History - New York City

Smithsonian - Washington, DC

National Gallery of Art - Washington, DC

Field Museum - Chicago, IL

National Museum of Anthropology - Mexico City, Mexico

South America

El Museo del Oro (Gold) - Bogata, Columbia

Europe

British Museum - London, England

Tate Modern museum - Bankside, London, England

Tower of London - England

Rijksmuseum - Amsterdam, Netherlands

Louvre Museum - Paris, France

Guggenheim - Bilbao, Spain

Museo Nacional del Prado - Madrid, Spain

Ufizzi – Florence, Italy

Vatican Museums – Rome, Italy

Naples National Archaeological Museum – Naples, Italy

Doge's Palace – Venice, Italy

Pergamon Museum – Berlin, Germany

The Hermitage – St. Petersburg, Russia

National Archaeological Museum – Athens, Greece

Africa

Egyptian Museum – Cairo, Egypt

Middle East

Topkapi Palace – Istanbul, Turkey

Asia

National Palace Museum – Taipai, Taiwan

Museum of Qin Terracotta Warriors and Horses – Xian, China

www.greatmuseums.org

Transportation Museums

Learning is a treasure that will follow its owner everywhere.

- Chinese proverb

The broad shoulders of the American transportation industry took a leadership role in the early 20th century. Our nation engineered, produced, operated, embellished and marketed the very finest in transportation. Manufactured in large quantities, our transportation became the symbol of the American fast-paced society. A brotherhood between government and industry fostered impressive growth, with new technology quickly overtaking the old, resulting in early retirement for many hall-of-fame modes of transportation. The burgeoning museums captured as many key trophies as they could afford, but sadly some slipped away. No examples are left of the "Flying Boat" Pan Am clipper, no Hiawatha Train from the Milwaukee Road, and the famous Flying Cloud clipper ship has long since gone to the briny deep. Putting things into perspective, transportation museums offer a marvelous setting for the public to appreciate the evolution of modes of travel.

Best-in-Class Transportation Museums

Transportation Museums –General Transportation Displays
- Henry Ford Museum–Dearborn, Michigan
- Forney Transportation Museum–Denver, Colorado
- Museum of Transportation–St. Louis, Missouri
- Smithsonian - National Museum of American History–Washington, DC
- Virginia Museum of Transportation–Roanoke, Virginia

Foreign Transportation Museums
- National Maritime Museum–Greenwich, UK
- National Railway Museum–York, UK
- The Railway Museum–Saitama, Japan

Railroad Museums
- California State Railroad Museum–Sacramento, California
- Colorado Rail Museum–Golden, Colorado
- Galveston, Texas Railroad Museum–Galveston, Texas
- Museum of Transportation, St. Louis Missouri
- National Railroad Museum–Green Bay, Wisconsin
- Illinois Railway Museum–Union, Illinois
- Railroad Museum of Pennsylvania–Strasburg, Pennsylvania
- Baltimore & Ohio (B&O) Railroad Museum–Baltimore, Maryland

Best-in-Class Transportation Museums (Cont.)

Tourist Railroads
- **Durango & Silverton Narrow Gauge Railroad & Museum**–Durango, Colorado
- **Rocky Mountaineer**–Vancouver, Canada
- **Skunk Train**–Fort Bragg & Willits Depot–California
- **Nevada Northern Railway**–Historical Operating Railroad Museum–Ely, Nevada
- **Cass Scenic Railroad State Park**–Eastern West Virginia
- **Cumbres & Toltec Scenic Railroad** - Antonito, Colorado | Chama, New Mexico
- **East Broad Top Railroad**–Orbisonia, Pennsylvania
- **Scranton Limited**–Scranton, Pennsylvania
- **Mt. Rainier Scenic Railroad**–Mineral, Washington
- **Mt. Washington Cog Railway**–Mt. Washington, New Hampshire
- **Pikes Peak Cog Railway**–Pikes Peak, Colorado

Airplane Museums
- **Smithsonian (National Mall)**–Washington, DC
- **National Air and Space Museum**–Steven F. Udvar-Hazy Center–Dulles Airport, Chantilly, VA
- **National Museum of the US Air Force** (military aircraft)–Wright-Patterson AFB, Dayton, OH
- **The Museum of Flight** (Boeing)–Seattle, Washington
- **Evergreen Aviation & Space Museum**–McMinnville Oregon (Spruce Goose)
- **Pima Air and Space Museum**–Tucson, Arizona
- **National Naval Aviation Museum** (military aircraft)–Pensacola, Florida

Ship Museums
- **Baltimore Maritime Museum**–Baltimore, MD
- **The Maritime Museum of San Diego**–San Diego, California
- **San Francisco Maritime National Historical Park**–San Francisco, California
- **Coast Guard Heritage Museum**–Barnstable, Massachusetts
  (Note: There are several Coast Guard Museums)
- **The Mariners' Museum**–Newport News, Virginia
- **Mystic Seaport**–The Museum of America and the Sea–Mystic, Connecticut
- **Ships of the Sea Maritime Museum**–Savannah, GA

Automotive Museums
- **Blackhawk Museum**–Danville (near Oakland), California
- **Auburn Cord Duesenberg Automobile Museum**–Auburn, Indiana
- **Harold E. LeMay Auto Museum**–Tacoma, Washington
- **National Automobile Museum** (The Harrah Collection)–Reno, Nevada
- **Gilmore Car Museum**–Hickory Corners, Michigan
- **Petersen Automotive Museum**–Los Angeles, CA

Special thanks to the many people who contributed to the transportation museums list, and beauty in transportation. Contributors in alphabetical order are: John Burkart, general plant manager, Chrysler Motors; Audrey Claxton, clipper and tall ship enthusiast and frequent passenger; Joe Doyle, chairman Rhinebeck Antique Car Show; Bill Droege, Model-A truck enthusiast, nine restorations; Jeffrey Erickson, past president Trans World Airlines (TWA); David Huelsing, American steam train enthusiast; Greg Knobbe, Mopar muscle car enthusiast, over 25 restored; Scott Safranski, Naval historian and model ship builder; Jim Strassner, Museum of Transportation St. Louis; Joe Vilmain, former vice president TWA; Bob West, past president Trans World Express.

Come along;
grow strong with me,
for us the best is yet to be.

–Paraphrasing Robert Browning

Chapter 10:

Tourism's Shining Future

One of the obstructions to tourism in the 20th century has been government barriers. I can bear witness to the damage done by political obstacles. Communism was a formidable impediment to all forms of travel and tourism. When the black cloud of the hammer and sickle blew away, nations reapportioned their budgets and priorities. I visited many countries that could ill afford funds for roads, national landmarks or tourist infrastructure. They spent precious budgets on military armaments to protect them from the Comunists; but that was yesterday and yesterday is gone. You and I can now take advantage of touring without major political turmoil, though few lesser pockets of unrest remain. Set your sights high, plan well and discover the wonders of the world.

The 21st century offers an impressive array of tourist choices for the urban traveler. Unprecedented cruise and tour selections fill travel agents' brochure racks. Online bookings of packages are offered daily to all points on the globe. For independent adventurers, you may now hand-tool a trip to fit your specific niche. Suppliers of family vacations coax children with bright colors and sounds, yet can provide a learning experience for the entire family. A boundless offering of leisure trips is at your beck and call.

A journey is best measured in friends rather than miles.

–Tim Cahill

Give the Gift of Exploration

Do, or do not, there is no try.
—Yoda (Star Wars)

First things first, take stock in your future! Find time to step away from daily routines and dream. Dream of jaw-dropping scenery with eagles, osprey and elk, of billowing clouds and sugar-like sand on tranquil islands. Visualize strolling tiny streets in grand imperial cities jam packed with architectural treasures. Dream of bright and breezy resorts that encourage you to lollygag around or discover harmony by walking hand-in-hand down a hiking trail.

The next step flows from dreaming to creating a trip that fulfills your expectations and gives the gift of exploration to you and the people who matter in your life. Begin with the end in mind — what take-away value will you keep? Will the gift of a voyage across the seas leave a legend etched in your memory? Will family and friends recall mouth-watering cuisine in a village restaurant, or the first time they saw the Parthenon majestically perched on the Acropolis? Will young minds visit old landmarks and set their lives on a path of discovery? "Start ahead, stay ahead" is more than a cliché; it's one of the building blocks for a young person's future lifestyle. It follows suit that early life vacations become, in a fashion, part of one's adult experience and helps mold your personality.

How often have you heard people say that when they were young, their parents took them on a family vacation to wonderful places full of fantastic sights? Their minds opened like a popcorn machine exploding with new treasures of travel discovery. Let them roll another language around on their tongue, learning new phrases for a permanent vocabulary. Sprinkle them with a little self-esteem so they might say "yes, I've been there." Let them watch a sports event in another locale, hike a trail, climb a mountain, ford a stream, and give them true appreciation of other cultures.

In 1970, I began my travel career as a reservation agent for TWA. The pay was low, but one perk overshadowed my financial woes. I received airline passes that included tickets for my parents. This was a moment in time where I took advantage of TWA benefits and sent my parents first to Kenya for an East African safari, then later in the year to Egypt and the Holy Land. It was an uplifting feeling to be able to say thank you to the two people who had given me my early wings. Later in life, I dreamed of my wife and three boys joining me on journeys to faraway places. Since then, they have enjoyed and been enlightened by adventures including Europe and a Rhine River cruise; two African safaris; Australia and New Zealand; China; Machu Picchu and the Galapagos, the Caribbean and numerous North American destinations. Many journeys also included my two sisters and their families, bringing us all together for adventure and laughter. My self-fulfilling prophecy is still in progress.

Before the curtain descends on the impressionable time of youth, give a gift that will last forever. If you are a parent or a grandparent, forgo the normal birthday and Christmas lists and present a travel odyssey that will enrich everyone's life.

Two of the greatest gifts we can give our children
are roots and wings.

–Hodding Carter

The world needs dreamers
and the world needs doers.
But above all,
the world needs dreamers who do.
–Sarah Ban Breathnach

Appendix:

All Countries Great & Small

Countries come in different shapes and sizes. Some are omnipotent world powers, while other tiny principalities have few people and fewer stop lights. Great nations strive to reshape the balance of power; little countries just want to balance their budgets. Over the ebb and flow of time, cultures, politics and natural terrain have carved out boundaries defining one country from another, but not without some misgivings. The creators of nations apparently adopted the hop-skip-and-jump approach to boundary outlines, thus giving map-makers a colossal world jigsaw puzzle.

Though there is no shortage of shifting boundaries, there seems to be a cornerstone of consensus for defining and counting countries. First, the League of Nations and later the United Nations established a roll-call in their organizations granting membership to most and denying very few. This political list of countries fluctuates slightly, generally settling at about 195 nations. For world politics the UN is a stalwart body, but to consider the full scope of countries on a list, political lines on a map do not fully describe what constitutes a country.

I discovered a better mouse trap, a better list and an all-encompassing set of rules when I was first introduced to the Travelers' Century Club. This non-political organization based in Los Angeles has strived to stay contemporary with changing national sovereignties and since the 1950s has published a yearly list. Today, by the numbers, it totals 320 countries. Yearly changes are announced to the membership in the January newsletter, adding or subtracting countries. Like the ancient Wonders of the World, other lists have appeared, but the TCC list has stood the test of time.

I first learned of the Travelers' Century Club while visiting Suriname in South America, having a nightcap on a terrace bar overlooking what appeared to be an enormous encroaching jungle surrounding the hotel grounds. Tropical birds provided background music and created a primeval illusion right out of Sir Arthur Conan Doyle's "The Lost World." A venerable member of our tour group, a retired army colonel, told me of a list and club in which members travel, sometimes together, and share information on countries found on their club's list. The colonel informed me that membership was restricted to travelers who had visited at least 100 countries. "How many have you visited?" the colonel asked. Once I saw the list and counted 89 countries – I was hooked … just 11 to go. This was a defining moment in my life; like a child following the pied piper, I spend the next years of my life gleefully traipsing around the world, running, stumbling but always thirsting for knowledge about faraway places with strange-sounding names.

No. 100 was the Land of the Morning Calm—Korea. Then 150 countries—many were added via Caribbean cruises. Oh, for Pete's sake, if 150 was possible…why not 200? And on and on until I landed on Lampedusa, an obscure island in the Mediterranean. I had completed my life-long goal. Nearly every year the Travelers' Century Club adds a country or so; and if I have not visited that new area of the world, I jump on a plane to explore the new country.

The last 40 countries were the hardest—I traveled sometimes alone, many times isolated and a few times in peril. Eminent travelers such as Dr. Alex Gushansky of Los Angeles provided insights to former Soviet enclaves as we bused across the bleak Karakum Desert toward Samarkand. When I needed a companion to travel into hostile lands, Bill Droege would find a way out of the Hudson Valley and journey into the unsettled Vale of Kashmir or join in a climb high above Machu Picchu. Such friends are nuggets of gold—colleagues for life.

Here, then, is the official Travelers' Century Club list. Please feel free to check off the countries you have visited, or just possibly, if you've reached the magical 100 you can join this unique travel club. www.travelerscenturyclub.org.

North America (6)
Alaska
Canada
Mexico
Prince Edward Island
St. Pierre & Miquelon
United States (continental)

Caribbean (30)
Anguilla
Antigua & Deps. (Barbuda, Redonda)
Aruba
Bahamas
Barbados
Bonaire
Cayman Islands
Cuba
Curacao
Dominica
Dominican Republic
Grenada & Deps. (Carriacou, Grenadines)
Guadeloupe & Deps.(Marie Galante)
Haiti
Jamaica
Leeward Islands, French (St. Martin)
Leeward Islands, Netherlands (Saba, St. Eustatius)
Martinique
Montserrat
Puerto Rico
St. Barts
San Andres & Providencia
St. Kitts & Nevis
St. Lucia
St. Maarten (formerly Netherlands Antilles)
St. Vincent & Deps. (Bequia, Canouan Grenadines)
Trinidad & Tobago
Turks & Caicos Islands
Virgin Islands, U.S. (St. Croix, St. John, St. Thomas)
Virgin Islands, British (Tortola, etc.)

Central America (7)
Belize (British Honduras)
Costa Rica
El Salvador
Guatemala
Honduras
Nicaragua
Panama

South America (13)
Argentina
Bolivia
Brazil
Chile
Colombia
Ecuador
French Guiana
Guyana (British Guiana)
Paraguay
Peru
Surinam (Netherlands Guiana)
Uruguay
Venezuela

Antartica (7)
Argentine (Palmer Peninsula)
Australian Antarctic Territory South Pole (Mawson, Davis, Macquarie, Heard)
Chilean (Palmer Peninsula)
Falkland Islands Dependencies (British Antarctica, Graham Land, So. Shetland, So. Sandwich, So. Georgia, So. Orkney)   F
rench Southern & Antarctic Territory (Kerguelen, Crozet, Amsterdam, St. Paul)
Norwegian (Queen Maud Land, Bouvet)
New Zealand (Ross Dependency)

Atlantic Ocean (13)
Ascension
Azores Islands
Bermuda
Canary Islands
Cape Verde Islands
Falkland Islands
Fernando do Noronha
Faroe Islands
Greenland (Kalaallit Nunaat)

Atlantic Ocean (Cont.)
Iceland
Madeira
St. Helena
Tristan de Cunha

Euope & Mediterranean (67)
Aland Islands (Mariehamn)
Albania
Andorra
Austria
Balearic Islands (Mallorca, Minorca)
Belarus
Belgium
Bosnia & Herzegovina (Sarajevo)
Bulgaria
Corsica
Crete
Croatia
Cyprus, Republic
Cyprus, Turkish Fed. State
Czech Republic
Denmark
Dodecanese Is. (Rhodes)
England
Estonia
Finland
France
Germany
Gibraltar
Greece
Guernsey & Deps (Alderney, Herm, Sark, Channel Islands)
Hungary
Ionian Islands (Corfu, etc.)
Ireland (Eire)
Ireland, Northern (Ulster)
Isle of Man
Italy
Jersey (Channel Islands)
Kaliningrad
Kosovo
Lampedusa
Latvia
Liechtenstein

Euope & Mediterranean (Cont.)
Lithuania
Luxembourg
Macedonia
Malta
Moldova
Monaco
Montenegro
Netherlands
Norway
Poland
Portugal
Romania
Russia
San Marino
Sardinia
Scotland
Serbia
Sicily
Slovakia
Slovenia
Spain
Spitsbergen (Svalbard, Bear Island)
Srpska
Sweden
Switzerland
Trans Dniester
Turkey in Europe (Istanbul)
Ukraine
Vatican City
Wales

Africa (53)
Algeria
Angola
Benin (Dahomey)
Botswana (Bechuanaland)
Burkina Faso (Upper Volta)
Burundi (Urundi)
Cabinda
Cameroon
Central African Rep.
Chad
Republic of Congo

Africa (Cont.)

Democratic Republic of Congo
Djibouti
Egypt
Equatorial Guinea (Rio Muni, Fernando Poo)
Eritrea
Ethiopia
Gabon
Gambia
Ghana (Gold Coast, British Togoland)
Guinea (French)
Guinea-Bissau
Ivory Coast
Kenya
Lesotho (Basutoland)
Liberia
Libya
Malawi (Nyasaland)
Mali
Mauritania
Morocco
Morocco,Spanish (Ceuta, Melilla)
Mozambique
Namibia
Niger
Nigeria
Rwanda
Sao Tome & Principe
Senegal
Sierra Leone
Somalia (Italian Somaliland)
Somaliland (Brit.)
South Africa
Sudan
Swaziland
Tanzania (Tanganyika)
Togo
Tunisia
Uganda
Western Sahara (Spanish Sahara)
Zambia (No. Rhodesia)
Zanzibar
Zimbabwe (So. Rhodesia)

Middle East (20)
Abu Dhabi
Ajman
Bahrain
Dubai
Fujeirah
Iran
Iraq
Israel
Jordan
Kuwait
Lebanon
Oman
Palestine
Qatar
Ras Al Khaimah
Saudi Arabia
Sharjah
Syria
Umm Al Qaiwain
Yemen

Indian Ocean (14)
Andaman-Nicobar Islands
British Indian Ocean Territory (Chagos Arch, Diego Garcia)
Christmas Island
Cocos Islands (Keeling)
Comoro Islands (Anjouan, Moheli, Grand Comoro)
Lakshadweep
Madagascar   Maldive Islands
Mauritius & Deps. (Agalega, St. Brandon)
Mayotte (Dzaoudzi)
Reunion & Deps. (Tromelin, Glorioso)
Rodriguez Island
Seychelles
Zil Elwannyen Sesel (Aldabra, Farquhar, Amirante Is.)

Asia (50)
Abkhazia
Afghanistan
Armenia (Yerevan)
Azerbaijan (Baku)
Bangladesh
Bhutan
Brunei

Asia (Cont.)
Cambodia
China, People's Rep.
Georgia
Hainan Island
Hong Kong
India
Indonesia (Java)
Irian Jaya (Dutch New Guinea)
Japan
Jeju Island (South Korea)
Kalimantan (Indonesian Borneo)
Kashmir
Kazakhstan
Kyrgyzstan
Korea, North
Korea, South
Laos
Lesser Sunda Islands (Bali,Timor, Indonesia)
Macau
Malaysia
Moluka
Mongolia, Rep.
Myanmar (Burma)
Nakhichevan
Nepal
Pakistan
Philippines
Sabah (No. Borneo)
Sarawak
Siberia (Russia in Asia)
Sikkim
Singapore
Sri Lanka (Ceylon)
Sulawesi (Celebes, Indonesia)
Sumatra (Indonesia)
Taiwan. R.O.C.
Tajikistan
Thailand
Tibet
Timor Leste
Turkey in Asia (Anatolia, Ankara, Izmir)
Turkmenistan
Uzbekistan
Vietnam

Pacific Ocean (39)

Australia
Bismark Archipelago (New Ireland, New Britain, Bougainville, Admiralty Islands)
Chatham Islands
Cook Islands (Rarotonga, Aitutaki, Penrhyn)
Easter Island
Fiji Islands
French Polynesia (Tahiti,Tuamotu, Austral, Gambier)
Galapagos Islands
Guam
Hawaiian Islands
Juan Fernandez Islands (Robinson Crusoe Island)
Kiribati (Gilberts,Tarawa, Ocean Island)
Line/Phoenix Islands (Palmyra, Fanning, Christmas, Canton, Enderbury, Howland)
Lord Howe Island
Marquesas Islands
Marshall Islands, Republic of (Majuro, Kwajalein, Eniwetok)
Micronesia, Fed.States of (Pohnpei, Kosrae, Chuuk,Yap,Caroline Islands)
Midway Island
Nauru
New Caledonia & Deps. (Noumea, Loyalty Islands)
New Zealand
Niue
Norfolk Island
Northern Marianas (Saipan, Tinian)
Ogasawara (Bonin, Volcano Island, Iwo Jima)
Palau, Republic of
Papua New Guinea
Pitcairn Island
Ryukyu Islands (Okinawa)
Samoa, American (Pago Pago)
Samoa (Apia)
Solomon Islands (Guadalcanal, New Georgia,Tulagi)
Tasmania
Tokelau Islands (Fakaofu, Atafu, Union)
Tonga (Nukualofa)
Tuvalu (Ellice Island, Funafuti, Vaitapu)
Vanuatu (New Hebrides Islands)
Wake Island
Wallis & Futuna Islands

This list is recognized by the world as the standard of countries and destinations that
are politically, ethnologically or geographically different.

Country Status
Rules Established by the Travelers' Century Club in 1970

1. Government/Administration: Any geographic area with a sovereign government or separately administered as a colony, protectorate, trusteeship territory, territory or mandate shall be considered as a separate country.

2. Enclaves/Continental Separation: Continental land areas having a common government or administration but which are geographically discontinuous either by reason of being separated by foreign land not under their control, by being located on separate continents, or by being separated by a natural body of water shall be considered as separate countries provided their population exceeds 100,000. Multiple fragments separated by the same foreign country shall only count for one country.

3. Federations: A geographic entity which is a federation of separate geographically definable entities, each of which is a separate republic/emirate/kingdom in its own right shall be counted as separate countries.

4. Islands/island Groups:
a. In island/island group not separately defined under section I shall be considered a separate country if, It is situated at least 200 miles from the closest continental portion of its administrating country; or Being located within 200 miles, it has a population exceeding 100,000 and is administered as distinctively separate state(s), province(s), or department(s).
b. Island groups that are parts of an island country within the definition of section I shall be considered separate countries if, They are situated at least 200 miles from the closest portion of the same island country; or Being located within 200 miles, they have a population exceeding 100,000 and are administered as distinctively separate states, provinces, or departments.

5. Disputed Status: Geographically defined areas which have historically had an independent identity and whose current political status is the subject of dispute shall be counted as separate countries.

6. Unpopulated/Unadministered Areas: Any area which is unadministered or has no resident population will not be considered as a separate country, except for the political divisions of the Antarctica.

7. Grandfather Clause. An area which is recognized as a country in the past may be retained as a country even if it does not fit any of the above criteria and any country that is deleted from the list will still count for the purposes of having reached the minimum number of countries required for membership or for the 150 or 200 country levels.

*Hi ho, Hi ho
It's off to work we go.*

–Disney Theme Song

Bonus:

Gig's Tips for Business Travel

This is a bonus section of the book that looks at business travel. If you have read the different chapters of this book, hopefully at this point you have accepted the challenge to create an extraordinary vacation. But I would be remiss if I did not discuss the world of commercial travel, as a matter of fact, business travel fills a whopping 66% of all airline seats. Men and women who venture out to sell, service, buy and consult, represent the core of revenue for the airline industry. Adding to the air transportation is the car rental market, lodging and general travel and entertainment necessary to support all those captains of industry—not to mention, the sergeants and privates. The business traveler actually subsidizes, to a large extent, the infrastructure of the hospitality industry.

After a fulfilling vacation, travelers don't seem to want to return home. On the other hand, road warriors on a business trip want to return back home as soon as possible to sleep in their own beds. The goal therefore is to make business travel as comfortable and convenient as possible. My agency works every day to service and protect our business travelers, which accounts for 75% of our revenue.

Most airlines provide a VIP club that is designed for the business traveler with all the necessary amenities. They come with a price tag, but for the road warrior this can be a welcome oasis. For the frequent traveler, car rental companies provide VIP or quick-service handling to get the traveler out of the airport and on the road. Hotels and other lodging facilities pride themselves in their express check-in or frequent traveler lodging programs.

Again, if the goal is comfort and convenience, these frequent flyer clubs can be very beneficial.

Here is a quick checklist for business travel that can be reviewed before each trip.

Pre-Trip

❑ Travel agents email newsletter focusing on current trends and late breaking events.

❑ Self-Booking reservation system providing airline reservations, seat assignments, car and hotel reservations, and corporate reporting.

❑ Or, call your favorite front-line travel agent who knows your special travel needs.

❑ **Briefcase with wheels and ID tags.**

   Inside the brief case:
   ❑ Electronic equipment; laptop, smart-phone, etc.
   ❑ Business documents, business cards, a passport if needed
   ❑ Reading materials (both business and personal)
   ❑ Airline eye shades, ear plugs and airline socks

❑ **Suitcase with wheels and ID tags.**

   Inside the suitcase:
   ❑ Business clothes to dress for success
   ❑ Most used items include: ample socks, undergarments, shirts or blouses
   ❑ Shoes (they are bulky so keep them limited)
   ❑ Standard toiletry items
   ❑ Medication (in carry-on or in brief case)
   ❑ Sunglasses
   ❑ Folding umbrella

Purpose of the Trip

❑ Sales, service, purchasing or consulting

❑ Seminars or meetings

❑ Regional or national conventions (or a big boondoggle)

Conventions and Conferences

You get back what you put into a convention. If you organize your questions in advance, you'll be prepared to ask pertinent questions. Conventions bring together the best of the best in your industry, along with the latest ideas, services or products. It is a great opportunity for networking, idea exchange, people updates and industry knowledge (or a big boondoggle). So be on time, smile and make the most of your business travel.

*Not all who wander
are lost.*

–JRR Tolkien

About the Author:

A Travel Explorer's Global Quest

A life well lived should be fueled by passion ... my passion is travel. I believe my wanderlust came in part from my parents. I learned about traditions from my mother, got courage from my father, and both encouraged me to see the world at an early age. My mother was an elegant lady with a respect for all people. My father, Dr. Jimmy Gwin, was a professor at the University of Maryland. In summers, my two sisters and I would pile into the family car with mom and dad, we'd sing for hours on the way to see other universities, staying in the dorms while dad attended seminars. I remember a tour of Corning Glass Center in upstate New York, the Carolina beaches of Cape Hatteras and my first rodeo near Boulder, Colo. By age 18, I had visited 42 states.

My first international travel was a paid, all-inclusive trip to Vietnam, courtesy of the U.S. Army. I served as a military police sentry dog handler, guarding Hawk missiles in a field battalion near Saigon. Battle zones are a maturing experience when you're 20, but all that put aside, the Vietnamese people and culture inspired my lifelong passion for travel.

After four well-spent years in college, I joined Trans World Airlines as a reservation sales agent, learning the ropes and airline codes while helping New Yorkers with their travel reservations. That was a sobering experience. It was a rush working in the fast-paced airline industry; it took me from crawl ... to walk ... to run in a matter of weeks. I received training that has held me in good stead for many years.

Some say if you wish upon a star, your dreams will come true. My star was Maritz Travel Co. in St. Louis, and my wish came true when I became a travel director for the largest incentive travel company in the world. For the first two years at Maritz, I escorted corporate travel groups to exotic destinations around the world. My very first day on the job, I flew to Honolulu, helped with check-in and assisted the chairman of the board of a global corporation.

Travel directors were like soldiers of fortune, landing in different countries almost weekly. Our groups ranged from 50 participants to 10,000. We hired top-notch guides, our hotels and resorts were always the best, and we ate at the finest gourmet restaurants—a great job for any young career. Then bad luck struck. I was promoted off the road and plunked into a desk job as a travel account executive. It was actually a great opportunity, and I dispatched my duties with great delight—planning and operating incentive trips and learning client needs. The last years were the most rewarding. My primary responsibility was as a product development director, working with corporations on site selection for their incentive trips. I traveled the world reviewing destinations and resort properties. The destination reports I submitted became standard operating procedure for the incentive industry.

I left Maritz to open Gwins Travel Planners in late 1979. The adjustment from large corporation to small travel agency was softened by the sheer joy of running my own ship. Gwins Travel stumbled and learned, and soon we grew to three offices. Thirty years later, we're still having fun and servicing corporate business and vacation clients alike. Last year we booked 44,000 trips.

Today I continue as owner and chairman of Gwins Travel, counseling with clients on travel destinations. I enjoy travel writing and speaking, and occasionally teach travel and tourism courses. Nothing is more fulfilling than helping people find the destination that suits their lifestyle; and yes, I still travel to faraway places with strange-sounding names.

Credentials: Bachelors Degree in Asian History - University of Missouri St. Louis; Associate Degree Travel and Tourism - Forest Park Community College; Certified Travel Counselor; Destination Specialist (all nine world regions); Bahamas Travel Agent Advisory Board 1998-99; Board of Advisors-Trans World Airlines; Board of Directors - Woodside Travel Trust; Founder and Chairman of Gwins Travel Agency - in its 30th year.

Honors: First Travel Agent to Visit Every Country in the World; Travel Industry Wall-of-Fame – St. Louis Community College-Forest Park; St. Louis 'Top 25' Small Business Award; Kirkwood Business Person of the Year; Historical Building Landmark Designation and Restoration Award-City of Kirkwood.

Organizations: The Explorer's Club; Travelers' Century Club; Tourism Cares

Media Highlights *American Express Persona Magazine* National Travel Writer; Contributing writer *St. Louis Post-Dispatch* Travel & Leisure section; Feature articles—*USA Today*, Associated Press, *Globe and Mail*, Examiner.com, *Stars and Stripes*; Freelance articles in 50 newspaper publications; Travel Specialist NBC-KSDK Television St. Louis, WGN Chicago; Radio Guest - CBC Canada, KMOX St. Louis; Keynote Speaker to over 200 organizations.

*If you would lift me up you
must be on higher ground.*

–Ralph Waldo Emerson

Acknowledgements

In my realm of life, I am blessed with people of value and substance. My parents gave their son a platform to stand on and encouraged me to climb any mountain, slay any dragon. My sisters Gailyn Gwin and Geniel Strock were loving cheerleaders and sounding boards for any of my ideas. Maritz Travel educated me into the corporate world, and Tom and Barb Wilson taught me the ways of a travel agent.

Tributes for writing and publishing go to Ron Cobb, John Frain, Ron Osborne, Donna Picataggio, Dan Poynter and Grady Jim Robinson.

Veterans of travel knowledge, who gave of their time and effort, include: Bill Altaffer, Paul Bickham, Jeffrey Bonner, John Bottchen, Brendan Bowers, Brooks E. Bowers, Gordon Branchfield, Glenn Detrick, Bill Droege, Phil & Bonnie Duyff, Al Geismar, Jack Grisham, Alex Gushansky, Bob Hoelscher, Christine Huffman, Jerry Kaminski, Dan Leeth, Eric Miller, Mark K. Morimoto, Hilary Nangle, Jim Patecha, Peter Raven, Ray Scott, Beth & John Tomasovic, Randy Wagner and Bob West.

Editing with wise council, goes to Marilyn Davis and Ron Cobb, who cleaned me up and sent me out ready to face the publishing world.

Yet, even with all these noble people, this book would never have been published without my beloved administrator – Christie Overy. Her determination and understanding gave me the strength to take a travel dream and develop it into a book.

I sincerely thank all of these fine people, plus many more not mentioned who contributed to this work. They truly helped me give the gift of exploration.

Index

Need Help Crafting an Extraordinary Vacation?

After reading **Travel Dreams Sold Here**, you may want to gather ideas for your next vacation. Remember, the choices in travel which include: Touring, Romance, Relaxation, Adventure and Special Interests. Decide upon your best possible trip, taking into consideration different modes of transportation, food and beverage options, and lodging.

If you prefer to have my staff and me at Gwins Travel help coordinate and book your next vacation, you may call or email us and we will be happy to talk with you. As a general rule, Gwins fees for most tours and cruises are absorbed by our suppliers, and therefore you'll pay the same price as you would if calling directly or going on line. Since my staff and I have traveled the world, we can help with the best destinations, tours and cruises. We will always try to find the best value and costs for your travel dollars.

Contact Information:

www.gwins.com/vacation

In Missouri:

212 N. Kirkwood Rd, Suite 100

St Louis, MO 63122

314-822-1957 · 888-325-1904

In Illinois:

418 W Bethalto Dr

Bethalto, IL 62010

618-259-1940 · 888-254-1844

or

www.gwins.com/gig

Gig Gwin, CTC/DS

111 N. Taylor Ave.

Kirkwood, MO 63122

Keynote Speaking for Meetings, Organizations and Clubs.

Should you or your organization have need of someone who can deliver a spellbinding, riveting, thought-provoking speech filled with travel tips and blending inspirational moments with light-hearted humor, well ... you might want to find Marco Polo.

That's a tall order, but on the other hand, I sincerely enjoy speaking to groups about the world of travel and the fascinating destinations that they can explore both state-side and abroad.

For example, one of my favorite topics is Uncovering the Gems of Travel. Here is an opportunity for people to discover great new vacation options plus a review of why we travel. I have given numerous speeches from the World's Ten Most Amazing Destinations to the Rivers of Africa.

You can be sure the audience and I always have a lot of fun.

Contact Info:
www.gwins.com/gig
Gig Gwin, CTC/DS
111 N. Taylor Ave.
Kirkwood, MO 63122
p: 314-822-1993